Table of Contents

Charts & Tables

Acknowledgments

This book is dedicated to everyone working toward a world in which good tasting, healthy, and environmentally sustainable food becomes a cornerstone of our democratic society. Many people contributed to the update of this book, which emerged as a much relied upon resource in educating the public during the last Farm Bill fight. I sincerely thank Marjorie Roswell for her ongoing support of Watershed Media, as well as the Garfield Foundation and the 11th Hour Project, who have contributed so generously to our work. I express my absolute admiration for our editor, Robin Rauzi. Emmett Hopkins labored over early revisions and left his mark on the "National Security" and "Who Will Grow Our Food" chapters. Hallie Detrick comfortably wore numerous hats: editor, fact checker, proofreader and production coordinator. Jane Mackay served as our line editor for the manuscript. Elanor Starmer helped reframe the "Family Farms to Mega Farms" and "Who Gets the Money" chapters. Thanks to Becca Klein, Marlena White, Kate Clancy and Roni Neff at the Center for a Livable Future and to Joel Kimmons of the CDC for their comments on the public health chapters. Michael Bomford of Kentucky State University set us straight on the complexity of energy issues. Randy Gray, my long-time tutor about USDA conservation programs, offered insightful comments on that chapter. Thomas Forster, Gus Schumacher and Michael Dimock shared their expertise on the emerging cross sections of public health and urban and rural agricultural partnerships. Martha Noble and Ferd Hoefner at the National Sustainable Agriculture Coalition frequently shared their ears and expertise, Martha drafting an update on the GIPSA rule that was later revised. Anti-CAFO activist Lynn Henning provided information about ongoing EQIP programs that continue to pay to keep industrial animal factories in business. Ben Lilliston and Jim Kleinschmit of the Institute for Agriculture and Trade Policy advised us on trade issues. Brise Tencer and Bob Scowcroft shared their experience on the "Organic's Fair Share" effort. I am indebted to the numerous organizations that follow these matters closely, including farmpolicy.com, Food and Water Watch, the Environmental Working Group, AGree, Dan Morgan and the German Marshall Fund, the Center for Rural Affairs, Institute for Agriculture and Trade Policy, Food Democracy Now, Roots of Change, and many others. Thanks to Chris Blum and Kris Costill for our updated cover and of course to our graphic designer Timothy Rice, who pulled everything together. I must always thank my wife, Quincey, and the staff and Board of Directors of Watershed Media who guide the ship on our yearly journeys. My humble and sincere apologies if I forgot anyone.

— Dan Imhoff, November 2011

I tell you frankly that this is a new and untrod path, but I tell you with equal frankness that an unprecedented condition calls for the trial of new means to rescue agriculture. If a fair administrative trial of it is made and it does not produce the hoped-for results I shall be the first to acknowledge it and advise you.

–Franklin Delano Roosevelt, March 16, 1933,
  New Means to Rescue Agriculture, speech to Congress

Men who can graft the trees and make the seed fertile and big can find no way to let the hungry people eat their produce. Men who have created new fruits in the world cannot create a system whereby their fruits may be eaten. ...The works of the roots of the vines, of the trees, must be destroyed to keep up the price, and this is the saddest, bitterest thing of all. ...A million people hungry, needing the fruit—and kerosene sprayed over the golden mountains.

There is a crime here that goes beyond denunciation. There is a sorrow here that weeping cannot symbolize. There is a failure here that topples all our success. The fertile earth, the straight tree rows, the sturdy trunks, and the ripe fruit. And children dying of pellagra must die because a profit cannot be taken from an orange. And coroners must fill in the certificates—died of malnutrition—because the food must rot, must be forced to rot.

–John Steinbeck, *The Grapes of Wrath*

The United States government's agricultural policy, or non-policy, since 1952 has merely consented to the farmers' predicament of high costs and low prices; it has never envisioned or advocated in particular the prosperity of farmers or farmland, but has only promised "cheap food" to consumers and "survival" to the "larger and more efficient" farmers who supposedly could adapt to and endure the attrition of high costs and low prices. And after each inevitable wave of farm failures and the inevitable enlargement of the destitution and degradation of the countryside, there have been the inevitable reassurances from government propagandists and university experts that American agriculture was now more efficient and that everybody would be better off in the future.

–Wendell Berry, *The Total Economy*, Citizenship Papers

Foreword
Don't Call It the "Farm Bill," Call It the "Food Bill"

Michael Pollan

Every five to seven years, the president of the United States signs an obscure piece of legislation that determines what happens on a couple hundred million acres of private property in America, what sort of food Americans eat (and how much it costs), and, as a result, the health of our population. In a nation consecrated to the idea of private property and free enterprise, you would not think any piece of legislation could have such far-reaching effects, especially one about which so few of us–even the most politically aware–know anything. But in fact, the American food system is a game played according to a precise set of rules that are written by the

The Farm Bill determines what our kids will eat for lunch in school every day. Right now, the school lunch program is designed not around the goal of children's health, but to help dispose of surplus agricultural commodities, especially cheap feedlot beef and dairy products, both high in fat.

federal government with virtually no input from any but a handful of farm-state legislators. Nothing could do more to reform America's food system, and by doing so, improve the condition of America's environment and public health, than if the rest of us were to weigh in.

The Farm Bill helps determine what our kids will eat for lunch in school every day. Right now, the school lunch program is designed not around the goal of children's health, but to help dispose of surplus agricultural commodities, especially cheap feedlot beef and dairy products, both high in fat.

The Farm Bill writes the regulatory rules governing the production of meat in this country, determining whether the meat we eat comes from sprawling, brutal, polluting factory farms and the big four meatpackers (which control more than 80 percent of the market), or from local farms.

Most important, the Farm Bill determines what crops the government will support–and, in turn, which kinds of foods will be plentiful and cheap. Today that means, by and large, corn and soybeans. These two crops are the building blocks of the fast food nation: a McDonald's meal (and most of the processed food in your supermarket) consists of clever arrangements of corn and soybeans–the corn providing the added sugars, the soy providing the added fat, and both providing the feed for the animals. These crop subsidies (which are designed to encourage overproduction rather than to help farmers by supporting prices) are the reason that the cheapest calories in an American supermarket are precisely the unhealthiest. An American shopping for food on a budget soon discovers that a dollar buys hundreds more calories on the snack food or soda aisle than it does in the produce section. Why? Because the Farm Bill supports the growing of corn but not the growing of fresh carrots. In the midst of an epidemic of diabetes and obesity, our government is subsidizing the production of high-fructose corn syrup. In effect, we're supporting both sides in the war on type 2 diabetes.

This absurdity would not persist if more voters realized that the Farm Bill is not a parochial piece of legislation strictly concerning the interests of agribusiness farmers. Today, because so few of us realize we have a dog in this fight, our legislators feel free to leave debate over the Farm Bill to the farm states, very often trading away their votes on agricultural policy for votes on issues that matter more to their constituents. But what could matter more than the health of our children and the health of our land?

Perhaps the problem begins with the fact that this legislation is commonly called "the Farm Bill"—how many people these days even know a farmer or care about agriculture? Yet we all have a stake in eating. So perhaps that's where we should start, now that the debate over the 2012 Farm Bill is about to be joined. This time around let's call it "the Food Bill" and put our legislators on notice that we're paying attention.

Michael Pollan is the author of *The Omnivore's Dilemma: A Natural History of Four Meals, In Defense of Food: An Eater's Manifesto,* and, most recently, *Food Rules: An Eater's Manual.* He is a long-time contributor to the *New York Times* magazine and is the Knight Professor of Journalism at the University of California at Berkeley.

Introduction

A Food and Farm Bill
for the 21st Century

Fred Kirschenmann

As the manager and co-owner, with my sister, of Kirschenmann Family Farms in North Dakota, I fully understand the challenges that farmers face in today's agricultural economy, as well as the additional challenges we will likely face in coming decades. I am also keenly aware of the impact farm policy can have on farmers. The farm policies we design now will likely determine whether we will continue to have a sustainable food system in the future.

Most farmers today, even on some of the smaller and mid-sized farms, must accumulate millions in capital to acquire land and equipment just to be able to farm. And even those who successfully get into farming find most of their cash receipts eaten up each year by the expenses they incur. Consequently, most farmers stay in business only by generating additional income through off-farm jobs and government subsidies.

This economic dilemma farmers face may seem of little consequence to the average urban/suburban citizen. But an enlightened food and farm policy is of considerable consequence to every citizen on the planet.

The 1996 Farm Bill, dubbed the Freedom to Farm Act, was intended to change that. By gradually reducing government commodity subsidies and allowing farmers to produce whatever they wanted, the 1996 Farm Bill backers assumed that farmers would make adjustments in response to market demand, enabling the government to get out of the subsidy game. For example, if farmers could not generate a net profit by producing corn at the available contract price, they would presumably plant different crops. Eventually the reduced supply would drive its market price up enough for those who did plant corn to make a net profit. Of course, it didn't work out that way.

Rational farmers know that when the price of corn goes down, producing less corn to drive prices up is not a real option. They know that their individual decisions to reduce corn acres in an effort to balance supply with demand will have little effect on supply or price. It will simply reduce their own income. When the price of corn drops, they will produce as much as possible as their only defense against economic disaster. Naturally, if the price of corn goes up, they will also produce as much as possible to make up for the income lost in leaner times.

The lesson here is that, as individuals, farmers cannot manage supply to coincide with demand. That can only occur through a comprehensive farm policy. Now, this economic dilemma farmers face may seem of little consequence to the average urban/suburban citizen.

But an enlightened food and farm policy is of considerable consequence to every citizen on the planet.

It is in everyone's best interest to have:

- **Stable societies.** We cannot have stable, secure societies without a food production and distribution system that supplies a safe and adequate diet to every person. Malnutrition and starvation breed terrorism and social unrest.

- **An ecologically restorative food and fiber system.** We cannot meet present and future food needs if we continue to undermine the health of the land, pollute and overuse our water, and destroy our biological and genetic diversity.

- **An economically and ecologically efficient food and fiber system.** True efficiency must address the use of energy, capital, soil and water, and community, as well as labor. Our policies must move us toward a system based on renewable energy, recycled wastes, and diverse farming systems and ecosystems.

- **A food and fiber system that encourages independent entrepreneurship.** Human capital is critical to a sustainable food system. Without an influx of young, entrepreneurial, creative, dedicated, wise, and imaginative farmers, we will have trouble facing the challenges ahead.

- **Regional food sufficiency and food sovereignty.** We need food and farming systems that share our limited planetary resources so that citizens in every region of the planet can become food self-reliant.

The era of industrial agriculture, which relied on abundant natural resources to fuel our production systems and adequate natural "sinks" to absorb its wastes, is rapidly coming to a close. Even business design specialists now recognize this. We have so overexploited most of the earth's natural resources and so polluted the natural environment that continuing on our present industrial agriculture course is simply no longer viable.

Even oil industry leaders acknowledge that the days of "easy oil" have passed. And since our industrial food system depends almost entirely on fossil fuels, we must make major course corrections. We currently produce most of our nitrogen (fertilizer) from natural gas and most of our pesticides from petroleum; our farm equipment is largely produced with petroleum resources. And, of course, petroleum fuels all of our farm equipment.

Industrial agriculture has also depleted our fresh water resources. According to Lester Brown of the WorldWatch Institute, agricultural irrigation uses 70 percent of those resources. Four-fifths of China's grain production depends on irrigation, as do three-fifths of India's grain production and one-fifth of U.S. agriculture. And ground water resources are rapidly declining—ten feet per year in China, twenty feet per year in India.

Climate change will continue to bring us more floods, droughts, hurricanes, tornadoes, hail storms, frost, and heat waves, making it extremely difficult to maintain today's highly specialized monoculture cropping systems, which require relatively stable climates.

These and other imminent challenges will force agriculture to transition from an industrial economy to an ecologically based economy. We must invent a new era of agriculture. As anthropologist Ernest Schusky has reminded us, humans have made three major transitions in the way we secure our food. First we employed hunting and gathering techniques. Then we invented agriculture and produced our food by domesticating plants and animals, using human and animal energy inputs to drive the system—the Neolithic era that lasted almost 10,000 years. In the 1930s we introduced a third era, which Schusky calls the "neocaloric era" because it depends almost entirely on imported caloric inputs—fertilizer, pesticides, antibiotics, growth hormones, feed additives, diesel fuel, and so on. We continue to use these "old calories"—that is, calories that nature has stored for billions of years—at a rapid rate, and since they are "old calories" they are not renewable.

Consequently we must very soon invent the "next era" of agriculture.

This shift will require innovative planning and policy making. Can we create a new agriculture that increases the availability of healthy, nutritious food in all regions of the planet yet uses one-fourth of the external energy inputs, requires less than half the water, and thrives in adverse climate conditions?

Pulitzer Prize winner Jared Diamond vividly reminds us that those civilizations that have correctly assessed their current situations, anticipated the coming challenges, and gotten a head start in preparing for them, were the ones that survived. Those that failed in that exercise, collapsed. Shaping public food and farm policies now that begin to address these issues will help prepare us for the day when we can no longer ignore them. The critique that Dan Imhoff provides on our current farm policy in the following pages, and his invitation for all citizens to become engaged in the food and farm policy debate, can begin to take us down this new path.

Fred Kirschenmann is a Distinguished Fellow at the Leopold Center for Sustainable Agriculture and president of Kirschenmann Family Farms, a 3500-acre certified organic farm in Windsor, North Dakota. He is past president of Farm Verified Organic and has served on the U.S. Department of Agriculture's National Organic Standards Board.

Preface to the Second Edition
Food Democracy

Delving into the Farm Bill can seem like visiting another country (if not another planet), with its foreign language and sometimes twisted logic. *Specialty crops,* for example, are what the USDA calls fruits, vegetables, and nuts—the foods that we are told to eat five to nine servings of each day. *ChIMPS* describes what happens when budget committees make a "change in mandatory program spending," taking away the funds that were promised for a program, such as permanently protecting wetlands or providing supplemental nutrition to low-income families. "Direct payments" are the redistribution of tax dollars to landowners, based on the historical harvest records of a property, regardless of whether the land is still being farmed or the owner has suffered income or yield losses. For the average citizen concerned about the food system, rural job creation, and stewardship of the land, it's a trip that's more frustrating than inspiring.

I confess, I am a reluctant policy wonk. But these are the issues of our times. If Americans don't weigh in on the Farm Bill, the agribusiness lobbyists will be more than happy to draft the next one for us as they have done for at least 30 years.

The Farm Bill that passed into law in May 2008 certainly did not give those who care about locally grown food and revitalized regional food systems or protected natural habitats within farming regions much to cheer about. The bill, like its predecessors, primarily insured that very big growers of a select few crops make—or at least don't lose—money. But the real winners are the commodity cartels, concentrated animal feeding operations, and gasohol producers that purchase corn, cotton, soybeans, wheat, and rice in buyers' markets. If there was a sea change in '08, it was a troubling one. Over 70 cents of every dollar allocated by the Farm Bill now goes to Food Stamps, known as SNAP (Supplemental Nutrition Assistance Program). In dire economic times, approximately 45 million Americans have come to depend on hunger assistance—almost three times the number of just a decade ago. If nothing else, this shocking shift exposes the shortcomings of our national food system, which, in theory, has prioritized making food cheap and plentiful.

The good news? There were incremental improvements, such as programs to enable low-income consumers to shop at farmers markets, help beginning farmers and ranchers, expand the research base of organic farming, and set up new businesses that add value to food by making things like cheese and yogurt or packaged cherries or carrots for school snacks. More money was allocated for conservation programs than at any time in recent history. (However, $500 million was ChIMPed from conservation programs by budget reconcilers in 2011 and $1 billion was stripped in 2012, an all too familiar occurrence.)

To me, the most encouraging development was that more Americans than ever tuned into the Food Bill debate. Erstwhile House Speaker Nancy Pelosi admitted, "The Farm Bill used to be my least-informed vote. Now I know more about it than I ever wanted to know. It's fascinating."

This book was intended to be a primer, a view of the Farm Bill from 30,000 feet. The goal was to increase political literacy on the subject, to translate the jargon, to tell people how to engage strategically with the webs of producers that actually put food on their tables. As this second edition goes out, there is a groundswell of Americans who already vote with their forks and food dollars. When they also learn to dig in politically, the food fight will begin to be a fair fight.

The Farm Bill is a tremendous opportunity: used correctly, it can incentivize an agriculture and food system that remedies rather than perpetuates many of today's problems. Absent any significant campaign finance reform, I can't help wondering what it would be like if eaters had their own political action committee or lobbying organization. An EAT Healthy PAC or a Food and Farm Patriots lobbying organization that could press for programs that truly are investments in family farmers, conservation, jobs and affordable, nutritious food for all Americans. What an engine for healthy people, healthy air and water, and healthy economies that might be. It would be subsidization with meaningful social obligation in return.

Fear of ominous leap for bird flu

Fatal disease suspected of making jump among several humans for the first time

By Donald G. McNeil Jr.
NEW YORK TIMES

Reacting to the death
day of an Indonesian
World Health Organizat
Tuesday that the case app
be the first example of t
flu jumping from humar
man to human.

But the health agency
cautioned that this did no
sarily mean that the virus

lungs, not in the nose and throat
as seasonal flu does.

The man who died Monday

ives away from corn-b
d the task of finding gasolin
s things work now, every g
n or domestic — gets a tax
at subsidy is effectively t
thanol by a tariff of 54 ce
mers see relatively little fo
nerican farm lobby is happy
his whole debate misses th
that they need alternative
forms of ethanol made fror
ol to become a true alternat
ivers, Congress must set ou
e, existing subsidies.

rious bills on Capitol Hill
es, gua
age gre
c etha
t-fuel co
It is n
cusing

> *"Our cattle eat the trash. Little animals stick their heads in bean cans . . . until they die.
> There's constant harassment of wildlife."*
> **WENDY GLENN**, on immigration's effects on livestock

Wilderness victim of immigration

WHY THE FARM BILL

Divisions Remain Among EU Leaders on Farm Subsidies, Budget

European leaders at a one-day summit
side London wrangled over how to accel-
ate their stuttering economies but failed
bridge a deep gap over European Union
ending or their position on global trade

and other agricultural countries to modern-
ize their economic systems in the face of
globalization.

Mr. Blair had hoped to dodge the trade
issue at the summit, and the divisive issue

tural subsidies, wants an end to the U.K.'s
€5.7 billion annual rebate.

At a postsummit news conference at
Hampton Court palace outside London,
Mr. Blair acknowledged that countries re-

bridge the budget gap, and leaders' positions seemed frozen. Outgoing German
Chancellor Gerhard Schröder warned that
a new German government would not allow higher spending, saying, "Germany

see rel
an farn
hole de
they ne
s of eth
become

Federal dairy advice questioned

Milk a key part of many dietary recommendations, but many can't drink it

By MIKE STOBBE
ASSOCIATED PRESS

ATLANTA — Americans
should drink three cups of milk
a day, the government says. Atlanta resident Kiesha Diggs ig-
nores that advice.

Diggs, who is black, is lactose-
intolerant, meaning she can't
easily digest dairy products.

say information on milk alternatives is sometimes buried

The
notch r
an adve
suit ain
ducers
with a
cause d
tose-int

Milk
the law
scaring
is not g

Many
eating e
bles, so

One group — which includes
some nutritionists, public
s and animal
— believes di-
lations should
problems and
nd them. The
ld clearly ex-
y groups that
eded calcium
nts like vita-
ables and oth-
ay.

s Joyce Guin-
for an organi-
mprove health
ck communi-

California to lose out in massive farm bill

Prairie Farmers Reap Conservation's Reward

By ELIZABETH BECKER

MEDINA, N.D., Aug. 23 — In the tawny summer landscape of the Dakota plains, where grasslands inter-rupt the crop sout

ed loans and production of well as the wh

turn their fields into grasslands that require little upkeep and become nesting and breeding gr ducks.

The subsidies help fam

ed States Fish and Wildlife Servic habitat and population evaluat

High Price of Oil Is Biofuel Boon

Continued From First Page
spokesman for ConAgra Foods Inc., which holds a minority stake in Changing World Technologies, says the company is in a "wait and see mode" with

Transport last year installed a 5-foot-tall diesel brewer that turns cooking oil into fuel for three of the company's trucks and several forklifts. It collects its own cooking oil from local restaurants and

Ethanol: Risi oil prices boo interest in sta

to boost his investmen
The tax would aid "
are behind the initiativ
Lundeen, a spokesma
fornians Against Highe
Khosla says his ph

Report slams U.S.-European trade subsidies

Oxfam says price-boosting

of legal challenges on both sides of the Atlantic, trade and agricultural ex-

United States' corn, rice and sorghum programs, while the 25-country Euro-

of $44.8 billion, on an annual basis.
Oxfam, a nongovernmental advoca-

acific
ornia
a Re-
from

MATTERS

Lawmakers give nod to $100 billion farm

Election-year measure seeks to satisfy every region, segment of country

pitol Hill would do just that ives, guaranteed loans and urage greater production of osic ethanol, as well as the lex-fuel cars, wh

the American fa
This whole know that they other forms of e ethanol to becon can drivers, Con inforce, existing
Various bill by providing ta

tion on working farms.
It is also one of the major pieces of social welfare legislation before Congress this year, increasing food stamps for work-le substitutes.

gallon of ethanol — x break of 51 cents. aken away for for- ents a gallon. Thus

welfare overhaul that has led to overburdened private soun ki th p

cent of the country's gross domestic product, convinced Con-

limit. The final compromise includes a limit of $360,000 but

er."
Lawmak

Corn Laws for the 21st Centu

President Bush's recent proposal to suspend the tariff on imported ethanol was dead on arrival in the House of Representatives. Ethanol is an important ingredient in gasoline and an alternative fuel in

incentives away from corn-b toward the task of finding gasolin

As things work now, every foreign or domestic — gets a tax bsidy is effectively t l by a tariff of 54 ce see relatively little fo an farm lobby is happ hole debate misses th they need alternative s of ethanol made fror ecome a true alterna , Congress must set on sting subsidies.
s bills on Capitol Hill g tax incentives gu

Costly natural gas future predicted

Despite bulging inventories, suppliers warn no guarantee that price will remain low

By BRAD FOSS

warns there is no guarantee that the nation's supply cushion will look so comfortable by the end of summer — let alone next winter, when consumption typically peaks.
If it is an unusually hot sum-

reason for the plunge in front-month natural gas futures since December has been weekly Energy Department data showing steady increases in the volume of gas stored in underground facilities across the lower 48 states.

1. We Reap What We Sow

Governments have long played a role in food systems. Thousands of years ago, palace grana-ries' stockpiles were distributed in times of need. Such policies may have been more a matter of self-preservation than altruism; passing out free bread, rice, or other staples goes a long way toward pre-empting rebellion.

Today, most countries accept that governments need to be involved in food production and hunger prevention. Just as a strong defense is regarded as national security, a diverse and well-developed agriculture is regarded as food security. In the United States, the Department of Agriculture is charged with this dual mission: support the creation of an abundant food supply, and ensure that all citizens receive basic nutrition. One of the primary mechanisms for this is legislation passed every five years known as the Farm Bill.

Unlike during the Great Depression, when the Farm Bill was first written, America is no longer a country interlaced with vibrant rural family farming communities. Today America is the world's leading industrial agriculture powerhouse. The U.S. Census identifies over two mil-lion farms, but 90 percent of the nation's farm output comes from only 300,000 mostly large-scale, highly mechanized operations.[1] Feeding their 310 million countrymen is just one part of the job assignment. The American farmer is also expected to counter the mounting trade deficit and feed the rest of the world (or so we are told) with a steady stream of exports. Now there's the addi-tional task of supplying crops for thirsty gas tanks, single-use packaging, and other products as a replacement for fossil fuels.

The path to reform ultimately leads to gov-ernment policy. As the adage says, we reap what we sow, and in that regard there may be nothing more important than the Farm Bill.

To promote this massive farm output, the government has embedded complex subsi-dies in various sections of the 700-page Farm Bill. Land payments, crop insurance, research assistance, export marketing, and many other programs serve to maintain an ample supply of certain foods and commodity crops. The scale of government intervention is such that talk of "free markets" is merely rhetorical. Conventional farmers stay afloat by farming the system, rather than growing what might best serve their particular tract of land or provide for more well-rounded healthy diets. If the government removes all financial risks from growing corn, offers generous tax breaks to ethanol producers and writes 6-figure checks to feedlot operators, for example, then farmers will plant corn and lots of it—even when the real winners are the agribusinesses and food manufacturers that buy it.

This plays out each spring, during what's called "the fight for dirt," when American farmers decide how much land to devote to each commodity crop. Corn wins easily, and is grown on upwards of 90 million acres of farmland, an area roughly the size of the entire state of Montana.

Then, because American farmers export 60 percent of the world's corn and 40 percent of the soybeans, these choices send ripple effects across global commodity markets. Farmers who grow corn, cotton, wheat, rice, or soybeans in countries without strong subsidy programs can be severely disadvantaged. According to Tufts University agricultural researcher Timothy Wise, the dumping of subsidized U.S. corn on the Mexican market, for instance, has cost that country's farmers as much as $200 per acre per year since the passage of the North American Free Trade Agreement in 1994.[2] An estimated 2.3 million small farmers in Mexico have been forced to look for other work in the burgeoning maquiladoras—manufacturing factories and sweatshops of U.S. corporations in cities like Jaurez and Matamoros—or in fields, orchards, vineyards, and slaughter plants across the border to the north.

Massive farm worker migration is just one of the social costs of what happens when a government subsidizes an oversup-

ply of corn. Others are harder to measure. For instance, most corn grown by American farmers isn't eaten by people. Instead, it is fed to animals in livestock warehouses and feedlots. It is fermented into ethanol (with the residual grains fed to animals), or turned into sweeteners and hundreds of other manufactured food ingredients. It contributes to a food system that relies heavily on farm chemicals, processing, packaging, and fossil fuels. The irony is that all this work conflicts with the government's other major task in overseeing the food system—establishing healthy dietary guidelines and doling out nutrition assistance to those who are hungry. It might seem that subsidizing an industrial food system would make food cheap and abundant for everyone. The reality, however, is that enrollment in Supplemental Nutrition Assistance Programs (formerly called Food Stamps) is at an all-time high. More than 44 million people in 2009 were recognized as living in "food insecure" households—the USDA's latest term for going hungry.[3]

What's more, all the mountains of cheap food haven't made us healthy, either. Indeed, our epidemic of obesity hits the poor hardest. Fresh fruits, vegetables and whole grains—the foods most recommended by USDA dietary guidelines—are largely ignored by Farm Bill policies. We have become overeaters of the wrong things, and many critics say that Farm Bill policies are at least partially at fault, and can play a dynamic role in reversing this crisis.

Today's global headlines reflect riots due to rising food costs, conflicts over growing crops for fuel rather than food, and disease outbreaks emanating from ever-larger meat-, milk-, and egg-producing animal factories. The number of people affected by and worried about these problems is growing—and, increasingly, they realize that the path to reform ultimately leads to government policy. As the adage says, we reap what we sow, and in that regard there may be nothing more important than the Farm Bill.

Figure 1

Effects Of Cornification

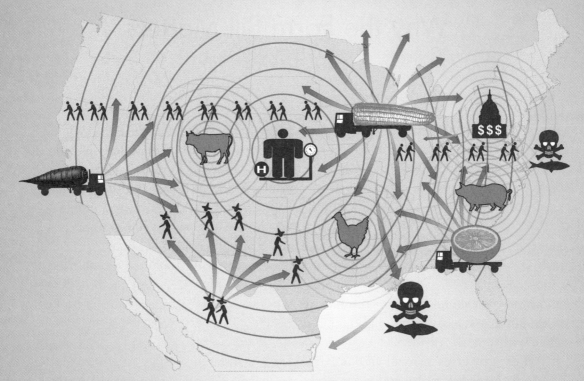

Taxpayer Subsidies. Direct payments and crop insurance totaling nearly $4 billion in 2009 help make corn the largest crop. Many small- and medium-sized farmers depend on subsidies to survive. Large operators use subsidies to get bigger.

Corn surpluses. 12.54 billion bushels were produced on nearly 90 million acres in 2010. Very little of the corn is actually fed to humans. Most goes to animal feed or is processed into starches, corn oil, sweeteners, or ethanol for our gas tanks.

Rural Exodus. The farmer replacement rate has fallen below 50 percent as younger generations flee the Corn Belt for the "Fruitful Coasts." There are seven times as many principal farm operators over the age of 65 as there are under 35. Many wonder if the United States may permanently lose the skills and productive farmland to remain an agricultural leader.

Concentrated Animal Feeding Operations. Confinement facilities, largely made possible and profitable through the low costs of subsidized feed, house tens of thousands of hogs, chickens, or cattle. Heavy concentrations of animal wastes, odor pollution, reliance on antibiotics, and dangerous workplaces are just a few of the many concerns.

Food Deserts. Monoculture specialization of corn and other grains for export is the reason we see "so much agriculture, so little food" in farming areas. Impoverished inner city areas, where access to supermarkets or farmers markets is limited or nonexistent, also become "food deserts."

The Obesity Crisis. The number of Americans who are overweight or obese climbed to 68 percent in 2008; the childhood obesity rate more than tripled between 1980 and 2008, from 5 percent to 17 percent. Lack of physical activity and poor nutrition—linked to subsidized and super-sized processed foods high in sugar, fats, and sodium along with soft drinks—lie at the root of the epidemic.

Food Miles. The average fresh produce item now travels approximately 5,000 miles from farm to table. California, Florida, and a number of other states (and a growing number of countries) supply the nation's supermarkets with fruits and vegetables. Relatively little of this "specialty crop" production is federally supported.

Immigration. Since the implementation of NAFTA in 1994, an estimated 1.3 to 2.3 million Mexican campesinos were forced to leave their lands and move elsewhere (the U.S. or Mexico) to attain employment. Subsidized U.S. corn, combined with the NAFTA trade agreement, has had a catastrophic effect on Mexican farmers.

The Dead Zone. Nutrient and chemical runoff from farms in the Corn Belt flow through watersheds that empty into the Mississippi River and create a "dead zone" in the Gulf of Mexico, harming fish and marine life. (There are dozens of agriculturally induced hypoxic zones around the world, including the Chesapeake Bay.)

2. Why the Farm Bill Matters

On one level, we could make this a very short read by simply stating that the Farm Bill doesn't matter, at least to the average citizen. It's a fully rigged game run by the immensely powerful farm lobbies and monopolies that profit mightily from how our food is grown, processed, marketed and distributed. No matter what we concerned citizens do to change an unfair and

As a result of the Farm Bill, citizens pay a national food bill at least three times: (1) at the checkout stand; (2) in taxes that subsidize commodity crop production; and (3) in environmental cleanup and medical costs.

unhealthy system for the better, we are inevitably going to fall short. There is simply too much money at stake in a corrupt political process to make any significant difference. Sadly, this may be all too true. The next Farm Bill may well end up propping up the industrial agriculture complex with billions of annual taxpayer dollars, as it has done for decades. But this issue is far too important to go down without a serious debate.

Here's why.

If you eat, pay taxes, care about biodiversity, worry about the quality of school lunches, or notice the loss of farmland and woodlands, you have a personal stake in the Farm Bill. If you're concerned about escalating federal budget deficits, the fate of family farmers, working conditions for immigrant farm laborers, the persistence of hunger and poverty, or how we value local and organic food, you should pay attention to the Farm Bill. There are dozens more reasons why the Farm Bill, and its attendant tens of billions of dollars, is critical to our land, our bodies, and our children's future. Some include:

- The twilight of the cheap oil age.
- The onset of unpredictable climatic conditions.
- Looming water shortages.
- Plummeting wild fish populations.
- An aging farm population and lack of young farmers.
- Expansion in production of biofuels and bioplastics.
- Escalating medical costs related to obesity.
- Direct payments to corporate farms regardless of economic need.
- 50 million Americans, at least 20 percent of them children, who don't get enough to eat.

The Farm Bill matters because it makes some big mega-farms scandalously rich as it drives family farmers out of business. It makes the ingredients of unhealthy food cheap and abundant and at the same time it produces a fragile rather than a resilient food system. It legalizes and supports polluting and destructive monoculture farming practices, then spends billions trying to put bandages on the damage. It artificially sets prices, while officials tout the virtues of "free markets" and "fair trade." Its consequences contribute to poverty, rural exodus, and famine.[1]

Although subsidies do provide a critical safety net in some years to family farms that continue to grow commodity crops, the big beneficiaries are absentee landlords, tractor dealers, and insurance companies that service farmers, as well as the corporate agribusinesses, grain distributors, animal feed operations, and ethanol producers that purchase subsidized crops. What started as an ambitious temporary effort to lift millions of Americans out of economic and ecological desperation during the Great Depression and Dust Bowl (supported initially by a tax on food processors) devolved over decades into a corporate boondoggle. As a result of the Farm Bill, citizens pay a national food bill at least three times: (1) at the checkout stand, (2) in taxes that subsidize commodity crop production, and (3) in environmental cleanup and medical costs related to the consequences of industrial commodity-based agriculture.

Most analysts, most farmers, and even many legislators agree that our present course leaves the nation unprepared for the urgent challenges it faces in the 21st century.[2] The silver lining is that Americans actually have a substantial food and farm policy to debate. Conditions for change are ripe,

Our challenge is not to abolish government support; it is, rather, to make certain we are investing in a viable future for our food system.

as market dynamics and public awareness rapidly align to create momentum against farm politics as usual.

Indeed, the Farm Bill matters because much needed funds can drive small-scale entrepreneurship, on-farm research, species protection, nutritional assistance, healthy school lunches, job creation, and habitat restoration. Our challenge is not to abolish government support; it is, rather, to make certain we are investing in a viable future for our food system. No one knows exactly how that change will unfold. But most observers agree that massive giveaways to corporations and surplus commodity producers must yield to policies that reward stewardship, promote healthy diets, enhance regional food production, support family farms, and make it easier for hungry families to eat healthy foods.

Figure 2

Course Correction

Americans deserve a Farm Bill that
addresses the challenges of the times.
Current Farm Bill programs shovel money to the largest producers and don't
properly support the small- and medium-sized growers, otherwise known as
the "agriculture of the middle." Our system is overloaded with animal products
and manufactured foods and short on
fruit and vegetable production.

With record budget deficits, rising
energy costs, an unpredictable climate,
and skyrocketing health costs due to
preventable nutritional diseases, we
can't afford not to act. Future Farm
Bills must look forward to ensure that
we have a farm population actively
engaged in growing healthy foods,
conservation incentives that protect our
natural resources from contamination
and overexploitation, research that
gives farmers valuable tools, and nutrition programs that ensure healthy and
affordable food for all.

Present Challenges

Consolidation and concentration in the
hands of a few corporate agribusinesses

Soil and biodiversity loss

Converging national health care crises

Childhood obesity on the rise

Chronic hunger and improper nutrition
that affects over 45 million Americans

Sprawl into prime farmland

Record budget deficits

World Trade Organization rulings
declaring U.S. export subsidies illegal

Devastated farm communities

Rapidly aging U.S. farm population

Escalating energy costs

Increasing dependence on commodity exports
and imports of "fresh" food

Water contamination and water shortages

Global warming

Increasing outbreaks of infectious diseases
related to confinement livestock production

Declining honeybee and native pollinator populations

Costly corn ethanol program

Solutions Proposed by Farm Bill Reformers

Limit payments to individual recipients to level the playing field for all farmers; Reform meatpacker regulations to break monopoly control of livestock industry; Protect small and mid-sized farmers

Make on-farm conservation efforts requirements of all insurance and subsidy programs; Make no net soil loss a goal of farm programs through fully enforced Sod Saver, Sod Buster, and Swamp Buster provisions.

Better align crop supports with most recent USDA "My Plate" nutrition guidelines

Launch nationwide farm-to-school, farm-to-college, and other fresh food distribution programs that also include a strong educational and fitness component

Maintain food assistance programs including improved access to healthy foods; Expand funding for SNAP-Ed and SNAP at farmers markets; Ensure that every American has access to affordable, healthy food

Greater funding to keep farm and ranchland in agricultural use and open space rather than subdivisions and sprawl

Make spending serve as true public investment with targeted results; Combine funding sources

Shift subsidies toward green payments such as the Conservation Stewardship Program that rewards farmers for environmental caretaking rather than overproduction of export crops

Investments and loans to revitalize and diversify rural sector; Rebuild livestock processing infrastructure

Add 100,000 new farmers and ranchers over the course of the next Farm Bill

Expand research into energy-effective farming systems and increase support for on-farm energy conservation and renewable energy infrastructure

Invest in value-added processing and flexible supports for more diversified local and regional "specialty crops"; Increase funding for efforts like the Fresh Fruit and Vegetable Snack program

Research alternatives to synthetic fertilizers; Increase incentives for farming systems that protect watersheds

Incentivize energy conservation, carbon sequestration, and pasture-based agriculture; Cap and trade

Expansion of grass-pastured livestock operations; Place a moratorium on new CAFO creation; Eliminate EQIP funding for CAFO waste management; Phase out non-veterinary usage of antibiotics in livestock

Expand wild habitat for native pollinators in and around farms; adapt new programs for beekeepers

End corn ethanol subsidies; Evaluate what role advanced biofuels play; Increase fuel efficiency

3. What Is the Farm Bill?

Every five to seven years, Congress drafts, debates, and ultimately passes a gargantuan package of legislation about food and farming. It gets a formal name–such as the Food and Agriculture Act of 1977, the Federal Agriculture Improvement and Reform Act of 1996, the Farm Security and Rural Investment Act of 2002, or the Food, Conservation, and Energy Act of 2008–but people generally refer to each as simply "the Farm Bill." Since its origins in 1933 as the Agricultural Adjustment Act, the bill has snowballed into one of the most–if not *the most*–significant legislative measures affecting land use in the United States.

The Farm Bill is an omnibus legislation because it addresses multiple issues simultaneously. However, modern Farm Bills traditionally have three primary thrusts: (1) food stamp and nutrition programs (now at least 72 percent of gross outlays), (2) income and price supports for commodity crops (about 22 percent), and (3) conservation incentives (about 6 percent). In addition to these, the Farm Bill directs and funds a wide range of other spending categories organized into "titles." These programs include trade and foreign food aid, forestry (because forests and woodlots are important components of farms), agricultural credit, rural development, research and education, marketing, food safety, animal health and welfare, and very recently, energy, and organic agriculture.[1] (See Figure 3, "How the Farm Bill Spends a Tax Dollar.") A number of policies, such as food assistance, conservation, agricultural trade, credit, rural development, and research are actually governed by both the Farm Bill and a variety of separate laws, which can be, and at times are, renewed or modified as stand-alone bills. (The Child Nutrition Act, the Clean Water Act, and the Food Safety Modernization Act are recent examples of stand-alone legislations that address food and agriculture issues.) Increasingly, though, Congress finds it advantageous to combine many of these laws into a single, mammoth reauthorization of multiple statutes at the same time they renew the farm commodity programs.[2] This omnibus nature of the Farm Bill keeps the public oblivious: it's nearly impossible for any one person to really understand the full extent of all that's actually covered.

Omnibus legislation: a law that addresses multiple issues simultaneously.

Although well over two-thirds of the Farm Bill budget is presently targeted toward the safety net nutrition programs (still widely known as "food stamps"), it is commodity subsidies, crop insurance, and "price supports" that are the heart of the legislation.[3] At their noblest, subsidy payments to farmers are intended to provide an income safety net in this economically and meteorologically volatile profession—thereby protecting the food supply and strengthening rural communities. Some programs genuinely invest in the long-term stability of the food supply and stewardship of the land. This was particularly true in the 1930s and 40s, when the bill's defining goals involved land idling and installing contour strips to prevent oversupply of crops and protect the soil in exchange for loans and price supports for storable foods.

But along the way, the Farm Bill became an engine driving surplus production of commodity crops and a gravy train for powerful corporations that purchased and traded them; the rules of the game changed and the public benefit aspects of its origins derailed. After modest reforms over five decades, political realities and global economics collided in the 1980s. Increased global trade, the call for less government spending, the concentration of food distribution and processing centers, and low commodity prices took their toll on the farm sector and rural communities. Corporate agribusinesses and mega-farms then succeeded in tilting subsidies completely in their favor. While control of today's agriculture is concentrated in a small number of corporate operations, the public perception of American agriculture is still rooted in the nostalgia in the father and daughter in Grant Wood's classic painting "American Gothic," the illustrations of Norman Rockwell, and the iconic images of the Western cowboy.

Many Americans believe, for example, that the tens of billions of dollars the government spends on agriculture primarily support farms where a husband and wife work from dawn to dusk growing crops, with roosters crowing from fence posts, and cows grazing on rolling pastures. The real picture is not so idyllic. Commodity payments primarily go to producers who grow corn and other feed grains, peanuts, sugar, wheat and other food grains, rice, cotton, soy, oilseeds, and dairy. Three in five farmers get no payments at all, while the top 5 percent of subsidy recipients (often producer cooperatives, Indian tribes, and large corporate entities) average about $710,150 each.[4] Another common perception is that Farm Bill subsidies that pay farmers not to grow crops have made soil erosion a relict of the Dust Bowl. Yet less than 10 percent of the USDA budget is linked to conservation practices;[5] according to the USDA Natural Resources Conservation Service, nearly two billion tons of cropland soil is still being lost every year.[6] Ethanol subsidies and generous crop insurance policies are encouraging an expansion of corn production and along with it risking a precarious escalation in soil erosion. One-half to two-thirds of agricultural counties in the U.S. have been designated as disaster areas in each of the last several years according to a 2009 USDA report.[7] This is simply unsustainable in the long term. There can be no farming without healthy soils.

The most frequently heard claim is that the Farm Bill underwrites the cheapest and

Figure 3

How the Farm Bill

Nutrition, Farm and Conservation Spending

Gross Outlays Averaged Over Ten Distinct Appropriations 2002–2012

5.70% Conservation $37.2 billion

0.17% Energy* $1.1 billion

6.80% Crop Insurance $43.9 billion

13.90% Commodities $89.9 billion

0.42% Exports $2.7 billion

72.89% Nutrition $470.2 billion

Source: Actual Farm Bill Spending and Cost Estimates, Congressional Research Service   *No data prior to 2008

Spends a Tax Dollar

Taking Food Stamps Out of the Equation

Gross Outlays Averaged Over Ten Distinct Appropriations 2002–2012

21.30% Conservation $37.2 billion

0.62% Energy* $1.1 billion

25.10% Crop Insurance $43.9 billion

1.50% Exports $2.7 billion

51.40% Commodities $89.9 billion

Source: Actual Farm Bill Spending and Cost Estimates, Congressional Research Service   *No data prior to 2008

most nutritious food system in the world. But today's beneficiaries are truly the large corporations and monopolies that trade grains and fibers and use and export "cheap raw materials" for livestock feed, ethanol, and mass manufactured foods. Ours is not necessarily cheap food, either. According to researcher Charles Benbrook, if food is assessed by the cost per calorie produced, rather than as a percentage of disposable income, more than 20 countries enjoy cheaper food systems than the United States.[8]

In essence, the Farm Bill has been hijacked by the powers dominating the industrial food system. What should be the government's best effort to invest in the finest food system possible for its people, instead has created a concentration of wealth and production that we are frequently told is simply too big to fail. Yet despite the dysfunction and missed opportunities, the Farm Bill still represents one of our best chances to create a truly vibrant system and culture of food production that compensates family farmers when markets fail them, cares for those most in need, and conserves invaluable soils, water resources, and natural habitat for future generations. More than anything, the Farm Bill is a snapshot of our democratic process in action, one that anyone who eats, votes, and cares about the present and future should pay close attention to.

Farm Bill Titles

The order and total number of Farm Bill titles varies from bill to bill. In the 2008 Farm Bill, the titles run as follows.

Title I - Commodity Programs
Title II - Conservation
Title III - Trade
Title IV - Nutrition
Title V - Credit
Title VI - Rural Development
Title VII - Research
Title VIII - Forestry

Title IX - Energy
Title X - Horticulture & Organic Agriculture
Title XI - Livestock
Title XII - Crop Insurance
Title XIII - Commodity Futures
Title XIV - Miscellaneous
Title XV - Trade & Taxes

Mandatory Spending

Programs with mandatory funding are generally assured, whereas programs with discretionary funding survive and perish at the hands of the Appropriations Committee. Certain program categories have achieved baseline levels of funding over the decades.

Commodity Programs (1930s)
Food Stamps (1960s)
Conservation (1980s)

Rural Development & Research (late 1990s)
Crop Insurance (2000)

Farm Bill Names

Each Farm Bill is actually a reauthorization of the programs dating back to the 1930s as well as the authorization of new programs.

Agricultural Adjustment Act of 1933
Agricultural Adjustment Act of 1938
Agricultural Act of 1948
Agricultural Act of 1949
Agricultural Act of 1954
Agricultural Act of 1956
Food and Agricultural Act of 1965
Agricultural Act of 1970
Agricultural and Consumer Protection Act
   of 1973

Food and Agriculture Act of 1977
Agriculture and Food Act of 1981
Food Security Act of 1985
Food, Agriculture, Conservation, and
   Trade Act of 1990
Federal Agriculture Improvement and
   Reform Act of 1996
Farm Security and Rural Investment Act
   of 2002
Food, Conservation, and Energy Act of 2008

Sources: The National Agricultural Law Center and the USDA Economic Research Service

Crop Subsidies at a Glance

Taxpayer-funded programs have taken most of the financial risks out of modern farming in America. Growers plant all they want and have a government security blanket to guaranteed income.

Direct payments—Landowners receive these payments according to historical land use—"base acres"—even in years of record income, even if they did not plant commodity crops that year. Direct payments are crop specific. Half of U.S. farms are ineligible for the $5 billion distributed each year because they don't grow commodity crops.

Counter-cyclical payments—These compensate farmers when the price of commodity crops drops below a target price established by Congress. Also tied to historical commodity base acres. Producers can even receive payments for crops they are no longer growing.

Marketing assistance loans—Producers take out these loans, using their commodity crops as collateral, then hold the crops to sell as prices rise. If prices fall below the loan repayment rate, however, the government will accept crops as payment. Producers may receive a loan deficiency payment, or LDP, to cover any gap between the market price and guaranteed price.

Dairy subsidies—The Milk Income Loss Contract (MILC) program compensates dairy producers when the average monthly price of milk falls below government targets. USDA purchases surplus dairy products to siphon off excess supply. Milk prices are also artificially controlled through marketing orders, which set minimum prices that handlers must pay for milk in specified areas. Restrictions on dairy imports also limit supplies to boost milk prices.

Sugar program—Quotas limit the amount of sugar that can be imported, and from where, to protect America's corn and beet growers. These can hurt unsubsidized farmers in other countries because putting the U.S. market off limits deflates prices.

Livestock supports—Environmental Quality Incentives Program offers hundreds of thousands of dollars in cost-share assistance to help Concentrated Animal Feedlot Operations to comply with clean air and water regulations. Food animal producers receive assistance through a suite of other programs: Livestock Compensation Program, Emergency Livestock Feed Assistance, Livestock Emergency Assistance Program, and the Livestock Indemnity Program.

Federal purchase programs—The U.S. government purchases surplus meat, eggs, dairy, vegetables, fruits, grains, and other farm products for distribution to the National School Lunch Program and various food assistance programs.

Crop insurance—Taxpayers pay about 60 percent of crop insurance premiums that cover nearly 80 percent of insurable acres. This system of risk-free farming is being rapidly expanded. Critics say it encourages expansion of crop production into highly sensitive marginal lands and is just another taxpayer financed income transfer.

Disaster assistance—Average Crop Revenue Election (ACRE) is a revenue loss guarantee. In recent years, the program has paid nearly $800 million per year to farmers enrolled in the program. The Supplemental Revenue Assistance Payments Program (SURE) reimburses total crop revenue loss for the entire farm. These can be supplemented with ad hoc emergency disaster funding.

Ethanol subsidies—Refiners get 45 cents for every gallon of ethanol they blend with gasoline, costing taxpayers $6 billion a year. Ethanol imports are hit with a $0.54 per gallon tariff and a 2.5 percent ad valorem tax.

4. Promises Broken:
The Two Lives of Every Farm Bill…

Every Farm Bill goes through two distinct phases. First comes the authorization of the bill itself–technically the reauthorization of the existing bill dating back to the 1930s along with the introduction of any new programs. The Senate and House Agriculture Committees negotiate a balance among the many competing interests served by the Farm Bill and provide directions on how taxpayer funding should be allocated. The result is essentially a set of promises made by Congress about the direction of U.S. farming and food policy.[1]

Some programs acquire "mandatory funding" status in the reauthorization process, a signal that support for these programs should be made available throughout the term of the legislation. Other programs receive "discretionary funding" status, meaning their fate rests on the Farm Bill's second phase–the yearly *appropriations* process.

The final say on whether a Farm Bill program actually receives money rests with the Agriculture Appropriations Subcommittees of the Senate and House Appropriations Committees. These subcommittees set spending levels and thus determine the yearly survival of the discretionary Farm Bill programs. But their powers don't end there. The Appropriation Subcommittees can also pass changes in funding to the "mandatory" programs. If Congress approves such changes through the annual Agricultural Appropriations legislation, the Farm Bill's funding directives for that year are overridden. *Flat funding* is one inside-the-Beltway term used to describe this process. *ChIMPS*, short for Changes in Mandatory Program Spending, is another. (So much for those supposed mandatory dollars promised for land conservation, organic agriculture research, or expanding farmers markets!)

Flat-funding: when the moneys authorized for certain programs are cut in the appropriations process.

As a rule of thumb, commodity price supports are the only untouchable spending categories in the appropriations process. If anything, commodity growers successfully lobby for more money, not less, through supplemental disaster payments in response to floods, droughts, market fluctuations, or other circumstances.[2] Programs that serve the broader public, however–conservation incentives, sustainable agriculture research funds, beginning farmer supports, farm-to-school distribution arrangements, even food assistance for mothers and children, and so on–are historically the first on the chopping block.

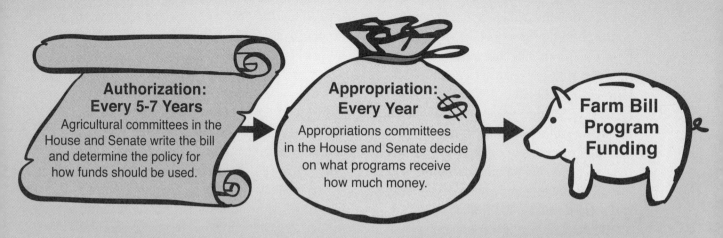

Figure 4

The Two Lives of Every Farm Bill

**Authorization:
Every 5-7 Years**
Agricultural committees in the House and Senate write the bill and determine the policy for how funds should be used.

**Appropriation:
Every Year**
Appropriations committees in the House and Senate decide on what programs receive how much money.

**Farm Bill
Program
Funding**

Flat funding, ChIMPing, and other forms of budget tinkering don't necessarily end with the annual appropriations process. In response to a projected deficit, Congress can also demand "budget reconciliation," forcing committees to recalculate their budgets and further decrease spending for mandatory and discretionary programs. After the 2002 Farm Bill passed, the reconciliation process tilted spending even further toward mega-agriculture, slashing at conservation and farm-to-school programs, while giving away billions in loan deficiency and counter-cyclical payments to compensate commodity growers for low market prices. Such cuts have long-lasting budgetary effects. When the baseline for a program is reduced in the middle of a Farm Bill, this can automatically trigger new lower spending levels in the next omnibus Farm Bill legislation.

The importance of the yearly money battles cannot be overstated. Regardless of promises in the Farm Bill, if no money is appropriated to carry out the work, the program is dead. A relatively recent example was the Conservation Security Program, which later morphed into the Conservation Stewardship Program (CSP) in 2008.[3] This initiative to reward farmers for environmental stewardship (rather than maximizing yields and acreage) was the primary concession offered to an alliance of conservationists and sustainable farming advocates during the 2002 Farm Bill negotiations. It was widely heralded as the best way to reform U.S. farm policies, with new supports based on green payments—financial incentives for landowners to maximize environmental benefits

Budget Reconciliation—a budget cutting exercise that can affect authorized program funding levels in the middle of a Farm Bill cycle.

like stable soil, clean water, and species protection. It represented a whole new conservation approach to farm support, by "rewarding the best and motivating the rest," and offering subsidies to a population of small producers long ignored because of the focus on commodity agriculture. Among other practices, qualifying participants had to actively prevent manure from polluting waterways, limit fertilizers from entering streams, minimize or eliminate pesticide use, improve energy efficiency, and set aside habitat for wildlife.

But flat-funding of conservation programs is sadly typical. The 2002 Farm Bill promised that CSP would have funding status equal to the Commodity Title and that all U.S. farmers would be able to apply for conservation related farm supports. That never happened. In fiscal year 2005, Farm Bill conservation programs were cut by nearly one-third, meaning that the backlog of qualified, under-funded applications to protect habitat on both agricultural and nonagricultural lands far exceeded support. Further slices to the CSP budget occurred in 2007, with $113 million taken from what had been promised. Things have only gotten more dire for the Conservation Title. The Environmental Quality Incentives Program funding was cut by nearly $300 million in 2010 alone.[4]

As deficit concerns escalated in 2011, budget appropriators slashed $500 million from conservation programs. The hemorrhaging continued in appropriations for 2012, when $1 billion was taken from so-called mandatory funds for CSP, EQIP, Wetlands Reserve Program, and other programs. On top of these cuts, renewable energy program budgets were reduced by nearly $300 million in 2012. Commodity subsidies suffered no such losses in 2011 or 2012, driving home the point that conservation programs are disproportionally ChIMPed compared to most other Farm Bill spending categories.

In addition to budget slashing, appropriations committees often assume interpretive legislative powers. For example, the Agriculture Appropriations Committee pushed back the implementation of the "mandatory" Country of Origin Labeling program (COOL)—established to inform consumers where their perishable foods originated—for four years, from September 2004 to September 2008. They also tinkered with organic standards by voting to allow non-organic-certified additives and ingredients in certified organic processed foods. Changes to the organic standards were ultimately dropped due to significant public resistance.

Authorization of the Farm Bill signals the beginning—not the end—of the annual *appropriation* struggles that continue through every five- to seven-year process. If any constituency (besides that of commodity producers) hopes to see promised Farm Bill funds, they must be prepared to fight tooth and nail every year.

Figure 5

Annual Agribusiness Lobbying

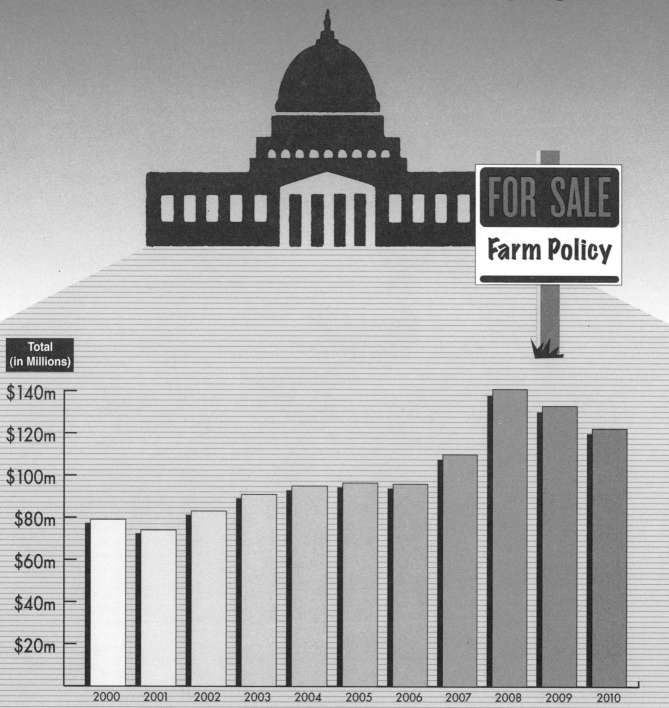

Total
(in Millions)

$140m
$120m
$100m
$80m
$60m
$40m
$20m

2000 2001 2002 2003 2004 2005 2006 2007 2008 2009 2010

FOR SALE
Farm Policy

Source: The Center for Responsive Politics

5. Where It All Started

The idea of a nation built by hard-working, God-fearing farmers taps a deep nerve in America. In 1801, when Thomas Jefferson became the United States' third president, 95 percent of the population of the young nation made their full-time living from agriculture. Jefferson envisioned the United States' democracy as orbiting around a citizenry of yeomen farmers. He wrote:

Cultivators of the earth are the most valuable citizens. They are the most vigorous, the most independent, the most virtuous and they are tied to the country and wedded to its liberty and interests by the most lasting bonds. I think our governments will remain virtuous for many centuries so long as they are chiefly agricultural.[1]

Half a century later, Abraham Lincoln extended this vision by establishing the railroad land grants, the Morrill Land Grant College Act of 1862, and the Homestead Act of 1862, all intended to spread independence, encourage settlement, and foster stability.

But as the decades wore on, wave upon wave of new settlers, bringing with them crops, domesticated livestock, and farming methods often not well suited to the land, exploited the continent's natural resources. By the early decades of the 20th century, more than half of the population had moved off the farm, and it was becoming clear that Jefferson's notion of an agrarian democracy was giving way to an urban industrial society with fewer and fewer farmers growing its food. For many, fewer people working in agriculture was a sure sign of prosperity as it meant a growth of manufacturing and service sectors of the economy.

America during the Great Depression was a hungry nation, whose most valuable natural resource—the soil—was literally blowing away in catastrophic fashion.

It took the Dust Bowl and the Great Depression to bring on total collapse of the agrarian-democratic ideal. By the 1930s, one in four Americans still lived on farms, but increasing numbers of tenant farmers and sharecroppers were being forced from their land or pushed into desperate poverty. Farm foreclosures had become commonplace. Drought, searing heat, dust storms, floods, monopolistic and unfair market practices also took a punishing toll. The nation's most valuable agricultural resource—the soil—was literally blowing away. On a single Sunday afternoon in 1935, for example, a storm barreling through the Texas Panhandle swept 300,000 tons of topsoil into the air—twice the volume of soil excavated during the entire construction of the Panama Canal.[2] It ravaged the countryside, choking people and animals, blanketing houses and cars. By most accounts, the United States was becoming a cauldron of civil unrest. In *The Grapes of Wrath*, John Steinbeck described the situation this way:

> *And the dispossessed, the migrants, flowed into California, two hundred and fifty thousand, and three hundred thousand. Behind them new tractors were going on the land and the tenants were being forced off. And new waves were on the way, new waves of the dispossessed and homeless, hard, intent, and dangerous...[3]*

Ironically, the farm crisis of the 1930s, like the Dust Bowl, had been triggered by overplanting. A decade of zealous and speculative field expansion, combined with technological advances such as tractors and nitrogen fertilizers synthesized from natural gas, resulted in chronic overproduction of most crops. Oversupply of crops also meant low prices. The growing disparity between low income levels in rural areas and the rising economic power in the cities created an ever-widening gap in American society.[4] The world was rapidly changing. While low crop prices directly benefited distributors, processors, and monopolists who were increasingly controlling the food system, the U.S. agrarian culture and economy were unraveling. In order to stay afloat, farmers and sharecroppers planted more and more acreage. But this just further oversaturated the markets, exacerbated land abuse, and dropped crop prices below what it cost to produce them. Total farm income decreased by two-thirds between 1929 and 1932. Six of every ten farms had been mortgaged to survive, and many did not make it. In the single year of 1932, five of every one hundred farms in Iowa were foreclosed and sold at auction.[5] In 1933, the price of corn plummeted to $0—as grain elevators simply stopped buying surplus corn altogether.[6] In Le Mar, Iowa, a group of angry farmers dragged a judge from his bench and threatened to hang him unless he refused to rule on cases that would result in a family losing its farm. Leaders of the mob were eventually jailed. This did not mean there were not some advantages to living in the country at this time, however. After the Wall Street crash, at least farm families could grow most of their own food, something urban folks could not do.

From these extraordinary circumstances, the first Farm Bill emerged and became one of the most ambitious social, cultural, and economic programs ever attempted by the U.S. government. On March 16, 1933, President Franklin Delano Roosevelt addressed Congress about this cornerstone of his New Deal agenda:

> *I tell you frankly that this is a new and untrod path, but I tell you with equal frankness that an unprecedented condition calls for the trial of a new means to rescue agriculture. If a fair administrative trial of it is made and it does not produce the hoped for results I shall be the first to acknowledge it and advise you.*

Administered by Secretary of Agriculture Henry A. Wallace, the early Farm Bill responded directly to a number of crises:

• Rock-bottom crop prices due to overproduction;

- Widespread hunger;
- Catastrophic erosion and soil loss due to prolonged drought and poor land stewardship;
- Unavailability of credit and insurance to subsistence farmers;
- Need for electricity, water, and infrastructure in rural communities;
- Unfair export policies prohibiting free and fair trade; and
- Increasing civil unrest.

Henry Wallace was a gifted lifelong farmer, a vegetarian, and a spiritual seeker, whose father had also served as a Secretary of Agriculture. Under Wallace's direction, the USDA blossomed into one of the largest arms of the government, with more than 146,000 employees and a budget of more than $1 billion. (USDA yearly budgets now reach well over $100 billion, but still less than 2 percent of the total federal budget.)

One of the driving principles of Wallace's administration was the creation of a farm support program based on a concept known as the "Ever-Normal Granary." This initiative took its historical precedent from ancient times, traceable to both Confucian China and the biblical story of Joseph.[7] The idea was straightforward, but politically controversial. The government would purchase and stockpile surplus crops and livestock during good years as a protection against dwindling supply in lean times. This helped to accomplish two important goals: (1) raising market prices for farmers by contracting supply; and (2)

distributing meat and grain products in times of need.

In addition, farmers participating in federally supported programs were required to idle a certain percentage of their historical base acreage, in an attempt to prevent overproduction. Author Michael Pollan explains how the early programs worked to regulate markets, such as the early Marketing Assistance Loan:

For storable commodities such as corn, the government established a target price based on the cost of production, and whenever the market price dropped below the target, the farmer was given a choice. Instead of dumping the corn into a weak market (thereby weakening it further), the farmer could take out a loan from the government—using his crop as collateral—that allowed him to store his grain until prices recovered. At that point he sold the corn and paid back the loan; if corn prices stayed low, he could elect to keep the money he'd borrowed and, in repayment, give the government his corn, which would then go into something that came to be called, rather quaintly, the "Ever-Normal Granary."[8]

Early Farm Bill programs were also attempts at maintaining fair markets by serving as a balance between farmers and large distributors. Because non-perishable commodities can be stored for a long time, large companies have the ability to withhold crops to keep prices high or flood commodity markets to artificially suppress prices. By increasing supply they can drive the price down when they want to buy commodities from farmers. Alternatively, they can drive the price up by making supply scarce when they want to sell. When commodity programs were first established, writes Scott Marlowe of the Rural Advancement Foundation International, the government acknowledged that without its intervention, companies could drive the price so low that it would be impossible for farmers to survive. Thus, early commodity programs were designed in part to counteract the domination of powerful corporations in agricultural markets.

Government involvement in the food system, however, did not begin and end with credit, price supports, and grain warehousing. Wallace's vision for farm policy included a range of departments and programs that, taken together, combined to make up an integrated food, farming, and stewardship platform. The Soil Conservation Service (originally the Soil Erosion Service and today the Natural Resources Conservation Service) addressed erosion control with alternative methods of tillage, cover cropping, crop rotation, and fertilization. In coordination with state agencies, more than 3,000 soil demonstration districts were established, primarily at the county level, to promote agricultural practices to combat Dust Bowl conditions. Participation in government subsidy programs required farmers to sign contracts agreeing to production control and conservation programs. Land-use incentives helped regulate crop acreage and maximize the fallowing and recovery

of fields. Programs were specifically tailored to assist sharecroppers and the rural poor. Credit and crop insurance programs met the early and late season needs of farmers. Research into plant and animal diseases along with new varieties and uses of crops led to critical innovations for farmers. Food relief and school lunch programs were part of an overall policy to provide a baseline of hunger and nutritional assistance for an extremely needy population.

Despite a demonstrated seven-times "multiplier effect" whereby every government dollar spent generated seven more in the overall economy, New Deal agriculture reforms were controversial from the outset.[9] Many farmers considered hunger relief both a shameful charity and a threat to free markets. Helping the needy was somehow perceived as un-American. As a consequence, in the early years of the Farm Bill, millions of young hogs purchased by the government to restrict supply (bump up prices) and feed the hungry never reached their intended beneficiaries. Instead they were slaughtered and dumped in the Missouri River. Likewise, millions of gallons of milk were poured into the streets rather than nourishing the famished.[10] Not until the term relief was dropped from the name of food distribution programs and replaced with the Federal Surplus Commodities Corporation were they ultimately accepted by powerful farmer coalitions. Surplus commodities could at last be distributed by the boxcar load to counties, schools, welfare agencies, charitable

NATION'S FIRST WATERSHED PROJECT

This point is near the center of the 90,000 acre Coon Creek Watershed, the nation's first large-scale demonstration of soil and water conservation. The area was selected for this purpose by the U.S. Soil Conservation Service (then Soil Erosion Service) in October 1933. Technicians of the S.C.S. and the University of Wisconsin pooled their knowledge with experiences of local farm leaders to establish a pattern of land use now prevalent throughout the midwest. Planned practices in effect include improvement of woodlands, wildlife habitat and pastures, better rotations and fertilization, strip cropping, terracing, and gully and stream bank erosion control. The outcome is a tribute to the wisdom, courage and foresight of the farm families who adopted the modern methods of conservation farming illustrated here.

Erected 1955

Coon Valley Wisconsin, 1930s

This historic photo documents the collapse of the Coon Creek Watershed in Coon Valley, Wisconsin during the Dust Bowl era. The valley was also the site of the first Farm Bill conservation programs.

institutions, etc.

In 1936, the Supreme Court ruled that initial programs to limit acreage and set target prices for upland cotton were unconstitutional, though marketing loans and deficiency payments (to boost farmer income up to a pre-set target price) were later upheld. Farmers themselves seem to have been conflicted about this emerging agricultural order. Historian Bernard DeVito wrote that "farmers throughout the West were always demanding further government help and then furiously denouncing the government for paternalism, and trying to avoid regulation."[11] A decade prior to the 1930s Farm Bill programs, H. L. Mencken said of American farmers, "When the going is good for him he robs the rest of us up to the extreme limit of our endurance; when the going is bad, he comes up bawling for help out of the public till....There has never been a time, in good season or bad, when his hands were not itching for more."[12]

Henry Wallace, meanwhile, moved on from Secretary of Agriculture to become vice president during the second term of Franklin Roosevelt, and his vision for an integrated farm and food policy was never completed. A genuine attempt had been made to enact policies that brought balanced abundance to the people, protected against shortages, and buffered farmers against losses with loan and insurance programs. And the two foundations of today's Farm Bill—nutrition assistance and aid to farmers—were firmly established.

Ultimately, however, these programs could not solve agriculture's looming challenge: overproduction in a rapidly globalizing and industrializing food system.

6. Family Farms to Mega-Farms

After World War II, a great deal of America's 5 million farms remained alike in many respects. They were similar in size with a fair degree of surrounding natural habitat, raising a diversity of marketable crops depending on the growing region, including livestock (for meat, dairy, eggs, and fertilizer), honeybees (for pollination and honey), and other products. Agricultural policy was likewise diverse: more than 100 commodities received some form of federal price support, mainly in the form of loans. All that would soon change in ways few could have ever predicted.

The technological and industrial capacities developed during the war were unleashed upon the civilian economy, and agriculture became one of the primary outlets. Tractors replaced horses, taking on tank-like power. Chemicals were concocted into a slew of pesticides, herbicides, and synthetic fertilizers. Squadrons of crop dusting planes were deployed in the Cold War effort to meet rising global demand for food. Plant breeding also evolved, creating high-yielding hybrid grains tailored to these shifts in chemical inputs and mechanical growing and harvesting. These unprecedented gains in farm productivity came to be widely known as the Green Revolution.

Farmers who had maintained wild or semi-wild borders around and between fields (in accordance with the best practices of former administrations), tore out shelterbelts, windbreaks, filter strips, and contours. Wetlands were drained and forests obliterated, often with direct technical assistance and financial aid from the USDA Soil Conservation Service.

Even as yields shot up, farming became more expensive to undertake, and not necessarily any more profitable, except for the largest operations. Between 1950 and 1970, according to agricultural historian Paul Conkin, the workforce in agriculture declined by 50 percent, while the total value of farm output rose by 40 percent.[1] Fewer people could harvest much more food–and this oversupply led to consistently low prices. Employment in the manufacturing and service sectors led to a time of unprecedented prosperity. In Washington, Congress struggled mightily to find an answer to the "farm problem": chronically low income across rural America.

Government policies provided an essential platform for these changes to take place. The Farm Bills of the New Deal era had opened the federal treasury's coffers to agriculture. Despite a few attempts to return to a free market system, the emergency measures of the 1930s and 40s gradually became institutionalized, and ultimately gave way to annual taxpayer support for an increasingly powerful farm lobby. For the next 50 years, the federal government maintained a system of production control and grain reserves along with loan benefits and price supports for farmers. Conservation programs continued, and in some cases were expanded. But with continual gains in output due to mechanization and industrialization, even taking land out of production did little to limit surpluses or raise prices. Farms were growing in size through consolidation and becoming more prolific, with yields steadily breaking records. Like other businesses, agriculture was also becoming more specialized. In the decades following World War II, it became increasingly rare even for family farmers to keep chickens, hogs, or dairy cows for market. With so many employment opportunities outside of agriculture in the booming postwar economy, many farmers left altogether or farmed part-time. Retiring farmlands provided for both the rise of agribusiness and an aggressive expansion of suburban housing developments around the country.

By the 1970s, government agriculture policy was being shaped by a controversial Secretary of Agriculture named Earl Butz, who, at the end of his career, earned a reputation for uttering offensive racial and religious insults, was convicted of tax evasion, and launched a campaign to drive the final nails into the coffin of the American family farm culture. In response to a rare period of surging prices and foreign demand, followed by a secret "Russian grain deal" in 1972, Butz decided that export markets were going to solve America's chronic problem of oversupply and low prices.[2] America would feed the world.

Under Butz, progress was measured by increasing yields, with little attention paid to any harmful effects of monoculture and the industrialization of agriculture. He spurred on farmers to "Get big or get out," "Adapt or die," and "Farm fencerow to fencerow." In addition to production loans, a new form of income compensation—deficiency payments to boost income when prices fell—was established. Larger operators were heavily favored in the new system. America's strategic grain reserves were nearly emptied out as the boom cycle continued. To add acreage, farmers leased lands or bought out smaller growers. Those who had maintained wild or semi-wild field borders (long encouraged by former administrations), tore out shelterbelts, windbreaks, filter strips, and contour terraces. Wetlands were drained and forests obliterated (often with direct technical assistance and financial aid from the USDA Soil Conservation Service). The rise of "clean farming" meant the loss of naturally buffered aquatic systems and non-cultivated habitat for native pollinators and beneficial insects. The American farm assumed a factory-like efficiency.

Animal agriculture epitomized this shift in farming as the animals were taken off the land and housed in windowless buildings by the thousands and tens of thousands. Rather than grazing on pasture, local forage crops, or local food waste, these animals in their factory-like

Figure 6

"Get Big or Get Out"
Fewer Mid-Sized Family Farms, More Mega-Farms

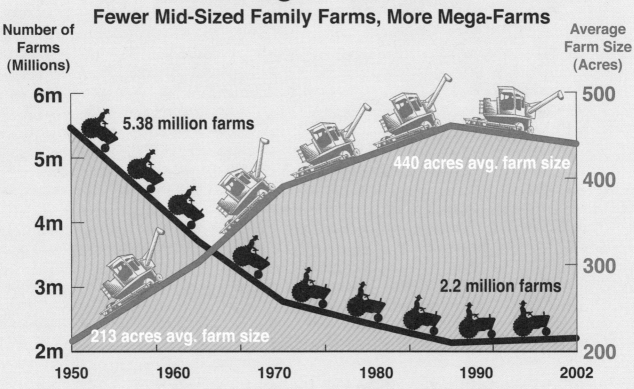

Number of Farms (Millions)

Average Farm Size (Acres)

5.38 million farms

440 acres avg. farm size

213 acres avg. farm size

2.2 million farms

6m — 500
5m — 400
4m — 300
3m — 200
2m

1950   1960   1970   1980   1990   2002

Source: USDA Economic Research Service: Structure and Finances of U.S. Farms: 2010 Family Farm Report

The "Green" Revolution

"The precolonial famines of Europe raised the question: What would happen when the planet's supply of arable land ran out? We have a clear answer. In about 1960 expansion hit its limits and the supply of unfarmed, arable lands came to an end. There was nothing left to plow. What happened was grain yields tripled.

The accepted term for this strange turn of events is the green revolution, though it would be more properly labeled the amber revolution, because it applied exclusively to grain—wheat, rice, and corn. Plant breeders tinkered with the architecture of these three grains so that they could be hypercharged with irrigation water and chemical fertilizers, especially nitrogen. This innovation meshed nicely with the increased "efficiency" of the industrialized factory-farm system…it also disrupted long-standing patterns of rural life worldwide, moving a lot of no-longer-needed people off the land."

—From Richard Manning, "The Oil We Eat"

Figure 7.

BIG AG

Market Share Controlled by Top Four Producers

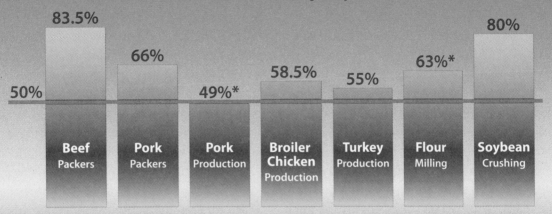

| 83.5% | 66% | 49%* | 58.5% | 55% | 63%* | 80% |
| Beef **Packers** | Pork **Packers** | Pork **Production** | Broiler Chicken **Production** | Turkey **Production** | Flour **Milling** | Soybean **Crushing** |

50%

Markets are considered concentrated if the share controlled by the top four producers exceeds 20 percent, and very highly concentrated if the share approaches or exceeds 50 percent.

Source: Hendrickson and Heffernan, Concentration of Agricultural Markets, April 2007. *Hendrickson and Heffernan, 2005.

warehouses had their feed brought to them, sometimes transported across vast distances. The heavy output of waste from such intensive concentrations of animals became a toxic liability rather than a replenishing fertilizer as it was spewed across the landscape, often finding its way into groundwater and stream channels. By the mid-1970s, Concentrated Animal Feeding Operations (CAFOs) were identified by the Environmental Protection Agency as point sources of pollution because of increasing concern over industrial agriculture's negative impacts on the country's rivers, lakes, and streams. Between 1980 and 2000, the percentage of U.S. livestock produced in factory farms increased dramatically. Nowhere

was this more astounding than in the pork sector, where the number of U.S. hog operations fell by a factor of almost 10, from just under 500,000 to about 60,000 between 1982 and 2006.[3] But the number of animals stayed roughly the same.

It could be argued that these mid-20th century changes in agriculture were serving a higher purpose. People all over the world were worried about an imminent shortage of global food stocks and potential famine. So the New Deal's Ever-Normal Granary programs of loan-based, county-by-county supply regulation, and grain reserves, were eventually phased out in favor of payments designed to reward farmers for maximizing crop yields. Farmers

6. Family Farms to Mega-Farms

specialized their operations and plowed up more acreage–even marginally productive lands. Debt leveraging became business as usual. And when prices inevitably plummeted once again, bankruptcies and foreclosures followed, along with a rise in depression, suicides, and rural outmigration.[4]

By the early 1980s, large grain handlers like Cargill and Archer Daniels Midland and other agribusiness giants were essentially writing the Farm Bills for their own benefit.[5] With the elimination of price floors and acreage controls, they got a steady oversupply of cheap commodity crops that they could trade internationally or process into value-added products.[6] There was money to be made in agriculture, to be sure, but not for the family farmer.

Despite a $20 billion program to boost farm income in 1985, 16 percent of farms were financially stressed. That year alone, about 300,000 farmers sold out and left agriculture entirely.[7] The big got bigger and the small and medium-sized independent farms–often referred to as the "Agriculture of the Middle"–disappeared.

The Butz era irrevocably changed the scale and face of agriculture. With the move from family farms to mega-farms, agriculture had become increasingly dominated by concentrated corporate interests in almost every sector. American farmers assumed a manufacturing mentality. They became low-cost producers of the industrial ingredients of modern food. As with manufacturing, econo-mies of scale allow the largest operations to spread fixed costs over a large swath of assets. And with industrialization came whole new sets of problems: carbon-intensive production; widespread environmental damage to soil, air, waterways, and marine life; the shuttering of entire farm communities; overuse of antibiotics and hormones in animal factory operations; disappearing grasslands, forests, and wetlands; and a rise in the number of endangered species and impacted fisheries.

During this time a sustainable agriculture movement also began to take root in America as a counter to the trend toward agribusiness. Inspired by the promise of living self-sufficiently on independent farms and concerned about an oil crisis, an estimated several million Americans went back to the land to work on farms, communes, and other arrangements during the late 1960s and 1970s. This "Back to the Land" movement was led by innovative, organic producers motivated around ideals of a clean environment, healthy food, and vital communities rather than profit and market domination as a reaction to an industrial food production system. Their efforts were unfunded by Farm Bill programs and based on sharing of information between growers. In the end, many back-to-the-landers found self-sufficient farm life extremely difficult or unsustainable without some sort of economic safety net–either strong markets or the type of taxpayer support that commercial farmers had received for decades. Ironically, many were replaced by yet another wave of rural refugees: immigrants from Mexico and Latin America unable to earn a living as farmers and farm workers in their respective countries. In the four decades after the sustainable agriculture movement began, those organic farmers that did remain succeeded in launching a modern food and farming revolution of their own. Organic products have become one of the fastest growing market segments in the food industry over the last decade, a movement that is now global and has finally been acknowledged with some degree of USDA Farm Bill funding and oversight.

Early in the 21st century the United States has more than 2 million farmers but only a quarter of them—450,000 operations—report sales of $50,000 or more.[8] Of course, food production doesn't only take place at the farm level. It involves increasingly complex systems for processing, marketing, and distributing, which according to the USDA Economic Research Service together consume 88 cents of every dollar spent on food. Less than 12 cents of every food dollar actually returns to the farm sector. The top three or four conglomerates in grain handling, corn exports, beef packing, pork packing, pork production, turkey production, broiler chicken production, and flour milling control at least 40 percent of their respective markets.[9] (See Figure 7, "Big Ag.") Oligopolies also dominate the crop insurance industry, the seed business, food retailing, food processing, fertilizer production, and ethanol manufacture, among many others.[10]

Even conservative financial institutions recognize that commodity subsidies have led to excessive corporate concentration that is failing rural communities. The Federal Reserve Bank of Kansas, hardly a liberal think tank, reported in 2005 that:

> *Commodity programs wed farming regions to an ongoing pattern of economic consolidation. It should not be surprising, therefore, that the very places that depend most on federal farm payments also happen to be places where economic consolidation is happening apace....Traditional programs simply do not provide the economic lift that farming regions need going forward.*[11]

In other words, what's good for mega-farms and mega-processors is usually not good for local and regional economies or their communities. The Federal Reserve Bank of Kansas also found that between 2000 and 2003, in nearly two-thirds of the counties that received heavy farm subsidies, the growth rate for job creation fell below the national average. A majority of heavily subsidized counties also lost population.

And so it goes: the lingering damage of Farm Bills under Earl Butz.

6. Family Farms to Mega-Farms

7. The Farm Bill's Hunger Connection

Even more controversial than government intervention in agricultural markets was the other half of the Farm Bill equation: public food distribution or financial assistance for the needy. Until 1932, that responsibility lay solely at the feet of local communities and charities. Critics of food assistance programs believed hunger relief would lead the country irreversibly toward socialism and the dole. Even as crop surpluses and global competition spawned record low prices, and displaced farmers and sharecroppers waged protests and joined the staggering unemployment lines during the Great Depression, no resolution appeared to the paradox of want in the midst of overabundance.

The Federal Surplus Relief Corporation, created in 1933 as part of the Agricultural Adjustment Act (the first Farm Bill), was charged with purchasing, storing, and processing surplus food to relieve the hunger stemming from unemployment and to stabilize prices for farmers.[1] Although the distribution of surplus food didn't always function perfectly, this legislation established a lasting connection between Americans' nutritional health and the nation's farm policy. Later in the Depression the government initiated the first Food Stamp program. Recipients purchased one dollar's worth of orange stamps for a dollar and exchanged them for any foods they wanted. In addition, they received 50 cents worth of blue stamps. Relief came in the form of these free blue stamps that could only be spent on select seasonally available government surplus foods–i.e., dairy products, eggs, fruits, vegetables, and wheat flour.

Having witnessed rural poverty first-hand on the presidential campaign trail, Kennedy signed an executive order in the early months of his administration that revived the food stamp program.

America's entry into World War II effectively wiped out agricultural surpluses and mass unemployment, and the New Deal food distribution and assistance programs were phased out by 1943.[2] Policymakers remained acutely aware, however, of the hazards of undernourishment. During wartime, 40 percent of draftees had been rejected from military duty because of malnutrition. Hunger was no longer simply a moral or social issue, but a threat to national security. With broad bipartisan support, the federal government passed the National School Lunch Act in 1946. As its name implied, the act established school lunch programs–which included distribution of surplus commodities–throughout most public schools. It remains one of the largest and most heavily relied-upon public food assistance programs, with 30 million children receiving meals every school day.

Otherwise, the strong postwar economy coupled with flagging political and public awareness of the lingering problem of hunger in the U.S., led the government to largely abandon food assistance programs for years. It wasn't until the late 1950s that John F. Kennedy and a few other senators picked up the torch for federal hunger and nutrition assistance. Having witnessed rural poverty firsthand on the campaign trail, President Kennedy signed an executive order in the early months of his administration that revived the Food Stamp program in select counties.

In the spring of 1961, unemployed West Virginia miner Alderson Muncy and his wife Chloe were driven 25 miles to a grocery store where they were met by Secretary of Agriculture Orville Freeman and a television crew. The Muncys ceremoniously received $95 in food stamps to feed their family, including 13 children, and the modern era of nutrition assistance was born.

Tensions remained high, however, between Cold War conservatives and Great Society liberals, over the acceptability of persistent income supplements to farmers on the one hand and government food giveaways on the other.

As in the Depression era, the initial 1960s food stamps were offered at a discount rather than given free of charge. This "copayment" arrangement was intended to dignify recipients and deflect the idea that it was an act of welfare. (Food stamps without restrictions seemed to some legislators too

Hunger in America. Among the first acts of the Kennedy administration was to reinstate the food stamp program, which eventually changed the nature of Farm Bill politics.

much like "free money" that could be used to buy whatever one wanted, even though alcohol, tobacco, and imported foods were ineligible.) As the decade wore on, however, a new political force emerged in Farm Bill negotiations. Nutrition and food assistance advocates—a.k.a. the "hunger lobby—began to wield power, trading votes with "farm-bloc" representatives, and ultimately gaining passage of the Food Stamp Act of 1964, expanding the program to reach 500,000 people. More importantly, the housing of responsibility and oversight of food assistance within the U.S. Department of Agriculture would prove to be an invaluable bargaining arrangement for the agency and key power brokers in future decades as Farm Bills evolved. Farm programs benefitted rural states with relative-

7. The Farm Bill's Hunger Connection

Figure 8

Hunger Safety Net for the Poor

$1.3 b

Other*
1.9%

8.8%

Women,
Infants,
Children
$6.5 b

3.4%

School
Breakfast
$2.5 b

13.6%

School
Lunch
$10 b

Food Stamp
Program (SNAP)
$53.1 b

72.3%

Average Annual Food and Nutrition Spending, FY 2008–2010

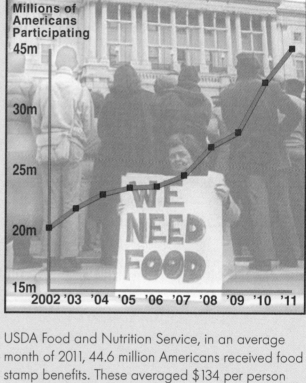

Food Stamp Rising Demand

Millions of
Americans
Participating

45m

30m

25m

20m

15m

2002 '03 '04 '05 '06 '07 '08 '09 '10 '11

Hunger in America. The Food and Nutrition Title is by far the largest Farm Bill spending category. Also funded by the Child Nutrition Act, food and nutrition programs make up over 70 percent of all USDA spending. There is a valid reason for this. The number of households classified as "Food Insecure," a technical term for going hungry, is experiencing significant increases every year. Supplemental Nutrition Assistance Program (SNAP) participation is also on a steady rise. According to the USDA Food and Nutrition Service, in an average month of 2011, 44.6 million Americans received food stamp benefits. These averaged $134 per person per month, an increase related to the stimulus package. Total spending for SNAP reached $68.2 billion in 2010 and even higher in 2011. The hunger crisis could be far worse than these figures suggest. Typically only 60 to 70 percent of eligible individuals actually register for and receive Food Stamps.

*Other programs include: Puerto Rico Grant, Special Milk Program, Child/Adult Care Food Program, Summer Food Service Program, Child Nutrition State Administration, Commodity Supplemental, Food Distribution on Indian Reservations, NSIP Elderly Feeding, TEFAP Emergency Food Assistance, Disaster Feeding, Charitable Institutes.

Sources: Supplemental Nutrition Assistance Program Data System, Time-Series Data; Annual Summary of FNS Programs

ly low populations. Nutrition assistance programs were increasingly popular among legislators representing large urban areas. These two lobbying forces would largely shape food and farm policies moving forward.

Hunger, nutrition, and civil rights advocates soon realized the potential for a further expanded Food Stamp program to provide a food safety net for the least fortunate in a country with huge class divides. Their cause was heightened in 1968 when a groundbreaking CBS documentary, "Hunger in America," hosted by Charles Kuralt, exposed appalling scenes of poverty and malnutrition across the country, among whites in Virginia, blacks in Alabama, Navajos in Arizona, and Latinos in Texas. Senators George McGovern, a liberal Democrat, and Bob Dole, a conservative Republican, spearheaded a special committee on hunger. Nutrition assistance soon became an integral part of Farm Bill politics, with both annual appropriations and direct payments to families steadily increasing. By 1971, powerful public interest lobbying organizations such as the Food Research Action Center (FRAC) and the Community Nutrition Institute (CNI) formed to defend these hard-fought gains during legislative negotiations.

Food Stamps (known since 2008 as the Supplemental Nutrition Assistance Program, or by its most recent upbeat acronym, SNAP) have been part of every subsequent Farm Bill, attempting to ensure that most low-income Americans receive a monthly stipend that affords them a low-cost nutritional-

ly adequate diet. By the mid-1970s, nearly 20 million Americans, or around 10 percent of the population, received assistance. In 1977, during the Carter Administration, Congress stopped requiring recipients to purchase stamps and distributed them for free. The program would come under assault at various times in subsequent administrations—during the Reagan Administration and in the Republican-led Congress of the mid-1990s in particular—with enrollment rising and falling along with the political perception of food assistance entitlements.

Today the Farm Bill's Food and Nutrition Title, which includes SNAP funding as well as other programs such as child nutrition assistance and emergency food distribution, is by far the largest chunk of money spent by Farm Bill programs. Over $75 billion was projected for SNAP in 2011, serving more than 45 million Americans. The stamps themselves (and much of the social stigma attached with food relief) are a thing of the past, having been replaced with plastic credit cards called Electronic Benefits Transfers, or EBTs.

One striking difference exists between the farm lobby and the hunger lobby. Thomas Forster, formerly with the Community Food Security Coalition in Washington, D.C., explains: "Along the way, benefits to farmers got subverted as the [crop] subsidies were increasingly channeled to the very largest producers, absentee landowners, and agribusiness and insurance corporations—often masquerading as family farmers. By contrast,

Figure 9

Struggling to Cope

Food Stamps Are A Lifeline for 45 Million Americans

Mother: Crystal S

They give me $376 in Food Stamps. To try to make it through a month you have to put cash to it; there's no way Food Stamps are gonna make it alone, it's not gonna work. With the money food stamps provide, I was able to feed her breakfast that morning. Without it what would she have eaten? She had cereal. She had milk. She didn't have to go without.

Mother: Shelly G

Let's say Welfare is giving me this money… every two weeks I get a check but I still have to make with these hands money. Because my kids still need to eat for those two weeks. So they say food banks… the food banks give you canned food. Who's gonna eat cans of tomato sauce? Nobody. I may do someone's hair and be able to get noodles with that tomato sauce to feed the kids, to feed myself.

Mother: Imani S

I was on my way to the overtime job that I was doing when I got my food stamps cut off. They had called me to work there for one day. So, I was thinking to myself, "Well, if I go down here this one day, are they going cut my food stamps off?" I really didn't know what to do. At the time I was walking through there, it made me think, "Was I going to get cut off again?" What kind of programs can the city do to help us stay on the food stamp program when we do extra work? I don't think it's fair for us to get reprimanded for doing something positive.

Mother: Melissa H

My son, he's already on the small side and he needs every bit of food that he can get to make him healthy, keep him healthy. He has failure to thrive. He has a bone deficiency that doesn't allow him to grow. He's only thirty pounds. And the kids know my food stamps got cut off. Because when they came home from school today, they didn't have their snacks. So they know that I didn't go to the market. I really didn't tell them why or anything like that, because I don't think they understand. But it affected them.

Source: Witnesses to Hunger Project, www.witnessestohunger.org. The Witness to Hunger Project allows mothers and caregivers of young children to document their experiences with hunger.

food policy has not been subverted from its original intent to serve as a hunger safety net for the poor."

While hunger advocates continue to fight to make sure food reaches populations in distress, a bitter irony remains: Farm Bill programs make sure Americans are fed, but not necessarily properly nourished. Addressing hunger is now widely recognized not simply as a matter of delivering calories. Rather it means providing consistent access to affordable nutrient-dense foods, including daily servings of fresh fruits, vegetables, and whole grains. Improving the diets of the more than 50 million Americans now classified as food insecure may be the largest challenge and opportunity for Farm Bill reforms in the decades ahead.

Indeed, SNAP plays a critical role in ensuring that basic nutritional (i.e., caloric) needs are met. Without food stamps, tens of millions of Americans–particularly children–could be suffering from hunger-related diseases. SNAP has demonstrably positive impacts on children, including: increasing their well-being, reducing or preventing food insecurity, reducing hospitalizations, improving birth outcomes, and raising test scores.

And yet, the program could be improved to better serve its recipients. It is important to recognize that SNAP does not reach all who need it or who are eligible for assistance. And it does not provide enough money to enable even purchasing the USDA's "Thrifty Food Plan" diet.[3] Perhaps most alarming, accord-ing to a 2009 study by Dr. Jay Zagorsky at Ohio State University, the longer an adult remains on SNAP benefits or food stamps, and the greater his or her dependence upon them for all food purchases, the higher the chance that he or she will become over-weight or obese.[4] The study found a link between food stamp use and weight gain, particularly among women, even after con-trolling for income and other factors. With extra body mass comes an increased vulner-ability to diabetes, hypertension, cardiovas-cular disease, and certain forms of cancer. While Dr. Zagorsky noted the need for more research in this area, his findings raise an important issue and highlight the potential benefits of improving SNAP.

Some reformers are taking a "carrot" approach, calling for an increase in pro-grams that double the purchasing power of SNAP recipients to buy fresh produce in farmers markets. Others argue for a "stick," such as eliminating the ability to use SNAP benefits to purchase sugar-sweetened bev-erages. The anti-hunger community has largely rebuffed any attempts to limit the free choice among Food Stamp recipients as an assault on personal dignity. Improving diets for SNAP recipients would not only increase their health and well-being, but also have economic ramifications. Economist Mark Zandi estimated that increasing food stamp budgets was one of the most effec-tive ways to stimulate a depressed economy. Every SNAP dollar spent generated a ripple effect of $1.73 throughout the economy.[5] Meanwhile, the health costs of overweight and obesity–including worker productivity declines–are estimated to be at least $164 billion annually.

Today, more than ever, we understand the link between the crops we grow, how their preparation or processing affects the nutrients they provide, and thus determines their long-term impacts on public health. The Farm Bill truly is a Food Bill. One of its stiffest challenges is to offer a basic nutritional safety net that meets the dietary guidelines recommended for all Americans, and at the same time involving the nation's farmers in providing that new future of food.

8. The Conservation Era Begins—Again

The 1972 deal to sell U.S. surplus grain to the Soviets—and subsequent commodity crop price spike—set off a decade-long fury of borrowing, speculation, and agricultural expansion (followed by the inevitable overproduction and price collapse). Particularly caught up in the euphoria were farmers in the Prairie Pothole Region, which spans parts of Iowa and Minnesota, the Dakotas, northeastern Montana, Saskatchewan, and Alberta. The Potholes Region—rolling hills and grasslands pocked by wetlands—is also called North America's duck factory, because up to 70 percent of waterfowl are hatched in this habitat. Farmers began draining wetlands to expand their harvest potential in the great plow-up inspired by the promise of new foreign grain markets.

Well-directed conservation efforts are arguably some of the very best tax dollars we can spend. When large continuous habitats are restored, they provide resilience against species loss, catastrophic weather events, and water shortages.

A prolonged drought in the Pothole region in the early 1980s laid bare the damage that had been done. The loss of vital habitat, combined with severe weather conditions, reduced the populations of ducks, pheasants, grouse, deer, and other species to record-low levels.

Legislators responded with the new conservation programs in the 1985 Farm Bill (formally the Food Security Act of 1985, but also frequently referred to as the "Environmental Farm Bill" or the "Environmental Act"). Funds were made available to enroll up to 37 million acres—approximately 10 percent of total U.S. farmed acreage—in the Conservation Reserve Program (CRP). This was, in essence, a contract with farmers to idle a certain amount of highly erodible land as set-aside acreage. That same Farm Bill included "Swamp Buster" and "Sod Buster" provisions. These "disincentive" programs immediately withdrew federal payments from farmers who drained wetlands ("Swamp Buster") or plowed up protected grasslands ("Sod Buster").

The global grain conglomerates hotly contested these conservation initiatives that had been championed by hunting, fishing and environmental groups, insisting that they would result in massive crop shortages. The next two decades, however, proved them wrong. Every year there were more farmers willing to idle fields than conservation funds available—and until the corn ethanol boom started in 2005, surpluses persisted and global commodity prices stayed low. According to Farm Bill conservation program expert Ferd Hoefner at the Sustainable Agriculture Coalition in Washington, D.C., in 2004, three out of every four farmers and ranchers applying to participate in Farm Bill conservation programs were rejected due to lack of

Conservation Milestones in the Farm Bill

1985 Conservation Compliance ("Swamp Buster" and "Sod Buster" provisions); Conservation Reserve Program; National Sustainable Agriculture Information Service (ATTRA); Low-Impact Sustainable Agriculture

1990 Sustainable Agriculture Research and Education Program; Integrated Farm Management Program; Wetlands Reserve Program; Water Quality Incentives Program; National Organic Program; Outreach Program for Socially Disadvantaged Farmers

1992 Beginning Farmer and Rancher Down Payment Loan Program; set-aside of loan funds for beginning farmers and ranchers

1996 Planting Flexibility; Environmental Quality Incentives Program; Farm and Ranch Lands Protection Program; Farmers and NGO representatives added to NRCS State Technical Committees; Fund for Rural America; Community Food Grants

1998 Initiative for Future Agriculture and Food Systems

2000 Insurance Non-discrimination Policy for sustainable and organic ag; Risk Management Education Program

2002 Conservation Security Program; Conservation Partnership and Cooperation; Wetlands Reserve Program increase; Increase in Value-Added Producer Grants to pay for local, sustainable and organic marketing and processing; Beginning Farmer Credit Reforms; Organic Farming Research; Organic Certification Cost Share; Farmers Market Promotion Program; Contract Agriculture Reform; Small- and Mid-Size Farm and Rural Research

2008 Conservation Stewardship Program; Biomass Research and Development

Source: National Sustainable Agriculture Coalition

funds. In fact, the 2004 backlog for conservation dollars exceeded the total funding available in 2005 by a three-to-one margin. Meanwhile, a study by the Natural Resource Conservation Service estimated an increase of nearly 26 million ducks and waterfowl in the Prairie Pothole region between 1992 and 2003, a success largely attributable to CRP land idling.[1]

After 1985, each successive Farm Bill added conservation programs. In 1990, the Wetlands Reserve Program (WRP) provided money to set aside and restore 1 million acres of wetlands.[2] While this could in no way compensate for the losses—500,000 acres per year—that had been occurring since the 1950s,[3] it targeted critical habitats for restoration that benefit a variety of species and protect the nation's aquatic systems.[4] Nearly 2 million acres of wetlands have been restored under the WRP, most under permanent or long-term easements. It is arguably the most successful and still among the neediest Farm Bill conservation programs.[5]

Pilot programs introduced in 1996 furthered the conservation emphasis. The Wildlife Habitat Incentive Program (WHIP) provides assistance for protecting sensitive species and restoring or maintaining critical habitats in farming regions. The Environmental Quality Incentive Program (EQIP) offers funds for a wide variety of environmental "improvements" and efforts to meet clean air and clean water regulations. Incentives and cost-shares cover measures such as soil erosion and air pollution reduction, forest replanting

Figure 10

Excess Demand for Limited Conservation Funds

Program	Year	Number of Unfunded Applications	Unfunded Application Dollars	Unfunded Application Acreage
Environmental Quality Incentives Program (EQIP)	2009	110,077	$1,361,337,261	No Data
Wildlife Habitat Incentives Program (WHIP)	2009	2,207	$34,764,187	No Data
Wetlands Reserve Program (WRP)	2005	3,204	$652,518,001	461,704
Grasslands Reserve Program (GRP)	2005	7,412	$981,070,482	4,970,528

Source: "Greenhouse Gas Mitigation and the USDA Conservation Programs," Agricultural Carbon Market Working Group, April 2011.

and thinning, and stream bank restoration. Thanks to lobbying from meat, egg, and dairy industries in the 2002 Farm Bill, however, hundreds of millions of precious EQIP dollars have been used to fund the construction of expensive manure lagoons, along with other dubious solutions to the problem of vast quantities of animal waste at industrial dairies, hog factories and feedlots.[6]

While demand for conservation programs has soared, funding remains modest, and such programs remain a prime target for the hatchets of appropriations committees and budget reconcilers. During the 2008 Farm Bill, the Wetlands Reserve Program, which mostly buys permanent easements to save and restore large swaths of critical habitat, suffered steep cuts, as did the Environmental Quality Incentives Program. For example, $500 million was slashed from conservation programs in 2011, while commodity spending at a time of unprecedented strong markets was left unscathed.[7] In addition, as markets for exportable commodities and biofuels strengthen, farmers are quick to beg release from land-idling contracts to cash in on high prices. So much for the social contract when there is money to be made.

Paying landowners to *not* grow crops may seem a counter-intuitive use of tax dollars unless it's viewed as a long-term investment in soil protection, habitat conservation, and the preservation of healthy water systems. In fact, well-directed conservation efforts are arguably some of the very best tax dollars we can spend. When large continuous habitats are restored, they provide resilience against species loss, catastrophic weather events, and water shortages. All of these efforts are vital to safeguarding our natural legacy for future generations, especially on lands being used for productive agriculture.

The market does not currently take into account all of the total costs of food production—known by economists as externalities. Conservation measures were in fact a requirement for all farmers enrolling in early Farm Bill programs, a policy well worth returning to. As the old saying goes, there is no free lunch. If we don't make the commitment to protect soils, streams, habitats now, we will surely pay later.

Paying the Polluters
Taxpayers Are Footing the Bill for Confined Animal Feeding Operations (CAFOs)

Massive dairies, mega–hog farms, poultry factories and battery operations, and other livestock feeding facilities house thousands (often tens or even hundreds of thousands) of animals, producing outputs of waste equivalent to the sewage volumes of small cities. Brother David Andrews of the National Catholic Rural Life Conference describes the problem as "a fecal flood."

The 2002 and 2008 Farm Bill Conservation Titles showered hundreds of millions of dollars on confinement animal factory feedlots (CAFOs), not only to clean up existing pollution, but also to fund new feedlots and expand old ones without accounting for their overall impacts on the environment. These Farm Bills mandated that 60 percent of the Environmental Quality Incentives Program (EQIP) budget be allocated to animal agriculture operators with the largest potential impact for remediation. This means preference is given to the most egregious bad actors, rather than healthy operations that might still have a need for improvements. In fact, CAFOs are eligible for up to 75 percent of costs up to $300,000 per owner (reduced from the 2002 cap of $450,000) to pay for hauling fees, building storage facilities for animal waste, and other costs of complying with regulations. Meanwhile, projects with organic production benefits are capped at $20,000 annually or $80,000 in any six-year period.

CAFOs first became eligible to receive EQIP funding at the same time that the Clean Water Act was expanded to address CAFO pollution issues. Thanks to hefty campaign contributions from agribusiness lobbies and the support of a few anti-pollution advocacy groups, Farm Bill conservation dollars are being diverted to build and fortify manure lagoons on corporate feedlots,[8] even as landowners eligible to protect wetlands, conserve invaluable habitat for wildlife, and provide other urgent environmental services are turned away due to a lack of funding.

Due to an abysmal lack of public data about the amounts of money distributed to CAFOs through the EQIP program, it is extremely difficult to understand the full scope of this government funded pay the polluter policy. Where information on specific contracts to industrial operations is available, it is troubling. In Becker County, Minnesota, for example, one producer received $285,500 through EQIP in 2003 to build a manure lagoon that was nearly 1 million cubic feet in size: approximately the size of 7 football fields 10 feet deep. In 2007, the average waste storage EQIP contract in Plymouth County, Iowa—one of the top hog-producing counties in the nation—was worth $89,174, more than twice the national average. And in Missouri, NRCS has approved a total of nearly $5 million in funding since 2003 for manure transfer payments alone—federal funding to move manure off the farm and out of the area because the operations produce too much waste to apply to surrounding cropland as fertilizer. In its book *CAFOs Uncovered* (2008), the Union of Concerned Scientists estimated that with just a paltry amount of information available to the public, the CAFO industry has received over $100 million per year in EQIP funding.

The issue raises a number of important concerns about the unwholesome connections between large livestock operations and Farm Bill subsidy programs.

1. **Taxpayer-funded CAFO infrastructure.** While enhancing water and air quality are indeed goals in the public's interest, should taxpayer funds be used to build the infrastructure for agribusiness to comply with regulations? Unfortunately, some politicians and even a few environmental organizations believe that the only way massive hog farms, beef, and poultry factory feedlots, and dairies will comply with regulations is if we pay them to do so. Construction loans and other financing mechanisms are one thing. These cost-share programs are corporate giveaways for some of the country's most horrendous polluters.[9]

2. **Compliance is not conservation.** EQIP funds come out of the Conservation Title of the Farm Bill. Misconstruing end-of-pipe factory farm pollution compliance as conservation is twisted logic. It's not benefiting the environment, but rather perpetuating environment-degrading

industrial dairies to deal with excessive manure output. Energy-capturing digesters represent an extremely valuable technology, particularly for small- and medium-scale operations, but they have proved to be extremely challenging to adapt effectively at an industrial scale. Many government funded digester programs have stalled out after consuming millions of taxpayer dollars. Others reportedly trap methane for nothing more than to use that energy to operate the digester. Proponents are calling this green power, but at the industrial scale, it seems more brown than clean.

feeding operations. In fact, a 2006 study by the United Nations Food and Agriculture Organization revealed that animal factory feedlots are a major contributor to climate change, generating even more greenhouse emissions than automobiles, and causing land and water degradation on a global scale.[10]

3. **CAFOs and energy production.** One of the largest emissions from CAFOs is methane, a potent greenhouse gas, which, when captured, produces energy. The limitation on incentive payments under EQIP is $300,000, unless USDA rules that the project is of "special environmental significance (including methane digesters)." Methane digesters convert animal waste in liquid manure lagoons into combustible fuels and residual solids and liquids. They are being installed particularly on

4. **Pasture operations deserve support.** While EQIP is used by many livestock and crop producers to carry out important environmentally beneficial practices, a disproportionate share of funds now flow to large-scale animal factories. This is a fundamental flaw in the policy and may jeopardize its goals and long-term effectiveness. EQIP funds can play an integral part in a healthful long-term solution to the CAFO crisis by shifting its support solely toward perennial, grass pastured, integrated livestock farms, the program's original intent.

Figure 11

Pay Now or Pay Later
Hidden Costs of Industrial Agriculture

WATER CONTAMINATION
Pesticides; Nitrates; Phosphates; Bacteria; Dead Zones

AIR EMISSIONS
Methane; Ammonia; Nitrous Oxide; Carbon Dioxide

BIODIVERSITY LOSS
Wildlife and Habitat; Hedgerow and Woodlot Loss; Bee Colony Decline; Vanishing Crops and Breeds

Above the Cost of Food at the Checkout Counter

SOIL LOSSES
Erosion; Loss of Organic Matter and Carbon Dioxide

HUMAN HEALTH
Pesticides; Asthma; Bacterial and Viral Diseases; Antibiotic Resistance; MRSA and E.Coli; Obesity

DISAPPEARING WETLANDS
Draining and Tiling; Dewatered Rivers; Impact on Species

Source: Based on Jules Pretty, "The Real Costs of Modern Farming," Resurgence, Issue 205.

Alphabet Soup: Deconstructing the Conservation Program Palette

Understanding Farm Bill conservation programs requires delving into a parallel universe of acronyms. First and foremost are the Natural Resources Conservation Service and Farm Service Agency—the NRCS and FSA—the conservation arm of the U.S. Department of Agriculture that administers programs.

Set-aside and easement programs such as the 1985 Conservation Reserve Program (CRP), 1990 Wetlands Reserve Program (WRP), Farm and Ranch Lands Protection Program (FRPP), and underfunded 2002 Grassland Reserve Program (GRP) pay landowners to take land out of production and restore functional grasslands and wetlands. They are either permanent buy-outs or long-term (30-year) contracts, and the most effective ones target large areas of contiguous and high-priority habitat.

Habitat building programs, which offer cost-share assistance to restore land and protect declining species, include the Wildlife Habitat Incentives Program (WHIP), Conservation Reserve Enhancement Program (CREP), and others.

Compliance-oriented programs like the Environmental Quality Incentives Program (EQIP) have more questionable conservation value. They often pay large amounts of money to polluting corporations, such as massive confinement hog and dairy farms, to comply with the Clean Water Act, Clean Air Act, and other regulations that most businesses have to abide on their own. However, to a lesser extent, EQIP has also been used to provide habitat for fluvial Arctic graylings, lesser prairie chickens, sage grouse, and bobwhite quail.

Stewardship-oriented incentives such as the Conservation Stewardship Program (CSP) combine both sustainable farming and long-term care for the land. The CSP encourages and supports conservation on farming and ranching operations of all types in all regions, and comprehensively addresses soil, water, wildlife, energy, and other resources as a basis of healthy agriculture rather than as side issues or through costly remediation.

9. Freedom to Farm and the Legacy of Record Payoffs

Rhetorically, the 1996 Farm Bill—known as "Freedom to Farm"—was supposed to signal the end of the subsidy era and a return to free-market agriculture not seen since the early days of the New Deal. It was passed by a Republican-controlled Congress in a time of strong crop prices, tight federal budgets, and on the heels of a World Trade Organization agreement where developed countries committed to eliminating their agriculture subsidies. Congress claimed Freedom to Farm would wean American agriculture off federal support over the following seven-year period. Instead, it triggered more than a decade of the largest agribusiness payouts in history, and is the main reason politicians and citizens alike cringe when they hear the words "farm subsidies."

Among heralded legislative improvements was the concept of the "decoupled payment." These subsidies were no longer linked, or "coupled," to growing a specific crop. Instead, decoupled payments rewarded landowners on the basis of their subsidy history—whether they were growing commodity crops or not. The intent of these "base acreage" lump payments was to afford farmers flexibility to transition to new crops and alternative approaches, while the sun slowly set on the Washington subsidy game.

Freedom to Farm triggered the largest government payouts in history, the opposite of its policy objective.

Freedom to Farm also eliminated the acreage set-aside requirements of past Farm Bills that served as both a soil conservation measure and a supply management strategy. In addition, the government shuttered what remained of its decades-old strategic grain reserve. With no county by county management of crop acreage, and no relief valve for surpluses, farmers now flooded markets with their entire harvests.

Phasing out subsidies did not go according to the script. With oversaturated markets, the farm economy swirled into one of its cyclical tailspins. Commodity prices plummeted and Washington reneged on the phase-out plan. The few preceding years of high crop prices had reduced the cost of commodity subsidy programs down to $3 billion to $4 billion per year. After the passage of Freedom to Farm, however, they soared to between $15 billion and $25 billion, ballooning with supplemental multi-billion-dollar "emergency market loss" bailouts on top of subsidies. These moves, originally intended to rein in government spending, shifted

Figure 12

Government Debt Is Your Debt
Budget Deficits and Surpluses, 1995–2012

DOLLARS IN BILLIONS (FY 2000 DOLLARS)

The End of Entitlements? The mounting costs of the prolonged wars in Iraq and Afghanistan, the global economic downturn, Medicare, Social Security, Bush-era tax cuts, and unexpected national disasters like Hurricane Katrina will force legislators to scrutinize all spending. The hard and honest truth is that—with the exception of record payouts for commodity producers—many programs have already been cut to the bone through the annual appropriations process. Unfortunately, the price of doing nothing to address the complex interrelated challenges of current food and farm policy in the long term may be unaffordable.

Sources: Budget and Economic Outlook: Historical Budget Data, January 2010, Congressional Budget Office. The Budget and Economic Outlook: Fiscal Years 2010 to 2020, Congressional Budget Office

*Projected

the advantage to buyers. The beneficiaries became an elite group of mega-farms along with the food processors, confinement feeding operations, grain distributors, and others that purchased the glut of corn, cotton, wheat, rice, and soybeans at prices that sometimes fell below what it cost to grow them.

By the turn of the millennium, the farm economy eventually rebounded, but the next Farm Bill, the Farm Security and Rural Investment Act of 2002, inked by President George W. Bush, continued the trend. In fact, it became the most lavish ever. The president boasted that this mammoth legislation "preserves the farm way of life for generations."[1] Onlookers across the country were appalled. The *Washington Post* called it "a shockingly awful farm bill that will weaken the nation's economy." The *Wall Street Journal* labeled it "a 10-year, $173.5 billion bucket of slop." North Carolina's *Greensboro News Record* deemed it "a gravy-train for mega-farms and corporations."[2]

The 2002 bill made permanent Freedom to Farm's temporary transition slush fund—decoupled payments—in the form of direct payments. They became an instant entitlement program that reeked more of 18th-century feudalism than present day democracy. Growers received direct payments just for owning land with a particular commodity production history. It didn't matter if they had lost money that year or even if they were planting commodity crops or not. Direct payments were also favored by

lenders financing the expansion of farming operations; and they were not limited by WTO agriculture guidelines. In addition, the blockbuster disaster bailouts of the late 1990s became normal budget items in the 2002 Farm Bill, this time as "counter-cyclical payments" that fluctuate depending on global market prices to insure farmers don't lose money in oversupplied markets. In fact, this type of deficiency subsidy to ensure farmers at least receive a pre-set target price based on estimated production costs had been around at least since the 1970s. Now the subsidies reached new heights.

To satisfy environmentalists and the outdoor "hook and bullet" constituencies, the 2002 Farm Bill also set a record for conservation spending—at least theoretically. This included a new program aimed at transitioning agricultural subsidies into green payments, the Conservation Security Program, along with new Grassland Reserve Program funds to protect rare remnant prairies and grassland habitats. But, as so often happens, these promises were eventually broken. Conservation programs wound up drastically underfunded (flat-funded or ChIMPed) during the annual appropriations process. As many as four out of five applicants were turned down for programs due to lack of support over the course of the 2002 bill. Ducks Unlimited and other conservation groups warned of another aggressive expansion into Prairie Pothole habitats that were previously uneconomical or impractical to farm, with

The Failure of "Freedom to Farm"

In 1996 when Freedom to Farm was passed conditions on the farm and in government were similar to what we see in 2011: farm prices were high and the federal budget was tight. Additionally, developed countries had just started feeling pressure from the WTO to eliminate subsidies. With that year's farm bill, Congress aimed to permanently phase out farm subsidies, but its plan backfired.

- In 1996, Freedom to Farm eliminates land idling requirements and the grain reserve program.

- The lack of idling requirements results in a combined increase of 15 million harvested acres of corn and soybeans between 1995 and 1997.

- Without a grain reserve program, farmers flood the market with their surplus crops.

- Due to oversupply, between 1996 and 1999 the price of corn falls by 50 percent, soybeans by over 40 percent.

- Farmers plant more acres to make up for low prices, which results in larger surpluses and even lower prices.

- Congress establishes disaster payments to supplement falling farm incomes.

- Congress makes disaster payments permanent in the 2002 Farm Bill, perpetuating the cycle.

Source: "Farm Subsidies 101 Fact Sheet," Food & Water Watch, February 2011

up to 22 million acres at risk to be plowed. These fears proved to be well warranted.

With so little money dedicated to environmental stewardship and diversified farming, the remaining incentive was to "farm the system" by planting as much as possible. The largest and most aggressive operators received the most benefits and used these land- and production-based subsidies to drive up cash rents and arable land values, exerting even more financial pressure on small and medium-sized farms and beginning farmers. For example, corn farmers received $2 billion in federal direct payments in 2007, a year during which they experienced record yields and strong prices,[3] most of it going to just 10 percent of the largest operations in highly concentrated geographic regions

Farmers now had a system exactly as they wanted it—the freedom to plant as much as they wanted, along with a litany of supports that guaranteed the government would bail them out if they experienced low yields, low market prices, unfavorable weather conditions, or crop failures because they planted on marginal lands. Countercyclical payments, crop insurance, disaster relief, other Farm Bill price supports, along with ethanol tax incentives virtually eliminated most risks for commodity agriculture operators. The concentration of power of corporate agribusinesses continues, at the expense of small and medium-sized farms and fueled by taxpayer dollars.

Farm Insurance Fraud is Cheating Taxpayers Out of Millions

P.J. Huffstutter

The federal investigator took the witness stand and described the crime scene: a sprawling field clogged with boulders, native grasses and knee-high sagebrush.

The defendant, a California farmer, had said the site was a 200-acre wheat field. But the investigator found no tilled soil, no tractors, no plows. In fact, she testified, she found no wheat.

The field was just a field—and a prime example, federal prosecutors allege, of a wave of agricultural insurance scams sprouting across the nation.

Such crimes are being perpetrated by farmers who fraudulently claim that weather or insects destroyed their crops to cash in on a government-backed insurance program. Some cheats never bother planting at all. Others sell their harvests in secret and then file claims for losses, collecting twice for the same crop.

One North Carolina tomato grower, armed with a camera and a party-size bag of ice cubes, created a mock hailstorm in his fields and swindled the federal government out of $9.2 million.

These growers—along with crooked insurance agents and claims adjusters—are using the program to bilk insurance firms and the U.S. government out of millions of dollars a year, according to prosecutors, industry officials and high-tech experts who review questionable claims for the U.S. Department of Agriculture.

Taxpayers are on the hook for many of those losses.

The federal government has been fighting back against such criminals, using satellite technology, advanced data-mining techniques and other tools to spot fraud. The penalties, too, have grown stiffer. These efforts have saved taxpayers at least $730 million over the last decade, by some estimates.

Critics, however, say that such high-tech oversight catches only the most egregious cases, and that insurance companies have little incentive to be more aggressive lest they lose lucrative federal subsidies to sell crop policies.

"Politically, it makes sense not to care too much, because otherwise the insurance companies get hauled up to Washington and read the riot act for not using taxpayer money efficiently to help out the poor farmer," said Bruce Babcock, director of the Center for Agricultural and Rural Development at Iowa State University.

The vast majority of U.S. farmers follow the rules, insurers and federal officials said. Bert Little, director of the data-mining group Center for Agribusiness Excellence, said that less than one-half of 1% of the farmers who take part in the program cheat the system.

"But that less than 1% represents a pretty big chunk of money, between $100 million to $200 million a year," said Little, whose Texas group is contracted by the federal government to analyze farm records in search of fraud clues.

By its very nature, farming is risky. The federal government created the Federal Crop Insurance Corp. and, in 1938, started selling policies to farmers to help them recover from the Great Depression. By the 1980s, the government was subsidizing farmer premiums to encourage participation, and Congress had voted to expand the program and turn it into a public-private partnership.

Washington handed over the selling and servicing of these rural policies to a tight-knit group of insurance companies, with some lucrative incentives. Lawmakers agreed the U.S. Treasury would still guarantee the riskiest policies. The government would also pay agents' commissions, cover some of the insurers' operating costs and continue to subsidize farmers' annual premiums. Today, taxpayers cover about 60% of these premiums.

The program ballooned, thanks to insurance industry lobbying and federal rules that make it tough for farmers to go without coverage. Although the amount of acreage covered remained relatively stable, the value of insured crops climbed to $78 billion in 2010 from $36.7 billion in 2001. Premiums, tied to the volatility of the commodity futures market, jumped in price. Agents' commissions, which are tied to crop prices and premiums, have tripled over the last decade.

The trouble, critics say, is that private insurers and their agents reap most of the benefits while the public still picks up the losses.

In 2009, taxpayers shelled out nearly $4 billion to the 16 insurers involved in the program, according to the USDA's Risk Management Agency, which administers the program. Of that, $1.5 billion was paid in commissions to an estimated 15,000 insurance agents. Because there were more gains than losses, the USDA said it retained $1.4 billion, some of which came from farmers' premiums.

Meanwhile, taxpayers paid $1.7 billion to subsidize farmers' premiums."

The net effect is that the industry keeps the most profitable customers and shifts the riskiest, least profitable customers to the taxpayers," Iowa State's Babcock said.

The insurance industry disputes the figures and argues that the government gets a good deal for its investment. Insurers said their profits are reasonable, given the expense and risk involved. Without them, industry officials said, the public would end up paying more.

"If a disaster struck, taxpayers would undoubtedly be called on to support agriculture," said Tom Zacharias, president of the trade group National Crop Insurance Services.

USDA officials agree that the program plays a crucial part in the broader economic safety net for farmers. But in the face of ballooning federal deficits and complaints from farmers about agent commissions, the USDA pushed through a plan last year that cuts $6 billion over the next 10 years and caps how much of the insurers' administrative costs the government will pay. More cuts to this and other farm subsidy programs, officials warn, could be coming.

"It's on the table. No doubt about it,

because everything is on the table," said Risk Management Agency Administrator William J. Murphy.

Complaints about fraud and waste have fueled calls for changes to the program. In recent years, criminal investigators have unearthed fraud in potato fields in Michigan, cotton farms in Texas and sweet potato plantings in Louisiana. In eastern North Carolina, federal officials have uncovered one of the nation's largest crop insurance scandals to date.

Twenty-two people so far have pleaded guilty in connection with a conspiracy to swindle at least $22 million by pretending foul weather had destroyed farmers' tobacco fields. Prosecutors said growers secretly sold off their harvested tobacco for additional millions. The conspiracy involved at least 14 farmers, three warehouse workers, two rural check cashers, two insurance agents and an insurance adjuster. That investigation, dubbed Operation Under the Barn, is ongoing.

At the federal courthouse in Sacramento, Stockton-area wheat farmer Gregory P. Torlai Jr. is on trial, accused of defrauding the Federal Crop Insurance Corp. and a private insurer of at least $400,000. Prosecutors said he filed phony crop information and lied about how many acres of wheat he planted in Lassen, San Joaquin and Contra Costa counties. To get the payout, prosecutors alleged, Torlai submitted dummied-up store receipts for seeds he'd never bought and filed insurance claims for land he'd never owned.

Torlai, 49, pleaded not guilty to the 17 counts. He and his attorney declined to comment. In court documents, defense attorney Donald Heller argued that Torlai didn't know he was making false statements in his insurance claims: He was simply following the instructions given to him by an independent insurance adjuster.

If found guilty on all charges, Torlai faces up to 30 years in prison and a $1-million fine.

Last month, as the trial progressed, prosecutors showed snapshots of Torlai's farm in Lassen County, about 200 miles northeast of Sacramento. They had been taken by Marla Fricke, an investigator with USDA's Office of the Inspector General. Torlai, a slender man with weathered skin, sat stone-faced, gripping his brass rodeo belt buckle, one leg bouncing nervously under the defense table.

Assistant U.S. Atty. Michael Anderson asked Fricke what she saw in the photographs.

"Native grasses, sagebrush and rocks," Fricke said. "Pits. Garbage put into those big pits. Normally, in wheat fields, you don't see garbage pits."

This article originally appeared in the February 6, 2011 Los Angeles Times.

10. The Beginnings of a Food Bill?

Throughout the 2007 and 2008 debates, Farm Bill negotiations were dominated by discussions about the country's exploding nutrition crises. A third of U.S. adults and 17 percent of children were classified as clinically obese. The ranks of citizens affected by *food insecurity* swelled to more than 50 million people. Nutrition programs, which already made up 50 percent of Farm Bill spending, were eventually awarded another $10 billion from Congress to boost consumption of fruits and vegetables and to increase benefits for the Food Stamp program over the next decade. In the midst of the greatest economic downturn since the Great Depression, record numbers of Americans were applying each month for government assistance, and SNAP received 80 percent of that increase.[1] Per meal allowances, also known as the Thrifty Plan, had not been updated in more than a decade and were given a modest raise.

With the nation entrenched in recession, the Food, Energy and Conservation Act of 2008 became largely a Food Stamp Bill.

With the nation entrenched in recession, the Food, Energy and Conservation Act of 2008 became largely a Food Stamp Bill. By 2010, with a huge infusion from the Stimulus Bill, the SNAP program would account for more than 70 cents of every dollar spent by USDA. Other gains in that nutrition package included:

- $1.26 billion increased funding for The Emergency Food Assistance Program (TEFAP), which distributes surplus foods primarily through food banks, emergency shelters, food pantries, and other nonprofit assistance centers. TEFAP also responds with food relief in the case of natural disasters.[2]

- $1 billion for the Fresh Fruit and Vegetable Program, to provide fresh fruits and vegetables as snacks to elementary school children, specifically those eligible for free or reduced-price meals.[3]

- Expanded use of Electronic Benefit Transfer cards (SNAP-style credit card) at farmers' markets.[4]

The 2008 Farm Bill also saw increased cooperation between nutrition advocates and regional food production promoters. They lobbied forcefully for grant and loan programs to invest in local food production networks. These included expanding upon previous pilot programs like Farm-to-School that help cafeterias purchase local food and produce and the

Farmers Market Promotion Programs that generate opportunities for local farmers and consumers alike. An important study mapped the country's *food deserts*,[5] impoverished areas where community access to healthy foods is critically limited if not nonexistent.

This merger of the public health and local food communities is an important evolution in Farm Bill discussions. It is leading to the creation of innovative urban and rural food distribution networks, with the broader goals of creating jobs, solving distribution and marketing challenges for family farmers, increasing public access to healthy foods, and fighting hunger. One victory involved just the insertion of regulatory language while adding nothing to the Farm Bill baseline. A Geographic Preference rule gives K-12 schools that receive federal funds from the school lunch program the flexibility to specify a geographic preference for their purchases: i.e., local vendors rather than simply the lowest cost producers.

For the first time, specialty crop farmers—growers of fruits, nuts, and vegetables—grabbed a slice of the Farm Bill pie. Nearly $1 billion was dedicated to research and marketing programs, including a dubious California media campaign to convince the public about the safety of pesticides applied to fruits and vegetables. Other specialty crop funds were more ingeniously directed toward increasing supplies of vegetables and fruits in school snacks and meals, and doubling the purchasing power of SNAP beneficiaries who buy fruits and vegetables at farmers' markets.

Some opportunities to fight hunger and improve nutrition were squandered, however. Despite heavy lobbying, many of these programs got miniscule budgets relative to their enormous public paybacks, including Community Food Projects, Value Added Producer Grants, Community Food Grants, and Senior Farmers Market Nutrition programs.

The organic industry also furthered its inroads into the Farm Bill. With upwards of $30 billion in food sales, and 4 percent of the food market,[6] organic farming is significantly under-served by grower supports and USDA research and data collection programs. Essential needs that could further boost organic production, such as farming research, insurance programs, and market data collection, have all been largely ignored by Farm Bill programs in the past. An organic coalition (led by the Organic Farm and Research Foundation in Santa Cruz, California) successfully lobbied for $78 million in research, $22 million to share the costs of organic certification fees, and $5 million for marketing. Unfortunately, over the life of the Farm Bill, the organic program fell under the EQIP program and the Natural Resources Conservation Service, not always a champion of chemical-free farming methods, and implementation has turned out to be spotty.

Despite promises of big budget increases, conservation efforts overall didn't gain much momentum. Even with 9 percent of the 2008 Farm Bill budget, these funds could not meet demand. The financial situation for conservation programs only worsened after so many were gutted during annual appropriations and budget reconciliation. Incentives to keep grasslands unplowed, plant buffer zones around sensitive streams, and reward farmers for environmental stewardship were awarded a modest increase under the renamed Conservation Stewardship Program extended through 2017. Meanwhile, the Wetlands Reserve Program and Environmental Quality Incentives Program all were heavily ChIMPed.

Worse, tacked on to the 2008 bill was a lavish $5 billion "Permanent Disaster Assistance" program.[7] This established a permanent fund to insure farmers who plant in vulnerable areas such as the Great Plains or Deep South that are highly prone to drought or flooding. Why is this such a problem? Agricultural scientists, as well as organizations such as the Environmental Working Group, have documented that these types of revenue assurance schemes, coupled with ongoing ethanol subsidies and soaring commodity prices, have led to a reckless expansion of crop acreage. According to the Iowa Erosion Project data, nearly one third of Iowa counties were experiencing unsustainable rates of soil erosion in 2009.[8] Carried along with the lost soils are heavy amounts of nitrate and phosphate fertilizers and other farm chemicals that travel watersheds, and in the case of the Mississippi River Basin, make their way to the Gulf of Mexico's expanding Dead Zone.

Increasingly, crop insurance programs are overtaking subsidies as a way of getting money to farmers. Although crop insurance sounds like it should be a service of the private sector, taxpayers cover at least 60 percent of the costs associated with these various weather and revenue warranties. Farmers now regard insurance as a vital component of the "farm safety net" to protect them in the case of crop failure or revenue loss. But the conservation requirements on insurance policies are weak to nonexistent. Record flooding on the Mississippi and Missouri Rivers, savage droughts in the Southwest, and cold, wet planting seasons are just a few weather-related disasters farmers contended with in 2011. However, without conservation requirements attached to crop insurance programs, one wonders how taxpayers can be protected from permanently bailing out the expansion of fields onto highly erodible, marginally productive, or disaster-prone areas.

Instead, the biggest tragedy in the Conservation Title might have been the elimination of the Sodsaver Provision, which would have denied federal crop insurance and disaster program payments to any landowner who converted native sod to cropland. What could have been one of the strongest conservation assurances to prevent risky and unstable plowing was eventually watered down. The final legislation was limited to only the Prairie Potholes regions of Montana, North Dakota, South Dakota, Minnesota, and Iowa—and only if the governor acted to put it in force. None did.

In the end, the agribusiness lobby got exactly what it asked for—a continuation of direct payments, counter-cyclical deficiency

GIPSA: The Fight to Restore Fair Competition to the Livestock Industry

For years, the U.S. meatpacking industry—the small number of enormous corporations that buy and slaughter nearly all of the country's livestock and poultry—has taken unfair advantage of America's independent family farmers and ranchers. They rigged the game to benefit huge feedlots and Concentrated Animal Feeding Operations (some of which they themselves own), and pay small poultry, hog or cattle producers less for their animals—even when the quality of the animals is exactly the same.

Meatpackers have also turned the job of raising animals, particularly swine and poultry, into a contract arrangement more like running a factory or sweatshop. The livestock integrators own the animals, and the contractors raise them to exact specifications; responsibility for mortalities and disposal of waste lies with the contractor. Smaller producers have either accepted corporate control, or have left the livestock sector altogether. The agency charged with regulating anti-competitive behavior in the meatpacking industry is called the Grain Inspection, Packers and Stockyards Administration—GIPSA. It's housed within the U.S. Department of Agriculture. Until recently, GIPSA has not performed its intended function of regulating fair markets. Congress gave GIPSA the power to prevent large corporations from using unfair contracts, price manipulation, self dealing, and other anti-competitive practices to gain monopoly control over the industry under the Packers & Stockyards Act of 1921. However, USDA did not issue regulations needed to implement the Act until 2010.

A coalition of family farmer and rancher, food justice and consumer groups lobbied Congress to require USDA to write new rules for GIPSA as part of the 2008 Farm Bill. As a result, USDA along with the Department of Justice examined the meatpacking industry to determine the extent of anti-competitive activity in livestock markets. A new set of rules was drafted. According to those new rules, packers would have to keep records detailing why premiums are paid. Contract terms would have to be transparent. Packers would be prohibited from retaliating against contract growers who voice concerns or seek improvements. The USDA would be required to more clearly define unfair and discriminatory practices.

The big meatpackers immediately pressured Congress and USDA not to finalize the rules, arguing that such changes would cost the industry and consumers billions. They demanded an economic analysis, a common stalling tactic. Congress has blocked USDA from implementing the new rules for fiscal year 2012. In the meantime, the meatpacking industry is marshalling all of its forces to maintain unfair domination of animal food production in the next Farm Bill.

The 2008 Farm Bill gave USDA more power to police anti-competitive behavior by meatpackers. Yet so far a minority of powerful meat and poultry industry interests have delayed these reforms, squashing any hope for a more diversified, competitive and fair food system.

payments, and marketing loans with a whopping increase of crop insurance and disaster relief. Efforts to reform income eligibility requirements or cap the amount of federal assistance an individual farming operation can receive were heartily rebuffed. And for the calloused and cynical, the 2008 Farm Bill also proved that no omnibus spending law gets by without absurd earmarks and giveaways. Budget hawk Mitch McConnell, the Senate's minority leader, championed tax breaks for racehorse owners in Kentucky. Timber magnates in the southeast as well as farmers in Alaska also lined up at the public trough.

The silver lining of the 2008 Farm Bill was that more concerned citizens tuned in to this debate, and voter disappointment at the lack of reform was palpable. Legislators who used to vote the party line or trade their support for future favors were forced to cast their ballots in the clear light. For many centrist Democrats in farm country whose main charge was to successfully bring home a generous Farm Bill to their congressional districts, however, the strategy to postpone reform backfired. Voting for this unpopular bill did not protect many of them from defeat in the 2010 mid-term elections.

Organic's Fair Share

By the year 2000, the organic food movement was reaping the benefits of two decades of pioneering work from farmers, retailers, and consumers across the country. While economic growth in much of the food industry remained static, the market for certified organic products was experiencing brisk yearly expansion. Annual sales of organic foods exceeded $25 billion by the time of the 2008 Farm Bill reauthorization, capturing nearly 4 percent of all food sales.

"Organic food was moving into the mainstream, but not in terms of federal support," says Bob Scowcroft, founder and former director of the Organic Farming and Research Foundation. "Our strategy was simple. We wanted our fair share of research dollars and other production support from national Farm Bill programs."

The fair share strategy was already eight years in the making, having started in the lead-up to 2002 Farm Bill. At that time organic farming was not included in the definition of "good farming practices" that qualified farmers for federal crop insurance benefits. With a legislative champion in their corner, an amendment was introduced to include organic farming under that provision. While it ultimately passed into law, there would be further reforms necessary to tailor crop insurance premiums to the high value of organic crops.

This small victory was symbolic of the growing influence of the organic food and farming movement on the political process. Organizational capacity had been steadily increasing over the years. Consumers had once generated over 300,000 public responses to defeat an attempt to allow sewage sludge, genetically modified organisms, and nuclear irradiation under the national organic standards. Groups such as the Organic Trade Association, National Organic Coalition, Organic Farming and Research Foundation, Organic Consumers Union, Center for Food Safety, National Sustainable Agriculture Coalition, grower cooperatives, and others presented a formidable voting block.

It helped to have sympathetic allies in Congress with aides willing to craft language that their legislators could champion. A bi-partisan "Organic Caucus" consisting of three Democratic and three Republican representatives was formed to drive the movement's legislative agenda. A primary focus was on research dollars to develop innovative strategies and markets for organically produced crops. The 2002 Farm Bill had introduced a modest pilot research program: $15 million over 5 years.

The Organic Caucus wanted to expand that research purse devoted exclusively to organic and sustainable agriculture to 2.5 to 3 percent of the $1 billion annual USDA research budget. (In the end, $78 million in research funding was devoted to organic farming over the course of the 5-year bill.) A second policy objective was to help farmers with third-party certification, a time consuming and costly part of verifying that something is actually grown without chemicals. (That effort netted $22 million over 5 years. Individual farms can receive up to 75 percent of certification costs with a $750 limit). Funds were also approved to assist farmers transitioning from conventional to organic production, a process that typically takes three years to complete.

Champions like Sam Farr (D-CA) and Tom Harkin (D-IA), ultimately pushed these programs into the law and budget. There is still a way to go to actually get organic's fair share of the farm bill budget. But in the short term there has been a push for crop insurance that takes into consideration organic's high cost and value in the marketplace, along with better market data collection to improve trending and forecasting. Finally conservation programs such as EQIP now recognize organic production as an environmental benefit.

One can expect the organic caucus to continue to leverage its share of Farm Bill funding and attention, and to focus on the real goal: having organic farming principles become the standard for agriculture in a country focused on health, a clean environment, energy conservation, and food security.

Lessons from the Organic Caucus

1. Assess Your Organizational Capacity

Be honest. How much time do you and your organization have to devote to the Farm Bill? Are there other NGOs you can collaborate with? Among the coalition, who has connections in Washington D.C.? Who has media skills? Can you forge a strategy together?

2. Who are your congressional allies?

Do you know anyone on the Agriculture or Agriculture Appropriations Committees? Can you find a sympathetic ear from a staff person who can help with the long, hard work ahead?

3. Create a Media Strategy.

Identify influential publications and key reporters on the national and regional agricultural policy beat, such as the *Washington Post, New York Times*, and *Politico*. Look for charismatic spokespeople—farmers, doctors, policy makers, school lunch coordinators—to carry your message to the media. Help reporters in your area tell Farm Bill stories (good and bad) that can influence local representatives and voters.

4. Generate funding to support your effort.

A combination of special events, corporate support, and grant writing can help you pay people, including interns, for the hard work that this Farm Bill lobbying entails. Budgets may include travel to Washington D.C.

11. Who Gets the Money?

Billions of Farm Bill dollars flow into America's rural communities each year to boost income for farmers, who continue to face an onslaught of financial, environmental, and agricultural challenges. But are the farmers and landowners who cash those subsidy checks the ultimate beneficiaries of these programs or are other interests being served? Following the Farm Bill money trail involves understanding the complex circumstances surrounding what it means to be a "farm." It also requires focusing in on why the government singles out so few crops for subsidies. Finally,

Out of the hundreds and even thousands of plant and animal species cultivated for human use, the Farm Bill favors just four primary groups: food grains, feed grains, oilseeds, and upland cotton. Most of these are either fed to cattle in confinement or processed into oils, flours, starches, sugars, or other industrial food additives—or ethanol.

it means drilling down into deep divides: family farms versus corporate mega-farms, producers versus buyers, commodity versus diversified agriculture.

Farm Bill funding is undoubtedly skewed toward a very narrow group of crops and the handful of congressional districts where those crops are grown. Of the $246 billion U.S. taxpayer dollars spent on commodity subsidies between 1995 and 2010, almost 70 percent went to the production of just five crops: corn, cotton, wheat, rice, and soybeans. Half of that money went to the eight states that produce most of those commodities.[1] Furthermore, the system is easily scammed. Although the 2002 Farm Bill prevented subsidy payments to farmers earning over $2.5 million per year, at least 2,702 individuals in this income bracket collected a total of $49 million in subsidies.[2]

Given these broad brush strokes, it's easy to demonize commodity farmers. Often cited in the news media is this statistic: the richest 10 percent of farm subsidy recipients take in almost three-quarters of payments. While the system certainly suffers from rampant abuse, those numbers must be unpacked to get a more accurate assessment of the financial state of the American farm.

The USDA identifies approximately 2.2 million farms in the country. In fact the agency's definition of a farm is quite broad: "any place from which $1,000 or more of agricultural products were produced or sold, or normally would have been sold, during the census year." When the USDA averages farm income, it includes a sizable category called "rural residence farms"–households that may own a cow or a few sheep, but do not list their occupation as "farmer." Only 23.5 percent of farms actually grow enough crops or animals to earn over

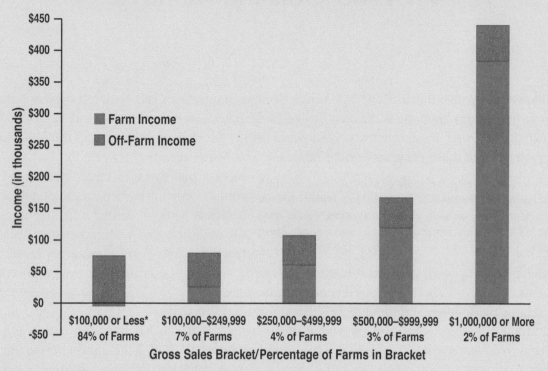

Figure 13

Only the Mega Farms Succeed
Average U.S. Farm Household Income 2005-2009

Income (in thousands)

$450
$400
$350
$300
$250
$200
$150
$100
$50
$0
-$50

■ Farm Income
■ Off-Farm Income

| $100,000 or Less* | $100,000–$249,999 | $250,000–$499,999 | $500,000–$999,999 | $1,000,000 or More |
| 84% of Farms | 7% of Farms | 4% of Farms | 3% of Farms | 2% of Farms |

Gross Sales Bracket/Percentage of Farms in Bracket

*Farm Income is average over 2006–2009 due to 2005 sampling error
Source: Agricultural Resource Management Survey, Economic Research Service, USDA.

$50,000 a year, and 31 percent are producing so little that they don't even clear $1,000 a year.[3] Such mini-farms generally do not receive subsidies and their households rely primarily on off-farm income–and yet these represent two-thirds of all "farms" surveyed by USDA. The paychecks these people get from other jobs are also taken into account when USDA tallies "average farm income." This makes it appear as if the majority of American farmers do not receive subsidies and have higher than average income.

Just a fraction–around 15 percent–of all farms generate most of the agricultural output, primarily because they have specialized in commodity crops. Family farms are a dying breed. Although the average American farm measures about 441 acres, farms of that size are in fact becoming increasingly difficult to find. While mega-farms and so-called "hobby farms" are on the rise, it is the medium-scale operations, with acreage between 50 and 2,000 acres, that are declining.

Focus on that slice of small and mid-sized

farms that comprise less than 10 percent of all operations—those that gross between $100,000 and $250,000 from farming and whose operators claim farming as their primary occupation—and a far different picture develops. According to an analysis of USDA farm data by Tufts University researcher Timothy A. Wise, in 2003, these commercial family farms earned an average net income of $30,000 a year from farming—more than half of which came from subsidy payments. Of all small- and mid-sized farms in this income segment, 82 percent received some sort of government payment. In other words, contrary to popular belief, a significant majority of family farmers receive benefits from farm programs and rely on them to keep their operations afloat.

Even as commodity prices reached record highs in 2007, family farmers continued to struggle. While corn prices increased 87 percent between 2003 and 2007, fertilizer costs jumped 67 percent. Fuel costs doubled. At the same time, counter-cyclical payments to small and mid-sized farms, which kick in when the market price of a crop falls below a set target price, dropped by half. As a result, small and mid-sized farms' net income from agriculture actually declined between 2003 and 2007, from $30,000 to $26,000. Farm households supplemented their income with an average of $31,000 from off-farm jobs during the period of Wise's study. Combined, household income was just barely above the U.S. average. Without the farm subsidies,

many of the small and medium-sized farms would border on poverty.

The elite group of mega-farms felt no such squeeze. These are the large commercial farms earning over $250,000 per year that control vast acreages, benefiting from farm payments tied to land ownership and historical production. According to Wise's analysis of USDA data, very large commercial farms were responsible for 44 percent of commodity crop production and received 32 percent of commodity payments in 2003. "The concentration of farm payments," Wise says, "is caused primarily by the concentration of land and production in the hands of a relatively small number of large farmers. It may be necessary to address the root causes of this concentration in order to meaningfully address inequities in U.S. farm programs."[4]

Even among those "wealthy farmers" at the top of the scale, however, the statistics can be somewhat misleading. Of the top 20 recipients of government farm and conservation payments between 1995 and 2010, none was an individual family farm. Instead, their ranks included corporations, Indian tribes or cooperatives that distributed payments among their members, and, to a lesser extent, conservation organizations.[5] It is important to keep in mind the type of agriculture—for both plants and animals—that our federal subsidy system has intentionally perpetuated. The farm sector has been converted to a manufacturing model, designed to provide buyers with a lowest-cost product. Labor is replaced with energy-intensive machinery and chemicals whenever possible. These are extremely expensive costs that are most economically beneficial when spread over a maximum number of acres or animals. Once invested in such a capital-intensive system, it is extremely difficult for an operator to make any significant change in the scale or approach to farming. In fact, as harvests and production become more and more efficient, the main response, as in manufacturing, is simply to try to grow the scale of the operation.

Scotty Pippin, The Prince of Lichtenstein, and Christmas Trees

It's understandable that we want to ease the plight of the family farmer. But, as we can see from the discussion above, drawing a line between what constitutes a family farm and a corporate mega-farm has become an extremely complicated issue. One recurring problem with farm subsidies is the lack of practical limits on how much a single farming operation can receive. Thanks to numerous legal loopholes, lax enforcement, and loose definitions of what it means to be actively engaged in farming, essentially no caps currently exist.

Starting in the 1970s, federal law technically capped subsidy payments at $50,000 per farm per year. But farmers and landowners easily circumvented this by morphing into multiple entities (sometimes referred to as Christmas trees), each eligible for payouts. In 1986 a nationwide scandal erupted when reports surfaced that the Prince of Liechtenstein had collected more than $2 million in cotton and rice subsidies as an absentee landowner. In response, Congress created the so-called three-entity rule. Under this provision, a farmer could collect $50,000 in subsidies in his own name, and, as half-owner, up to $25,000 for each of two other entities.[6]

But since those limits were enacted in 1987, new subsidy programs have proliferated and new loopholes have further eroded subsidy caps. Farmers and landowners creatively form complex family partnerships with associated limited liability companies that grow new tentacles into the subsidy gravy train. Lawyers and accountants opportunistically exploit these loopholes, offering "payments limitations planning" services that stretch the legal definitions of "actively engaged in farming." According to a report in the *Atlanta Journal-Constitution*, for example, in 2005 at least 195 U.S. farming operations—or more accurately, landowners—collected more than $1 million each from taxpayers.[7] That same year, 100,000 farms nationwide received between $25,000 and $100,000 each.

Under the 2008 Farm Bill, direct payments are capped at $40,000 for an individual or twice that for a married couple where both spouses are actively engaged in the farming operation. Current law defines this as a contribution of 1,000 hours of labor on the farm or involvement in its management. However, the vague and largely unenforceable regulatory standard for "actively managing" farm operations has foiled lawmakers' attempts to target payments to working farmers. Counter-cyclical payments are capped at $65,000 ($130,000 for an actively engaged couple). Loan deficiency payments and marketing loan gains are not capped. So, you can see, incentives can add up considerably. It's one thing supporting a family farmer. It's quite another subsidizing the expansion of a mega-farm operation that puts family farmers out of business.

European princes haven't been the only sources of indignation. The "Scotty Pippin Rule"–drafted after the multimillionaire NBA basketball player's farm subsidy receipts made headlines in 2002–determined that no one with an adjusted gross income over $2.5 million, of which less than 75 percent came from farming, could receive program supports. But enforcing such rules has become a bureaucratic nightmare and the payment system is easily scammed. In 2004, a Government Accountability Office (GAO) study found that USDA Farm Service Agency field offices failed to use their own tools to determine eligibility at least half of the time.[8] A lot of non-farmers receive subsidy payments. According to a 2006 report by the *Washington Post*, the federal government paid $1.3 billion between 2000 and 2006 in rice and other crop subsidies to landowners who did no farming at all.[9] Included in this group were subdivision developers who bought farmland and advertised that prospective homeowners could collect subsidies on their new backyards.

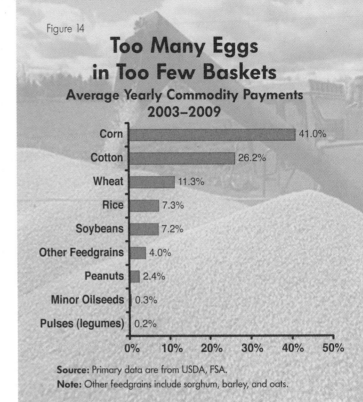

Figure 14

Too Many Eggs in Too Few Baskets
Average Yearly Commodity Payments 2003–2009

Commodity	Percentage
Corn	41.0%
Cotton	26.2%
Wheat	11.3%
Rice	7.3%
Soybeans	7.2%
Other Feedgrains	4.0%
Peanuts	2.4%
Minor Oilseeds	0.3%
Pulses (legumes)	0.2%

Source: Primary data are from USDA, FSA.
Note: Other feedgrains include sorghum, barley, and oats.

Congress members past and present have also been beneficiaries, sometimes raking in sizable yearly payments. According to the Environmental Working Group, 24 members of Congress or their immediate family members received farm subsidies between 1995 and 2010, some totaling millions of dollars.[10]

The True Beneficiaries

The goals, strategies, and rules for today's Farm Bill subsidies represent a complete departure from the price-stabilization policies that dominated the first four decades of Farm Bills. In general, the government purchased grain from farmers during harvest time when it was plentiful and sold it off when grain was more scarce. Other programs, such as land

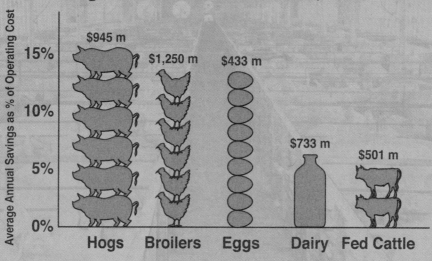

Figure 15

Factory Farms at the Public Trough

Savings from Below-cost Feed, 1997–2005

Average Annual Savings as % of Operating Cost

$945 m

$1,250 m

$433 m

$733 m

$501 m

15%

10%

5%

0%

Hogs Broilers Eggs Dairy Fed Cattle

Sources: Broilers, hogs from Starmer, Witteman and Wise (2006) and Starmer and Wise. Eggs, cattle, dairy from Union of Concerned Scientists. Dairy estimate based on 2002-2003 data only.

set-asides, also helped manage supply, boost prices, and impose some fundamental soil conservation practices.

These programs were slowly dismantled beginning in the 1970s, when globalization began to shape the political and economic agenda. The U.S. encouraged its farmers to plant fencerow to fencerow to generate exports. By 1996, the grain reserve program was eliminated by a Republican dominated Congress. With the government out of the supply management game, farmers once again planted as much as they could, hoping to get ahead. The result was deflationary oversupply. In the ensuing years, the market price of corn fell to an average of 23 percent

below the farmers' cost of production. As rural communities foundered, a flustered Congress instituted so-called "emergency payments" in 1998 to help keep farmers afloat. Those payments were made permanent in the 2002 Farm Bill.

With that move, the U.S. completed its shift away from policies designed to stabilize commodity prices for farmers to a system that encourages low market prices and then attempts to make up the difference with subsidies, revenue insurance, and disaster assistance programs.

In the meantime, the companies that buy commodity crops have been riding high. According to Timothy Wise, Tyson, the country's largest chicken producer, saved nearly $300 million a year in the decade after the 1996 Farm Bill because it could buy chicken feed at a price lower than what farmers (and the government) paid to produce it. Smithfield, the world's largest hog producer, saved nearly the same amount. In total, the top four chicken companies saved more than $11 billion in the decade after the 1996 Farm Bill, while the top four hog giants saved nearly $9 billion on their feed costs. (See Figure 15, "Factory Farms at the Public Trough.")

Big processed-food manufacturers have also fared well following the dismantlement of USDA supply management programs that attempted to regulate fair minimum prices for farmers. According to a 2011 paper by Food & Water Watch and Public Health Institute, corporations like Coca Cola reap huge capital benefits when high fructose corn syrup (HFCS) is made cheap and abundant. That's because just 2 cents of every consumer dollar spent on soda returns to the pockets of farmers who grow the corn that becomes HFCS. The remaining 98 cents goes to the beverage manufacturers and marketers. The authors report that soda companies have saved an estimated $100 million each year on their corn bill since supply controls were dismantled. Going back to the 1980s when HFCS began to replace cane sugar as a sweetener of choice, those total savings reach $1.7 billion.[11] Another sticky issue is that farmers who grow the perishable produce so necessary for a balanced diet have been kept out

of the subsidy game for decades. With 20,000 miles of waterways, nearly 80,000 farms, and over $30 billion in annual on-farm revenues, California tops all states in terms of agricultural sales, yet 90 percent of its growers receive no subsidies. (California contributes more than 12.5 percent of the total U.S. agricultural market value and nearly half of all fruits, nuts, and vegetables, yet its farmers receive less than 10 percent of commodity payments).[12] Florida is another prolific food producer, with extensive citrus, row crop, dairy, and calf-breeding operations. Yet only 10 percent of Florida's farms and ranches receive direct subsidies.[13] According to the Environmental Working Group, if farm payments were based on overall contributions to the nation's food and fiber supplies rather than the narrowly targeted commodity groups, five other states with large, but mostly unsupported, farm sectors would immediately benefit: North Carolina, Pennsylvania, Washington, Oregon, and Colorado.[14] Other regions traditionally left out would also get their due on par with their food and fiber output: all of New England (from Maine to New Jersey); the mid-Atlantic (from Georgia to Maryland); most of the upper Midwest; and states scattered across the South and West.[15]

Conclusion

In understanding the subsidy game, it's often more important to know who ultimately benefits from policies, rather than who directly gets the money. The real win-

11. Who Gets the Money?

ners in the subsidy explosion of the last decade and a half have been the animal feedlot operators and the largest corporate mega-farms, along with input suppliers like Monsanto, a host of service industry providers, and the big grain traders: ADM, Bunge, Cargill, and Dreyfus. Small and mid-sized growers depend on subsidies to stay afloat, sometimes even in big years; meanwhile big industrial growers thrive. Isn't there a better system to qualify who actually needs support and under what conditions?

The answers may require a fundamental shift from 20th-century policies that encourage overproduction and low prices. Rather, policies should be reoriented toward a complete economic system, one that helps qualifying family farmers earn a fair price for their products, caps payments, rewards environmental stewardship, incentivizes more diversified and resilient food and farming systems, and recognizes the value of family farms as key drivers of community health and economic development.

Subsidy Tracking

1. Over 60 percent of farm program payments went to the largest 12 percent of farms in 2008.

2. In 2009, 305 farm operations each received $200,000 or more in direct payments, in part because they were structured so that five or more partners or members of a farm business were eligible to receive the payments.

3. In 2006, 4.6 percent of individuals receiving program payments reported adjusted gross income of between $200,000 and $500,000, whereas 2.3 percent of other tax filers reported income at this level.

4. Corn farmers had record yields in 2007, yet received $2 billion in federal direct payments (income supplement checks).

5. In 2006, under a separate loan deficiency payment (LDP) program, farmers—predominantly corn growers—pocketed an estimated $3.8 billion more than was needed to make them whole under the government's price floor.

6. The USDA paid out nearly $1.2 billion between 2000 and 2005 on agricultural subsidies for Mississippi Delta farmers, most of whom are white. Only a fraction of that sum went to rural development projects to build up the economy of the region, where the population is predominantly black.

7. From 2003 to 2006, the USDA Farm Services Agency overpaid a number of individuals who reported income in excess of the statutory $2.5 million Adjusted Gross Income Maximum. Of the 1.8 million individuals receiving farm payments, 2,702 payments were made to beneficiaries with an AGI of $2.5 million or more. Over the four years reviewed by the Government Accountability Office, FSA overpaid almost $49.4 million to ineligible farming recipients.

8. In 2010, 1 percent of farming entities received over 20 percent of all direct payments. The same year, 10 states received nearly two-thirds of all direct payments, yet produced only one-third of all agricultural GDP.

9. American taxpayers foot the bill for storage of cotton and peanuts to the tune of $57 million per year, money that could be wisely invested in research or infrastructure programs.

10. Cotton subsidies are a particularly egregious form of corporate welfare, funneling about $3 billion a year to fewer than 20,000 planters, who tend to use inordinate amounts of water, energy and pesticides.

1-3 — Government Accountability Office, "Reducing Some Farm Program Payments Could Result In Substantial Savings," GAO-11-318SP Section II: Other Cost Savings and Revenue Enhancements; 4-6 — Dan Morgan, "The farm Bill and Beyond," Economic Policy Paper Series, The German Marshall Fund; 7 — U.S. Government Accountability Office, "Federal Farm Programs: USDA Needs to Strengthen Controls to Prevent Payments to Individuals Who Exceed Income Eligibility Limits," October 2008; 8-9 — Rep. Earl Blumenauer, "Growing Opportunities: Family Farm Values for Reforming the Farm Bill," p. 7; 10 -- Michael Grunwald, "Why the U.S. is Also Giving Brazilians Farm Subsidies," *Time Magazine*, April 9, 2010

11. Who Gets the Money?

12. Who Will Grow Our Food?

"If we are not careful, we could lose the farm and the food system on our watch." That drastic warning came from A.G. Kawamura in 2005, when he was secretary of the California Department of Food and Agriculture.

Kawamura was not only alluding to how important forward-thinking policy is to the food system, but also to the fact that people who grow food for a living are becoming a dying breed. Already, agriculture is greatly diminished in terms of economic measures: it represents just 1.2 percent of U.S. Gross Domestic Product; services make up 77 percent and manufacturing 22 percent of GDP.[1] It's becoming a forgotten career path as well.

Principal farm operators over age 65 now outnumber those under 35 by a ratio of more than seven to one.[2] Over the next 20 years, 400 million acres of agricultural lands—an area roughly five times the size of all our national parks combined—will be transferred to new owners.[3] But who will be those new owners? Youth continue to migrate out from the corn-rich "heartland" and leave agriculture altogether. Many interested younger Americans simply can't afford the costs of entry into farming. Others won't accept the economic instability of the job. Meanwhile, each year the United States edges toward becoming a net importer of foods; already we import more than $80 billion in agricultural products each year.[4] (See Figure 16, "U.S. Food Trade on the Rise".)

> *Principal farm operators over 65 years of age now outnumber those under 35 by a ratio of more than seven to one. Over the next two decades, 400 million acres of agricultural lands—roughly five times the amount of land set aside in our national parks—will be transferred to new owners.*

In short, we don't have enough people becoming farmers, and we're starting to import food to fill the gap. And yet few people are debating our flagging national food security with the fervor expressed about oil imports or manufacturing jobs shipped overseas.

Even our domestic foods are processed and distributed by an ever-smaller group of corporations.[5] Today, the majority of our food supply is in the hands of foreign producers or CEOs—as opposed to family farmers and a diverse corps of processors and regional distributors.

With just 2 percent of the U.S. population producing food for the remaining 98 percent, the efficiency of the existing food system is staggering. In 1900 it took 147 hours of human labor to grow 100 bushels of wheat. By 1990 that number had shrunk to 6 hours. Similarly, in 1929 it took 85 hours of human labor to produce 1,000 pounds of broiler chickens, but by 1980 the same could be produced with less than 1 hour of labor.[6] Imagine someone processing 1,000 pounds of chicken meat in less than an hour. It can be hard to comprehend the scale, mechanization, and infrastructure of a system that can produce 9 billion meat chickens every year.

While such efficiency is impressive, it comes with costs and trade-offs. Fewer hours of labor means fewer farmers. Fewer farmers means more consolidation, less diversity of crops, vacated rural communities, and reduced food security.

100,000 New Farmers

In 2010, U.S. Secretary of Agriculture and former Iowa governor Tom Vilsack introduced the idea of using Farm Bill programs to add 100,000 new farmers (an echo of a Clinton-era program to add 100,000 police officers to the nation's streets). Given population trends, however, these newcomers would barely begin to replace the aging farming generation. Still it's a step in the right direction. More farmers and food systems workers could mean a new generation of stewards of the land and a vessel for the skills and traditions of agriculture that are at risk of being lost. A concerted new farmer program could help to increase the number of small and mid-sized farms, boost food entrepreneurship, and reverse poverty in rural areas. Job creation—increasing the number of farmers—seems certain to be central to future Farm Bills. It will surely become part of Farm Bill rhetoric to justify ongoing agricultural policies as well, especially as budget constraints take center stage.

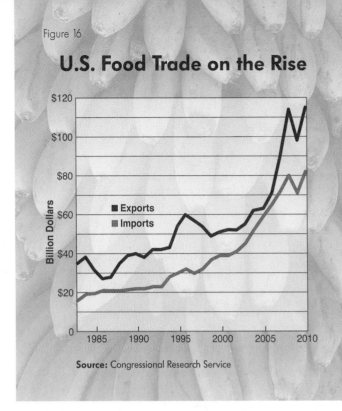

Figure 16

U.S. Food Trade on the Rise

Source: Congressional Research Service

The push for more farmers is finding support in the surging nationwide interest in local food production. These local food systems cover a great deal of ground: farmers who grow food; school and institutional cafeterias that purchase it; processing facilities that add value to fruits, vegetables, and meat and dairy products; chefs and agropreneurs developing new cuisine and products around local foods; new markets and distribution networks that link producers and eaters. Rebuilding local or regional food systems does not mean an end to international food trade, as some often suggest. It merely means restoring some geographic and seasonal balance to food production. In an era of growing populations and increasing climate uncertainty,

12. Who Will Grow Our Food?

Beginning Farm Programs Initiated by Recent Farm Bills:

Beginning Farmers and Ranchers Individual Development Accounts (BFRIDA) pilot program: Pilot program that provides beginning farmers of limited means with business and financial education and matched savings accounts.

Beginning Farmer and Rancher Development Program (BFRDP): Small-budget program that funds education, extension, outreach, and technical assistance initiatives for beginning farmers and ranchers.

Office of Advocacy and Outreach: Established by 2008 Farm Bill as a coordinating tool for all beginning and minority farmer programs.

Outreach and Technical Assistance for Socially Disadvantaged Farmers and Ranchers program ("Section 2501"): Provides grants to organizations that assist minority farmers in owning and operating farms and participating in agricultural and USDA-specific programs.

The Beginning and Socially Disadvantaged Farmer and Rancher Contract Land Sales Pilot Program: Guarantees federal loan to retiring farmers who self-finance the sale of their land to beginning or socially disadvantaged farmers and ranchers.

Conservation Reserve Program Transition Incentive Program (CRP TIP): Creates incentives for CRP contract holders to sell or lease to beginning or minority farmers.

Source: Compiled by the National Sustainable Agriculture Coalition

food producers will be more closely interconnected than ever before.

The Food Hub

One example gaining traction in Farm Bill circles is the Regional Food Hub. This is a centralized facility where local produce and animal products are aggregated, stored, processed, and distributed. There are already more than 100 operational food hubs around the country, with large clusters in the Midwest and Northeast. The average food hub generates $700,000 in annual sales, along with an estimated 13 jobs. This means new marketing opportunities for local farmers, as the average food hub is supplied by 40 small and mid-size farms.[7] Food Hubs are a prime example of applying new approaches to management, technology, marketing, and infrastructure to revitalize traditional food production arrangements. Farmers receive a fair price for their products and consumers value the quality of their food and the experience of interacting with and supporting local farmers.

There are other signs of hope for the next generation of farmers. Innovative partnerships are combining local, state, and federal programs to establish revolving loan funds and forgivable loan funds to help new growers get started. The 2002 and 2008 Farm Bills contained several provisions to assist beginning farmers and ranchers—and USDA leaders have shown a renewed interest in young farmers. Yet many of these programs initiated by the recent Farm Bills, such as the Beginning Farmers and Ranchers Development Program (see "Beginning Farm Programs Initiated by Recent Farm Bills" sidebar) either remain underfunded or are still sitting on a shelf waiting to be enacted.

To keep agriculture healthy into the future, subsidies will need to benefit the young and beginning farmer as well as the older, well-established or corporate farmer. Direct Payments–because they are based on historical baselines and not current farming practices–lock potential farmers out of the system unless they can afford to purchase land already receiving payments. An alternate payment scheme that better rewards hard work, crop yields, and conservation practices would draw more beginning farmers into the trade.

What's On Your Plate?

Consumers could do their part in local farm job creation by eating their daily recommended allotment of fruits and vegetables. The USDA has estimated that only one in five Americans actually eats five daily servings of fruits, nuts, and vegetables. Depending on the season, many Americans increasingly rely on farmers from other countries to keep them supplied year round with tomatoes, apples, and berries. According to a 2006 USDA study, if Americans increased their consumption of fruits and vegetables to meet the USDA dietary recommendations, the U.S. would need an additional 13 million acres of "specialty crops."[8] That's more than three times what the country currently devotes to fruit and vegetable production and slightly more than all the acres in California currently under crop, orchard and vineyard production. One has to wonder what an impact that would have on new farmers and emerging food hubs around the country.

Figure 17

Young Farmer Deficit

Share of Beginning Farmers by County

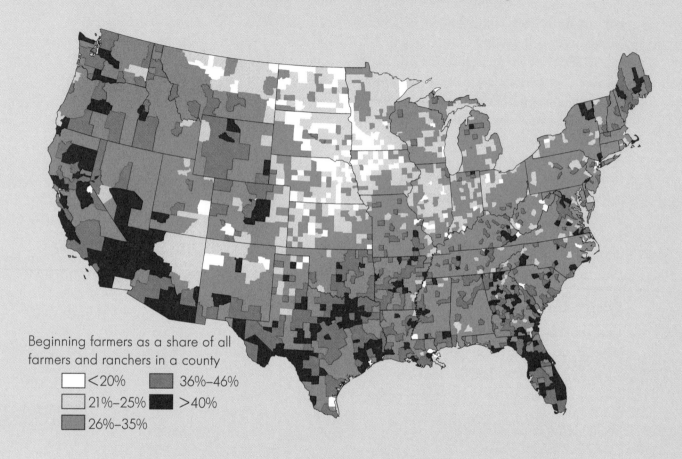

Beginning farmers as a share of all
farmers and ranchers in a county

- ☐ <20%
- ☐ 21%–25%
- ▨ 26%–35%
- ▨ 36%–46%
- ■ >40%

As the average age of farmers continues to rise, so have concerns about a pending farmer shortage and diminished innovation on the farm. There are several reasons that fewer people are choosing to become farmers: the cost of entry is very high, the lifestyle is difficult, and it has become increasingly hard to make a living as a farmer. This map shows just how few beginning farmers there are in the United States. However, it is important to keep in mind that beginning farmers are not necessarily young farmers. In fact, in 2007, 32 percent of beginning farmers were 55 years old or older.

Source: ERS tabulations based on the 2007 Census of Agriculture (USDA, NASS).

Beginning Farmer Incubator Programs

At a time when American farmers are aging and mega-farms are gobbling up medium-sized operations, the Agriculture and Land-Based Training Association (ALBA) has a bold mission: bringing new faces to agriculture. This is no small task. Farming remains one of the most challenging professions, requiring experience, planning and business skills, startup capital, and access to land.

ALBA is dedicated to breaking down those barriers to becoming a farmer. Every year, 25 people graduate from its rigorous farmer education program in the Salinas Valley—referred to as the nation's Salad Bowl because nearly two-thirds of all leafy greens are grown in this one valley. Farm Bill dollars, nonprofit foundation grants, and a burgeoning organic produce distribution business provide the funding for ALBA's farmer incubator project.

"The Beginning Farmer Rancher Development Program (BFRDP), established in the 2008 Farm Bill, is vital fuel for the economic engine resulting from beginning farmers' work," says Gary Peterson, executive director of ALBA. "Taxpayers should be proud of the results. There is a huge return on investment from these dollars, and a waiting list of people interested in this program."

To enter the ALBA farmer incubator program, students must first complete a six-month basic training, which includes 150 hours of farm training and field days, culminating with writing a farm plan and applying for a plot of ALBA's land to cultivate. Each year, up to 40 students farm on ALBA's

land during many stages of their training.

ALBA is designed to nurture a beginning farmer for seven years. After that, the training and below-cost land rentals end. Graduates have to make it on their own in the marketplace and pay the going rate for land rentals.

Many of their graduate growers are finding success. "One of the real strengths of this program is the direct marketing we are able to do with the quality organic produce that is being grown by our students and graduates," says Peterson. ALBA Organics, the organization's distribution arm, purchased $1.5 million worth of organic produce from present students and program graduates in 2010. Those fruits and vegetables supply the cafeteria systems of Stanford University, University of California Santa Cruz, and other large buyers.

ALBA also focuses on a sector of the farming population often overlooked by many policy programs: low-income, primarily Hispanic communities. These are farmers like Guilebaldo Nuñez, who grew up on farms in Mexico. Nuñez entered the ALBA program in 2004, with the desire to learn organic farming, initially leasing three acres. "At ALBA I really improved my techniques," says Nuñez. "I attended several educational events regarding organic farming and leadership that have been an important contribution to my success, because I had always focused on improving the quality of my products. Selling healthy products makes me feel good as a farmer and as a person."

Today Nuñez Farm leases 13 acres at ALBA and sells organic produce (his, and that of other ALBA farmers) at 13 farmers markets in the Bay Area. He owns two tractors and recently installed two large high tunnels, or hoop houses, to help him grow winter crops. Annual sales have expanded consistently. His business sustains five full-time jobs and nine part-time jobs including seven family members employed on his farm. The Beginning Farmer Rancher Development Program is a testament to how long it can take to transplant a Farm Bill program from inside the DC Beltway into the ground. It took 15 years—three Farm Bill cycles—from the time it was first floated as a marker bill on the House floor, until it was finally championed by representatives, written into law, and funded by the Appropriations Committee. The Beginning Farmer Rancher and Development Program is a relatively small budget program that effectively addresses an urgent issue for the future of food production. Yet like more than 30 other such programs, it currently has no baseline for spending past 2013.

13. The World Trade Organization and the International Community

The programs and policies set out in each Farm Bill don't exist in a domestic bubble. They also affect, and are affected by, global food demand, shifting prices, and, increasingly, international trade agreements. Most nations are both food importers and exporters, out of necessity, economic globalization, and dietary affluence. Yet conditions for farmers vary widely, especially between northern industrialized countries—where a small number of subsidized producers grow most of the crops—and the developing world—where farming is far less mechanized and employs large percentages of the population, often at subsistence levels.

The World Trade Organization's Agreement on Agriculture, an international convention forged between 1986 and 1994 to establish the rules of trade between countries, attempts to level a highly uneven economic playing field for farmers throughout the world. Agricultural subsidies and trade barriers such as tariffs, while designed to boost income and carve out markets for producers at home, can have a disruptive effect on prices in the

Brazil successfully argued that U.S. direct payments to cotton farmers were "trade distorting." These payments, the dispute panel found, artificially depress global prices and stimulate overproduction, thereby costing Brazilian cotton farmers millions of dollars in sales.

international arena. Many Farm Bill programs are specifically designed to pay for some of the costs of growing cotton, corn, and milk or to shield domestic cane and sugar beet producers from other lower-cost producers. Yet the United States also exports 20 percent of its agricultural output. So Farm Bill programs that promote the overproduction of corn, cotton, wheat, soybeans, rice, meat and dairy products can glut the market, undermine prices, and harm competing farmers in other countries.

Market distortions caused by agriculture subsidies in wealthy countries served as a point of bitter contention up until commodity markets heated up in 2007. Nobel Prize–winning economist Joseph Stiglitz explains: "When subsidies lead to increased production with little increase in consumption, as is typical with agricultural commodities, higher output translates directly into higher exports. Higher exports translate directly into lower prices for producers. And lower prices translate directly into lower incomes for farmers and more poverty among poor farmers in the Third World."[1]

The dumping of heavily subsidized commodity crops on international markets remained one of the key tripping points as the latest Doha round of world trade negotiations started and stalled over the past 15 years. The farm lobby, with its tremendous power, continually trumped both the U.S. trade position and domestic concerns about rising deficit spending as payment programs inflated between 1996 and 2007. This points to the perhaps irreconcilable tensions between an export-driven farm economy designed to "feed, clothe, and fuel the world" on the one hand, and the dire need for a new agricultural order on the other: one that promotes fair markets so that countries can feed their people to the greatest extent possible while still continuing to trade.

The United States agreed to pay the Brazilian Cotton Institute $147.3 million per year for "technical assistance and capacity building."

The Madness of Cotton

Writing about U.S. cotton export supports in particular, Joseph Stiglitz asserts, "seldom have so few done so much damage to so many."[2] Frustrated by America's continual refusal to reform its cotton program, Brazil brought a case before the World Trade Organization arguing that U.S. market deficiency payments and export subsidies to cotton farmers were "trade distorting." On March 3, 2005, a World Trade Organization Appeals Panel upheld a ruling against the United States, concluding that market loans and export subsidies to U.S. cotton farmers (part of 2002 Farm Bill programs) artificially depressed global prices and stimulated overproduction, thereby costing Brazilian cotton farmers hundreds of millions of dollars in sales.

The 2005 Appeals Panel ruling allowed Brazil to respond through "cross-sectoral retaliation." This meant that it could compensate for the losses in its cotton industry by imposing tariffs on American goods such as food, electronics, pharmaceuticals, and technology. The U.S. filed another appeal, and in August 2009, the World Trade Organization once again ruled in Brazil's favor, authorizing them to impose import tariffs on American goods and intellectual properties to the tune of $820 million. Rather than expose U.S. technology, pharmaceutical and biotech firms to costly economic reprisals, the two countries reached an interim agreement in April 2010.

The United States agreed to pay the Brazilian Cotton Institute $147.3 million per year for "technical assistance and capacity building." Nearly $150 million is a lot of money—much more than several Farm Bill program budgets combined—and public outcry over this deal was immediate and forceful. In June 2011 a defiant House of Representatives voted to eliminate these payments to Brazil, threatening to put the U.S. out of compliance with the WTO's ruling. The result could mean significant economic payback by Brazil against, for example, biotech giants like Monsanto and Pioneer, whose patented genetically engineered seeds are popular among Brazilian commercial growers.

Of course, the United States is not alone in subsidizing its agriculture in ways that distort free trade. Japan, South Korea, and many European governments (France, Norway, Switzerland, and other Group of 10 nations) have been propping up farm sectors for decades–often to a far greater extent than the U.S. does. Theoretically, open markets should help to "float all boats" and create a more prosperous world for all. But trade negotiators of developed countries appear to be deadlocked in a high-stakes game of "chicken." No one wants to be the first to cut its commodity growers off from production supports.

"Most countries recognize that some level of financial support and tariffs are necessary to promote food security," explains Ben Lilliston, of the Institute for Food and Agriculture Policy in Minneapolis. "Countries need to be able to protect and support domestic food production. Developing countries need to be able to support their farmers, and at the same time, protect their farm economy from dumping which has traditionally come from U.S. and European based agribusiness corporations." The WTO's Agreement on Agriculture already established rules to govern farm protection and supports. Referred to as the "Three Boxes" (see Figure 18, "WTO's Three Boxes"), these (now-expired but still functioning) categories offset limits on agricultural supports depending on how much they distort trade. "Amber Box" subsidies, which fund cheap exports or encourage

overproduction, are the most limited: to 5 percent of total production (either on a specific crop basis or across all agricultural output) for developed countries; 10 percent for developing countries. Current U.S. Amber Box payments include counter-cyclical price compensation programs, certain loans, and irrigation subsidies. "Blue Box" subsidies are direct payments to farmers that have production limiting characteristics, such as links to land set-aside requirements. These have per-nation ceilings. "Green Box" payments are "minimally trade distorting" and are currently unlimited under WTO rules. Green Box payments support conservation, rural development, renewable energy, and other investment programs. The U.S. currently includes direct payments and disaster relief payments under the Green Box, along with numerous conservation supports. Over the life of the 2008 Farm Bill, commodity prices have been well within WTO Amber Box compliance as deficiency payments have fallen in response to rising prices. A few reasons explain the surge: greater demand for meat and animal protein in emerging economies, an expanding use of biofuels, and crop failures due to extreme weather events. At the same time, the U.S. commodity supports are shifting to crop and revenue insurance rather than subsidies.

"The drive to cut budgets means that we can likely expect commodity programs to be reformed in the next farm bill." Says IATP's Lilliston. "What will emerge—some variation

Figure 18

WTO's Three Boxes

Box	Status	Payment Type
Amber	Trade Distorting	• Export credits • Commodity subsidies
Blue	Questionable	• Counter-cyclical payments • Other direct payments
Green	Non-trade Distorting	• Rural development • Green Energy • Conservation

Source: Forum on Democracy and Trade

Trade Talk Timeline

In late 2001 the World Trade Organization began a series of talks—the Doha Round—to assist developing countries by reducing government subsidies and opening markets for agricultural and manufactured goods.

Nov. 2001, Doha, Qatar: The latest round of WTO trade talks starts two months after the 9-11 attacks. Developing countries complain about subsidies, and U.S. cotton payments in particular.

Sept. 2002: Brazil sues the United States through the WTO appeals process, claiming cotton subsidies lower world prices by encouraging overproduction and excess exports.

Sept. 2003, Cancun, Mexico: Talks disintegrate as poor countries protest refusal of affluent countries to reduce or eliminate farm subsidies.

Sept. 2004: WTO rules in Brazil's favor. The United States is required to halt a few direct payment subsidies immediately and to reduce or eliminate certain major subsidy programs.

March 2005: WTO Appeals Panel rules against the United States and sets a timeline for action.

Oct. 2005: Trade negotiators from Washington propose significant subsidy cuts if Europe lowers tariffs and developing countries open markets wider to U.S. exports. No changes materialize.

July 2006, Geneva, Switzerland: Talks are suspended with affluent countries, United States in particular, criticized over their continuation of subsidies.

Aug. 2009: WTO arbiter rules that Brazil can take countermeasures against the U.S., up to 143.7 million dollars annually, including suspending international property right protection for such things as genetically engineered seeds.

Aug. 2010: The U.S. and Brazil reached an agreement in which the U.S. Commodity Conservation Corporation would pay the Brazilian Cotton Institute $143.7 million annually for technical assistance until a resolution is reached.

Source: Partially sourced from Dan Chapman, Michael Dabrowa, "Cotton Bailout: An ocean apart, but interwoven, record U.S. exports dampen world cotton prices," *The Atlanta Journal-Constitution*, October 8, 2006.

of crop/farm/disaster insurance–could also end up being costly, and it is unclear whether it would be WTO compliant."

The U.S. Farm Bill's counterpart across the Atlantic, The European Union's Common Agricultural Program (CAP), has committed to shifting trade distorting export subsidies into the WTO's Green Box. Under the "Decoupling 2013" plan, all tariffs and export refunds on agricultural goods are to be eliminated by 2013. (Whether France and other countries ultimately comply remains highly questionable.) The U.S. could follow Great Britain's lead and promise to phase out Amber Box subsidies altogether by transferring supports to its already established green payments plan, the Conservation Stewardship Program (CSP). Great Britain's "Environmental Stewardship" program is intended to phase out trade-distorting subsidies and begin paying farmers for the public services they provide, such as wildflower meadows and bird habitats, the restoration of traditional hedgerows, enhanced animal welfare, food safety, and food quality. As mentioned above, supports that promote conservation and rural development fall under the WTO's Green Box category, and are unrestricted.

Totally Un-COOL ?

In other respects, World Trade Organization rulings can work against environmentalist ideas in the Farm Bill. The 2002 Farm Bill, for instance, established Country of Origin Labeling (COOL), to tell consumers about the origins of perishable foods. Are those mangos from Mexico? Garlic from China? But meat packers put up a fuss. Ground beef often contains varying grades and cuts often from different countries, and all those would have to be on the label. Meat products remained immune from country of origin labeling through the 2002 Farm Bill; however, COOL was reauthorized and put into effect in 2009.

Canada and Mexico immediately filed a challenge within the WTO. Both countries export live animals across the U.S. border for fattening, processing, and distribution and they argued that COOL stigmatized their products as being of foreign origin, even if they were processed in the United States. In an initial ruling in November 2011, a WTO dispute panel found the U.S. COOL program in violation of international fair trade rules.

In effect, the WTO determined that the ultimate consumers of animals were not American citizens but concentrated animal feeding operations and meat packing houses. According to Ferd Hoefner of the National Sustainable Agriculture Coalition, these "consumers" are primarily multinational corporations that objected to the COOL rule in the first place because they don't want consumers to know the exact origins of their products.[3] Other groups objected that the WTO was over-ruling the national requirement to label something as fundamental as where food comes from. COOL may once again resurface as an issue in its third straight Farm Bill debate.

Conclusion

The effects of America's food policies and subsidies absolutely spill over international borders, and at the same time, international trade rules have profound ramifications on domestic fronts. As demands on the world's productive agricultural regions intensify due to rising populations, changing climatic conditions, and increasingly scarce fossil fuels, these interactions and stresses will intensify. In fact, the need for closer collaboration between countries may become more important than ever. While these rules can conflict and lead to international games of chicken over trade, there is a more direct path. The Farm Bill can begin to more closely align with trade goals established in 1995 by supporting rural development, conservation, public health and nutrition, energy security, and other related public benefits. Continued rising crop prices offer a perfect opportunity to shape a new bargain on international trade. Reduced or restructured farm subsidies could then open new international markets for other sectors of the economy. It could also lead to job creation here and abroad and a more level playing field for all farmers.

Who Pays for Dumping? Farmers in Developing Countries

Timothy A. Wise

Brazil and the United States may have settled, for now, their long-running WTO dispute over U.S. cotton subsidies but the issues it raised remain. After all, Brazilian producers were not the only ones hurt by U.S. dumping of its highly subsidized cotton on world markets, which not only took market share from competing producers, it depressed the international price for all producers.

How much does agricultural dumping cost farmers in developing countries? I recently completed a study for a Woodrow Wilson Center project that highlights just how high the cost of dumping can be. I benefited from the somewhat controlled experiment represented by U.S.-Mexico agricultural trade under the North American Free Trade Agreement (NAFTA). I call it a controlled experiment because NAFTA liberalized agricultural trade dramatically over a short period of time, Mexico imports most basic grains and meats almost exclusively from the United States, and Mexican farmers grow many of the crops that compete with the imports. In such a case, one can easily see the increase in U.S. exports, the drop in Mexican producer prices, and it is reasonable to assume that the U.S. export price is the reference price for these products in Mexico.

Using one of the definitions of dumping listed by the WTO (GATT Article VI Sec. 2.2), we estimated the extent to which U.S. export prices to Mexico were below U.S. farmer costs of production (plus transportation and handling). We looked at the nine-year period 1997-2005. We began in 1997 because the agricultural provisions of NAFTA were mostly implemented and the 1996 U.S. Farm Bill, which had a price-depressing effect on most major crops, had taken effect. We ended the period in 2005 to avoid the confounding effects of the speculative commodity price boom, which began in late 2006. We simply calculated the extent to which Mexican producer prices were lowered by U.S. dumping, and then estimated how much more Mexican producers would have earned if they had received non-dumping prices—at least high enough to cover U.S. costs of production.

Mexico was indeed flooded with imports, they were exported by the United States at prices below production costs, Mexican prices fell dramatically, and production declined in many cases.

The eight products studied all saw significant growth in U.S. exports, from

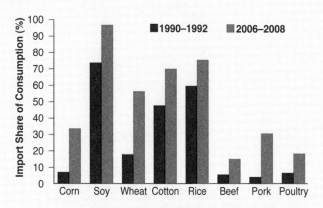

Mexico's Rising Import Dependency

Import Share of Consumption (%)

■ 1990–1992 ■ 2006–2008

Corn　Soy　Wheat　Cotton　Rice　Beef　Pork　Poultry

Source: USDA FAS Production, Supply and Distribution Online, 2009.

the 159 percent increase in soybean exports to the 707 percent increase in pork exports. All eight products showed positive dumping margins—5 to 10 percent for the meats, 17 to 38 percent for the crops. For all eight products, real producer prices in Mexico fell dramatically, with real 2005 prices 44 to 67 percent lower than their levels in the early 1990s. Mexican production fell for all the crops except corn, and rose significantly for meats, reflecting the rising demand for meat-based protein in the Mexican diet. Import dependency increased dramatically for all products.

What was the cost to Mexican producers of these dumping-level prices? We estimated the nine-year cost at $12.8 billion (in 2000 US$), $1.4 billion per year. To put these numbers in context, the annual losses are more than 10 percent of the value of all Mexican agricultural exports to the United States (including beer, which Mexico, oddly, classifies as its most important agricultural export). The losses from U.S. dumping surpass the total value of Mexico's annual tomato exports to the United States, widely touted as Mexico's biggest NAFTA success story in agriculture.

Not surprisingly, corn farmers suffered the highest losses. U.S. exports increased 413 percent, arrived at prices 19 percent below production costs, and real producer prices in

Mexico declined 66 percent. We estimated losses to Mexican corn farmers of $6.6 billion over the nine-year period, over $700 million per year. These losses amount to $99/hectare per year, a crushing blow to struggling smallholders.

Given how sluggishly the Mexican economy has performed under NAFTA, these are also crushing losses for Mexico. An estimated 2.3 million people have left agriculture in a country desperate for livelihoods. And food dependency has risen dramatically, which cost Mexico dearly when commodity prices spiked between 2006 and 2008.

Timothy A. Wise is Deputy Director and Researcher with the Global Development and Environment Institute at Tufts University.

U.S. Dumping on Mexico 1990–2005

	United States Exports to Mexico (1000 mt)			Mexican Losses from Dumping 1997-2005
	1990-92 (Pre-NAFTA)	2006-08 (Post-NAFTA)	Growth %	2000 US$ Millions
Corn	2,014	10,330	413%	6,571
Soybeans	1,410	3,653	159%	31
Wheat	360	2,515	599%	2,176
Cotton	49	312	531%	805
Rice	129	806	524%	67
Beef	54	204	278%	1,566
Pork	27	218	707%	1,161
Poultry	85	396	363%	455
Total Losses				12,832

Sources: USDA-FATUS, IATP, Starmer et al. (2006), SAGARPA Constant 2000 US$

14. New Zealand: Still Subsidy-free After All These Years

In 1984, the government of New Zealand announced the unthinkable. Faced with mounting deficits and spiraling inflation, the country abandoned the extensive programs that had been cushioning farmers with as much as 40 percent of their total income through the 1970s and early 80s.

At the time, New Zealand's farmers faced a crisis not radically different from the shocks that hit U.S. agriculture during the 1970s and 80s. Rising oil prices had triggered inflation, and farmers were finding it difficult to recoup fair prices on the open market. Great Britain, historically New Zealand's most secure trading partner, had joined the European Union, and was realigning its trading relationships. No longer privy to special status as a Commonwealth nation, New Zealand's agricultural exports were cast into the already overflowing basket of the global economy.

New Zealand's farm leaders brought national attention to the need for urgent subsidy reform.

The New Zealand government initially responded the way most developed countries do: by shoveling cash and incentives at the farm sector in the hope that boosting production would also boost farm income. Tax breaks, fertilizer subsidies, price supports, low-interest loans, disaster relief, weed-eradication payments, special training programs, and other farmer-friendly incentives unfortunately all funneled toward the same disappointing result. They generated oversupply, which in turn, depressed commodity prices.

New Zealand farmers were quick to catch on to the flawed logic. They dubbed the "livestock incentive scheme"—a direct payment program to help farmers increase the size of their herds—the "skinny sheep scheme."[1] (Alas, even a pasture-rich country falls victim to such fundamental laws as stock-carrying capacity. There are practical limits to the number of sheep that can be productively placed on the land.) One farmer sarcastically named his newly purchased boat "the SMP," after the "supplementary minimum prices" subsidy, the backbone of the country's farm supports.[2] Apparently the country's subsidy programs helped pay for it.

It was New Zealand's farm leaders who brought national attention to the urgent need for subsidy reform. It had become obvious to them that farm support programs weren't boosting prices, but were overburdening the national treasury. In 1982, the country's leading farm organization, the Federated Farmers of New Zealand, advocated a partial overhaul of the subsidy

A Subsidy-free View. Almost 30 years after New Zealand's Labor Party shut down an extensive agricultural support program, the farm sector is overachieving. Sheep stocking numbers have declined but have been replaced with a diversity of activities. Agricultural productivity, while averaging 1 percent growth per year in the subsidy era, has reportedly grown 5.9 percent per year since 1986 when farm supports were abandoned.

system. Then in 1984 the country's Labor Party won a landslide victory, and included in their sweeping economic restructuring was the elimination of nearly all agriculture programs. While certain safety net programs remained in place, New Zealand's farm sector was forced to go it alone.

By most accounts, the six-year transition was rocky, especially for farmers paying off loans for equipment and improvements. Farm income plummeted. Land and livestock prices fell. Some farmers committed suicide. An estimated 1 percent, or 800 farmers, were forced to leave the land. But that toll was far lower than the 8,000 farmers or 10 percent that had been anticipated. Sheep farmers, the most heavily subsidized before the reforms, bore the brunt of the impact. But by the early 1990s, land values, commodity prices, farm profitability, and other indices had stabilized or even begun to show steady improvement.

According to most reports, rather than a collapse of agriculture, New Zealand's shift has led to an energizing transformation of the food and farming sectors. Profitability, innovation, and agricultural diversity have returned to farming without extensive subsidies. While approximately 90 percent of New Zealand's total farm output is exported, most of the food consumed inside the country is grown domestically. The total number of sheep has fallen, but weight-gain and lambing productivity have increased. Similar efficiencies emerged in other areas. New Zealand's dairy industry was earning more foreign exchange than sheep farming by 2000, and its production costs were among the lowest in the world. Barely in its infancy in the pre-1984 era, New Zealand has developed a thriving wine industry.

What's more, a whole new generation of New Zealanders has entered the farming industry—a generation that has little experience with, or expectation of, subsidies. In a 2001 BBC News interview, Alistair Polson, chairman of the Federated Farmers of New Zealand, offered this advice to farmers in the developed world: "Get off the subsidy gravy train as soon as possible."[3]

One might argue that New Zealand represents a unique case because of its abundant resources, relatively small population, and geographic diversity. Another sound argument can be made for the country's social safety net, which includes public health care, education, and other services. But with the country now entering its third full decade without subsidies, it's clear the policy is not "experimental" or part of an ongoing trial.

While countries around the Pacific and around the world are emptying government coffers with output incentives, subsidized water and power, and countless other programs for their farm sectors, in New Zealand current government financial support for farmers is less than 1 percent of its average farm income.[4] Farm output and farm income are on the rise. Agriculture contributes slightly more to the overall economy than it did during the subsidy era and has taken on a culture of creativity and entrepreneurship.[5]

The chief architect of New Zealand's free market initiative, Roger Douglas—initially vilified—has been knighted.

What could agriculture look like with far fewer subsidies and direct payments? New Zealand presents a 25-year case study with a surprisingly positive ending. Many countries are taking notice.

Why New Zealanders Don't Like Subsidies

- Resentment among farmers, some of whom will inevitably feel that subsidies are applied unfairly.
- Resentment among nonfarmers, who pay for the system once in the form of taxes and a second time in the form of higher food prices.
- The encouragement of overproduction, which then drives down prices and requires more subsidization of farmers' incomes.
- The related encouragement to farm marginal lands, with resulting environmental degradation.
- The fact that most subsidy money passes quickly from farmers to farm suppliers, processors, and other related sectors, again negating the intended effect of supporting farmers.
- Additional market distortions, such as the inflation of land values based on production incentives or cheap loans.
- Various bureaucratic insanities, such as paying farmers to install conservation measures like hedgerows and wetlands—after having paid them to rip them out a generation ago—while those farmers who maintained such landscape and wildlife features all along get nothing.

Removing subsidies, on the other hand, forces farmers and farm-related industries to become more efficient, to diversify, to follow and anticipate the market. It gives farmers more independence, and earns them public respect. It leaves more government money to pay for other types of social services, like education and health care.

Excerpted with permission from Laura Sayre, "Farming without subsidies? Some lessons from New Zealand," *The New Farm*, March 2003.

WEDGE

ISSUES

15. Political Wedge Issues

It would be naïve to imagine that the Farm Bill could be radically overhauled during any single negotiation cycle (New Zealand style). Considering everything at stake—our health, our food, our environment—one might think that the forces opposing corporate industrial food and farming (conservationists, family farm advocates, anti-hunger groups) could constitute a united front for change. But more often than not, reform groups have remained divided, winning important concessions for their own special interests only to make an unsatisfactory system slightly less bad. At the same time, the agribusiness and food industry lobbies are unconstrained, farm states wield too much power, and entitlement programs are too entrenched. One resource economist described Farm Bill negotiations as a "fully rigged" game.

Reformers must learn to build bridges that lead to integrated solutions that address deep systemic problems.

At least three times in the last 80 years the Farm Bill has undergone true seismic changes. In 1961, the food stamp program was reinstated in the early days of the Kennedy Administration. Commodity growers and an emerging Congressional anti-hunger caucus eventually made common cause, tying agricultural output to a food safety net for the poor. In the mid-1980s, conservation resurfaced as an important Farm Bill priority. Environmental and wildlife advocates successfully lobbied for stewardship incentives that went beyond simple erosion control. In the 1980s and 1990s, a wave of deregulation reforms dismantled a long-standing federally run supply management system and replaced it with the subsidy supports so favorable to corporate agribusinesses and industrial food processors that we have today.

It remains to be seen which, if any, of the current issues might truly rattle the next round of negotiations, including:

- The need to significantly reduce the national debt burden;
- Mounting health care costs due to adult and childhood obesity;
- Rising costs and eventual limited availability of fossil fuels;
- Diminishing sources of fresh water;
- Brazil's victory in the World Trade Organization cotton case against the U.S.;
- Major push for income limitations on farm program eligibility and caps on total subsidies per recipient;
- Extreme weather events due to climate chaos;
- Emerging local food movements.

As an old saying goes, cultural shifts usually precede policy changes, which come slowly and idiosyncratically, often taking years and multiple Farm Bill cycles for even a single issue or new program to take root. Successful wedge interests become pilots and, later, programs with mandatory budgets and perhaps titles, over time demanding more money, sometimes raiding the till from other programs. Revoking them becomes difficult, even long after they've stopped being relevant, appropriate, or effective. Sometimes agribusiness simply co-opts programs, keeping the language of public benefit but funneling money to corporate agribusinesses and megafarms. (Using conservation money to finance pollution compliance on feedlots or giving renewable energy subsidies to capital-wealthy corn ethanol plants comes to mind.) The most recent movement underfoot entails replacing subsidy programs with federally funded crop insurance policies that would guarantee income based on historic crop prices.

Still, a food and farm policy earthquake could start along any one of multiple rumbling fault lines in the coming years.

Government Deficits. With the implications of trillion-dollar deficits weighing on the nation, conservatives and liberals alike are looking at ways to trim the fat. The USDA's food and farm programs, while just a small percentage of total government spending, are always a target of discontent about government pork. Decades of taxpayer giveaways to millionaire landowners have made farm programs enormously unpopular. Yet the need

for investments in conservation, research, regional food production, nutrition, renewable energy, and other priority areas makes supporting food and agriculture more important than ever. It might be time to look to other agencies that also have a stake in a healthy food system—such as public health or defense or energy—to contribute a fair share.

Energy. With rapidly fluctuating oil markets and the costs of food production on the rise, energy issues will dominate Farm Bill debates well into the future. The corn-based ethanol industry has enjoyed enormous growth thanks to twenty years of generous tax incentives, federal mandates, and other subsidies—now totaling as much as $6 billion per year. This has been more of a corn policy than a responsible energy policy. Finally the tide is turning against public support for corn-based ethanol. Energy efficiency measures need to take the place of growing crops to replace liquid fuels. Efforts to reduce energy-intensive and polluting nitrogen fertilizer must become national priorities.

Health Care. Perhaps the most influential lobbying force poised to weigh in on Farm Bill discussions is the health care community. With the annual medical costs of the obesity crisis now at $150 billion and predicted to reach $350 billion by 2018, the health care community is a sleeping giant about to awaken and throw around significant influence and resources behind food and farm policies. Will the health care community demand an agricultural policy that pushes healthier diets? Will it join forces with other movements calling for

Figure 19

Turning Points in

Nutrition

1939 In the wake of the Great Depression millions struggle for food and the nation launches an experimental food stamp program

1943 Experimental food stamp program ends

1946 The National School Lunch Program is launched amidst concerns for the security of a malnourished nation

1943–1961 After the experimental food stamp program ends, food stamps cease to exist for nearly twenty years

1961 Inspired by his encounters with poverty on the campaign trail, John F. Kennedy begins a new experimental food stamp program on his first day in office

1964 President Lyndon Johnson establishes a national food stamp program

Conservation

1936 The Soil Conservation and Domestic Allotment Act promotes soil conservation and profitable use of agricultural resources

1947 The Federal Insecticide, Fungicide and Rodenticide Act requires all pesticides to be registered and labeled but does not address environmental or human safety concerns

1950 Agriculture begins to shift towards industrialization

1950 Farmers rapidly increase the use of synthetic fertilizers. Misapplication leads to major pollution problems

1965 Food and Agricultural Act of 1965 authorizes a long-term plan to retire some farmland from crop production

On the Farm

1933 The first Farm Bill, officially titled "The Agricultural Adjustment Act of 1933" establishes minimum commodity prices and acreage reduction incentives

1942 To assuage fears of economic hardship, Congress guarantees price supports for twenty farm commodities at 90 percent of parity for two years after the legal end of World War II

1954 The Agricultural Act of 1954 establishes a government-run grain reserve program

1954 Earl Butz is appointed Assistant Secretary of Agriculture and promotes industrial farming

1961 The Kennedy Administration revives acreage controls, sets price supports close to market prices, and pays farmers for significant land retirement. Surpluses that had plagued farmers and government for years largely subside

1930s	1940s	1950s	1960s

Historical Context

1930 21.5 percent of the employed population works in agriculture

1931 Dust Bowl begins

1939–1943 Approximately 4 million people rely on food stamps

1947 International Harvester begins commercial production of cotton-picking machines

1950 16 hours of human labor are required to produce 100 bushels of corn, down from 147 hours of labor for 100 bushels in 1900

1960–1969 Output per worker on American farms increases by 82 percent

1965 More than half the corn in the U.S. is shelled mechanically

Food and Farm Policy

1977 President Jimmy Carter eliminates the requirement of purchasing food stamps in order to receive benefits

1981 After demonizing people who relied on public support to survive during his campaign, President Ronald Reagan makes significant cuts to food stamp benefits

1996–2001 A series of Congressional and local government actions restrict food stamp eligibility and coerce those who are eligible not to claim benefits

2004 The method of redeeming food stamp benefits shifts from coupons to "Electronic Benefit Transfer" or EBT cards

2008 The name of the food stamp program is changed to the "Supplemental Nutrition Assistance Program" or SNAP

2011 More than 45 million Americans rely upon SNAP benefits to eat

1972 The use of DDT is banned in the United States

1985 Congress begins requiring farmers to implement approved soil conservation systems in order to receive certain USDA benefits

1996 The Federal Agriculture Improvement and Reform act of 1996 eliminates acreage reduction programs

2002 Provisions for organic and local food systems are added to the Farm Bill

2008 Congress increases conservation program spending by nearly $4 billion

2010 Conservation programs receive lower than promised levels of funding. For example, funding for the Environmental Quality Incentives Program is cut by $270 million

1971 The Nixon administration limits land diversion payments to $55,000 per farm operator, but many farmers find loopholes.

1972 A major grain deal with the Soviet Union absorbs accumulated surpluses and wheat prices skyrocket

1985 The Food Security Act of 1985 effectively ends the minimum-price program for commodities and eliminates the government-run grain reserve program

1998 The U.S. government makes emergency payments to farmers because of low market prices.

2002 The Farm Security and Rural Investment Act of 2002 makes counter-cyclical and direct payments permanent

2011 The price of corn doubles between June 2010 and February 2011 as demand for ethanol increases. Prices of soy and wheat increase 60 percent each as supply decreases when farmers replace these crops with corn

1970s	1980s	1990s	2000s	2010s
1970 Five percent of the employed population works in agriculture	**1980** Food stamp enrollment reaches 20 million	**1990** A mere three hours of labor is required to produce 100 bushels of corn	**2000** 1.9 percent of the employed population works in agriculture	**2010** Food stamp enrollment reaches 40 million
1970 Japanese food scientists develop High Fructose Corn Syrup	**1980** Routine dosing of antibiotics becomes standard practice in livestock production	**1994** Food stamp enrollment reaches 27 million	**2007** Great Recession begins	

regional food production, non-toxic farming methods, grass-fed livestock and closer links between farmers and consumers?

Religious Communities. The faith-based community is yet another constituency whose influence could be significant. Issues of fair trade, hunger, the concentration of ownership, conditions of animal confinement, global hunger, and climate change have surfaced as moral concerns. Broader participation among congregants and faith-based organizations could greatly expand citizen input into food and farm politics, particularly outside traditional agricultural regions.

Climate Change. Scientists have warned for more than a decade that the planet's climate is changing. These changes appear to be having a direct bearing on farming: heavy storms, searing drought, and unpredictable weather patterns are becoming the norms of modern agriculture. At the same time, agriculture contributes an estimated 8 percent of America's greenhouse gas emissions. Worldwide, the food system's contributions are much higher. Methane emissions from concentrated livestock production, nitrous oxide from fertilizer use, and carbon dioxide from livestock and equipment all contribute to a global food system that is literally heating up the planet. The future requires a long-term transition toward production that uses less energy, raises fewer grain-fed animals, offers resilience against flooding and drought, and sequesters carbon.

Local Food Systems. A movement has been long afoot to increase the appreciation of and access to locally produced foods. Farmers markets, Community Supported Agriculture, Farm 2 School, Farm 2 Institution, and many other innovative developments are connecting local farmers and consumers now more than ever. Health providers are writing vegetable prescriptions for overweight patients, farmers market vendors are accepting SNAP electronic benefits, consumers are seeking out regional produce. Local food production is being expanded to increase regional food security, create jobs, and give school children an understanding of where their food comes from. City governments and regional food councils are even weighing in with their own platforms and principles that they hope can shape future Farm Bill funding priorities.

The more citizens learn what is at stake, and to an even greater extent, have a clear picture of the kind of agriculture and food system they want their elected officials to support, the better our chances for reform. But reformers must also learn to build bridges that lead to integrated solutions that address deep systemic problems such as the loss of diversity in the farming system or over-reliance on fossil fuels to produce food. Only by creating a fully healthy food and farming system—economically, ecologically, and socially—will citizens also gain full health. It is also essential to keep in mind that the Farm Bill is an ongoing process. It will require our ongoing attention long after the next version becomes law.

16. Public Health and Nutrition: Building 21st Century Food Systems, Fighting Chronic Disease

In recent years, the public health community has tuned in to the importance of agriculture and the Farm Bill. The American Public Health Association, the Centers for Disease Control, the American Dietetic Association, the Johns Hopkins Center for a Livable Future, and hundreds of other organizations all view crop choices, farming practices, animal welfare, and regional food security as key issues in promoting good health. The obesity epidemic may have been the catalyst, but now pesticide exposure, antibiotic-resistant pathogens in livestock, and air and water contamination are all coming to be seen as public health priorities. Many are looking to the Farm Bill for solutions to obesity, inadequate nutrition, and environmental health hazards.

The obesity epidemic may have been the catalyst, but now pesticide exposure, antibiotic-resistant pathogens in livestock, and air and water contamination are all coming to be seen as public health priorities.

Today, many Americans don't consume a healthy diet, despite benefiting from one of the world's most technologically intensive food and farming systems and spending a smaller percentage of income on food than many other nations. Here are just a few of the symptoms of our unhealthy national farm and food policy:

- Nearly one in three U.S. kids and teens are overweight or obese.[1]
- Only 2 percent of 2- to 19-year-olds meet all five federal requirements for a healthy diet.[2]
- The food industry spends $17 billion a year marketing to children. The Federal School Lunch Program spends less than $10 billion per year to feed our children in the public schools.[3]
- The average American consumes 44.7 gallons of soft drinks annually. (This includes diet sodas but excludes noncarbonated sweetened beverages, which would add another 17 gallons per person per year.)[4]
- Nearly 15 percent of Americans are "food insecure," or experience "relatively low food security," USDA shorthand meaning that they are often not certain where their next meal will come from.[5]

Figure 20 · Got Cheese?

U.S. Per Capita Cheese Consumption

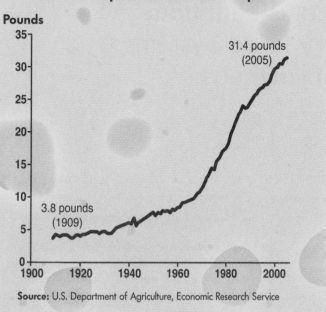

Pounds

31.4 pounds
(2005)

3.8 pounds
(1909)

Source: U.S. Department of Agriculture, Economic Research Service

• Nearly 24 million people ages 20 years and older have diabetes.[6]

Is the Farm Bill a Fat Bill?

In 2001, Surgeon General Richard Carmona sounded a public health alarm, declaring that U.S. obesity rates–double those of the early 1970s–had reached "epidemic" dimensions.[7] A year later, researchers tallied that two out of every three adult Americans were clinically overweight. This included 31 percent of adults between the ages of 20 and 74 who were medically obese, raising their susceptibility to chronic ailments such as heart disease and diabetes. Perhaps most troubling, 17 percent of children and adolescents are now obese–triple the number of the early 1970s.

(See Figure 24, "Overweight and Obesity on the Rise"). A November 2009 United Health Foundation report estimated that the obesity crisis, if unchecked, will add $344 billion annually to America's already skyrocketing health costs by 2018.[8]

It would be convenient to pinpoint a single bad actor in this unfolding public health tragedy. Unfortunately, a smorgasbord of influences is driving the country's excessive weight gain. Insufficient exercise. Meals more frequently eaten on the run or outside the home. High-calorie processed foods in school cafeterias. Stress and lack of money. Under-consumption of fruits and vegetables. Super-sizing of portions. Inability to resist foods that are high in sugars, fats, and sodium. A genetic predisposition known as the "thrifty gene" that causes some humans to gorge on available foods regardless of the nutritional consequences.[9] Exposure to endocrine disrupting chemicals dubbed *obesogens,* which researchers believe alter our ability to control body weight by changing metabolism and increasing fat cell development.

And just more food. According to the USDA Economic Research Service, in 2000 the aggregate food supply provided 3,800 calories per person per day. Adjusting for spoilage, waste, and other losses, the USDA estimated actual daily caloric intake at just under 2,700 calories per person per day.[10] The study reports that these added food calories primarily come from refined grain products, processed carbohydrates, processed sugars, fats, and oils. On average, for example, Americans consume 152 pounds of caloric sweeteners every year: 32 teaspoons per person per day.

Saturated fats are also adding to dietary imbalance. These include high-fat meats, coconut and palm oils frequently added to processed foods and vegetable shortening, as well as whole milk and high-fat dairy products. Responding to the obesity crisis, the USDA's most recent Dietary Guidelines for Americans 2010 came out with this analysis:

> *On average, Americans of all ages consume too few vegetables, fruits, high-fiber whole grains, low-fat milk and milk products, and seafood and they eat too much added sugars, solid fats, refined grains, and sodium. SoFAS (solid fats and added sugars) contribute approximately 35 percent of calories to the American diet. This is true for children, adolescents, adults, and older adults and for both males and females. Reducing the intake of SoFAS can lead to a badly needed reduction in energy intake and inclusion of more healthful foods into the total diet.*[11]

Nutrition After the Food Pyramid Era

So what is the Farm Bill's role in the obesity crisis? Some critics give it primary blame, because of its hefty emphasis on subsidizing commodities—animal feeds, high fructose corn syrup, and soybean oil—rather than fruits, nuts, and vegetables. Others are quick to point out that there is no causal connection

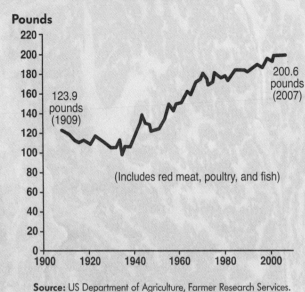

Figure 21

Eat Meat?

U.S. Per Capita Meat Intake

123.9 pounds (1909)

200.6 pounds (2007)

(Includes red meat, poultry, and fish)

Source: US Department of Agriculture, Farmer Research Services.

between crop subsidies and obesity; even if commodity supports were eliminated, the cost of processed foods would only increase marginally, and farmers would continue to grow corn and soybeans.[12] Rather, they argue that it is the food processing and distribution system—heavy on convenience, packaging, marketing—that has spurred a cultural shift toward unhealthy eating habits.

Still, we cannot be too quick to dismiss how badly USDA agriculture policies are out of alignment with its nutritional recommendations. This is not a minor disconnect. It's more like two trains on separate tracks running in completely different directions.

In early 2011, USDA replaced its ever-evolving Food Pyramid with My Plate, an

16. Public Health and Nutrition

easy-to-use graphic representation of the food groups recommended the agency's Dietary Guidelines. My Plate's message is clear: a healthy plate should be at least half full of fruits and vegetables and another quarter should comprise whole grains. If there was a matching USDA Subsidy Plate, however, its message would be: fill your plate with animal proteins and processed foods. Nearly two-thirds of the corn, over half of the soybeans, a great deal of the cottonseed and cottonseed meal, and even some of the wheat produced in the U.S. is fed to livestock. According to the Physicians Committee for Responsible Medicine, the meat, egg, and dairy sectors were the beneficiaries of the majority of the $246 billion in subsidies provided to U.S. food producers between 1996 and 2009.[13] (See Figure 22, "MyPlate/AgSubsidyPlate.") Until the ethanol industry began gobbling up more than one-third of the corn crop in 2007, an oversupply of corn and soybeans was a boon to animal feeding operations. Feed is one of the largest costs of these food factory operations, and when it's cheap and abundant, so are meat, high-fat dairy, and eggs—the same foods the USDA instructs us to eat in moderation.

On one hand, the USDA has been encouraging a switch to low-fat milk and low-fat dairy products over the past few decades. On the other, USDA's commodity subsidy programs have steadily supported an oversupply of milk. As low-fat milk products gain popularity, cheese has proven to be a profitable outlet for surplus milk fat.

In fact, cheese is now the top source of saturated fat in the U.S. diet. The average American eats 33 pounds of cheese every year, almost a three-fold increase from the 1970s. It's layered on burgers, sandwiches, and pizzas, sometimes with cheese in the crust or cheese sauce on top. A single ounce of many cheeses can pack as much saturated fat as a glass of whole milk.[14]

During the 2008 Farm Bill reauthorization, numerous reports surfaced about how much the cost of fruits and vegetables had risen over the past three decades relative to processed foods—particularly sweetened beverages.[15] The need to improve the affordability of fruits and vegetables dominated reform discussions in 2008, resulting in numerous USDA programs to educate consumers, broaden access to produce, fund healthy snack programs for public schools, and dedicate nearly $1 billion in support for specialty crop growers.

In fact, the different cost ranges between highly processed foods and nutrient dense fruits and vegetables may have more to do with the nature of their production chains than with Farm Bill subsidies per se. Fruits and vegetables can be expensive—especially when they are eaten out of season or shipped great distances. In general, produce is perishable and requires far more handling than storable commodity crops. Consumers are also increasingly turning to pre-processed produce—bagged spinach, baby carrots, salad mixes—that add value and cost to items. While Farm Bill subsidies may have no

Figure 22

MyPlate

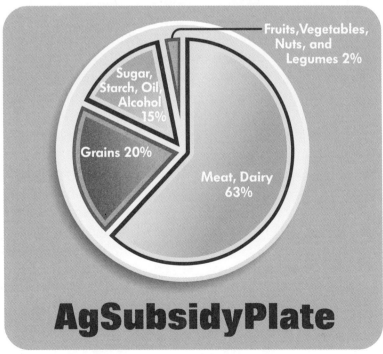

AgSubsidyPlate

Source: USDA's MyPlate Homepage; "Agriculture and Health Policies in Conflict: How Food Subsidies Tax Our Health," Physicians Committee for Responsible Medicine.

tangible direct bearing on the high costs of fresh produce, current and future Farm Bill programs could markedly improve the conditions for growers of specialty crops. Some key barriers to expanded production of fruits and vegetables include specialized equipment and labor, higher production costs, lack of proximity to processing plants or markets for fresh produce, difficulty accessing credit, and insufficient public demand for fruits and vegetables. That would mean tilting the balance of subsidies more in the direction of the USDA dietary recommendations to encourage all sectors of society to eat more fruits, vegetables, whole grains, and nuts.

From Hunger to Health—The 21st Century Safety Net

The Farm Bill's Nutrition Title has grown from an effort to distribute surplus crops during the Great Depression, into the largest food assistance program in the country. For more than 45 million people, or 1 out of 7 Americans in 2011, the Supplemental Nutrition Assistance Program (SNAP) often meant the difference between going to bed hungry and receiving minimal nourishment. Food stamps (SNAP), Women, Infants, and Children's (WIC) vouchers, and free and subsidized school meals all enhance the well-being of low-income Americans. To its great credit, the antihunger lobby has heroically defended the country's hunger safety net in Farm Bill after Farm Bill, attaining the necessary votes to "do no harm" to food assistance programs that essentially counter an entrenched national commitment

to low minimum wages. The antihunger lobby has also worked to de-stigmatize food assistance. An innovative debit card style system (Electronic Benefits Transfer, EBT) has replaced paper coupons and can even be used in approximately 10 percent of the country's 7,000 farmers' markets.

The biggest challenge may be that the Thrifty Food Plan, which sets the SNAP Program's upper cap for monthly benefits at $1.40 per person per meal, does not provide recipients with enough money to eat a balanced healthy diet. Likewise, the working poor disproportionately rely on foods that are loaded with sugars, sodium, and saturated fats. This is not necessarily out of dietary preference as much as the economic pressures that many Americans face. The easiest-to-prepare products in supermarket aisles often turn out to be those that are mass produced and made from heavily subsidized crops: frozen prepared foods, dairy products, baked goods. According to Adam Drenowski, professor of epidemiology at the University of Washington, the poor in particular are gaining weight and getting sick because unhealthy food is cheaper and often more available than healthy food.[16]

Admirable efforts were made in the 2008 Farm Bill to shift the mission of nutrition programs from simple hunger relief to making healthier foods available to the public. The Farmers Market Promotion Program set aside at least 10 percent of its funds to put SNAP benefit EBT machines in markets. The Senior Farmers Market Nutrition Program offered coupons for fruits and vegetables, honey and fresh herbs. A SNAP-Ed program dedicated $1 billion for promoting and better understanding healthy eating behavior among food stamp recipients. Healthy Incentives Pilot programs were set up to determine whether outreach campaigns actually encouraged greater consumption of fruits and vegetables. The Fresh Fruit and Vegetable Program funded an increase in the volume of healthy snacks in public schools.

In upcoming Farm Bills, legislators must find ways to realign crop subsidies. Public health demands more federal attention to nutrient-rich foods and less to feed crops and commodities. The good news is that this can be a very powerful job-creating opportunity–engaging young farmers, creating regional food hubs, bringing up a new generation of chefs and food entrepreneurs. As a starting point we can make proper nutrition the top priority of the of school lunch programs that feed 30 million children every day and are so important in the development of lifelong eating habits.

Food Deserts: So Much Agriculture, So Little Food

The lack of Farm Bill support for produce crops makes growing healthier foods a far

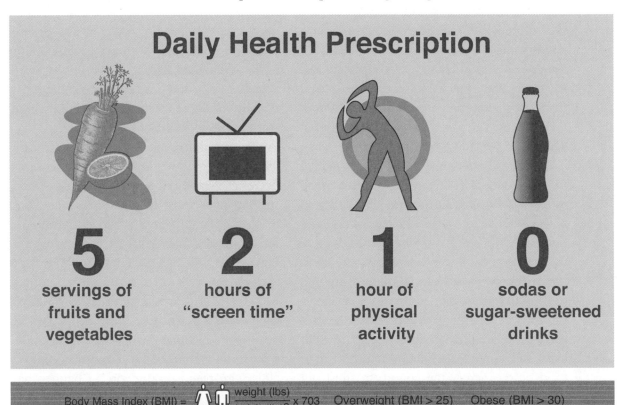

Daily Health Prescription

5
servings of fruits and vegetables

2
hours of "screen time"

1
hour of physical activity

0
sodas or sugar-sweetened drinks

Body Mass Index (BMI) = $\dfrac{\text{weight (lbs)}}{\text{height (in)}^2}$ x 703   Overweight (BMI > 25)   Obese (BMI > 30)

riskier proposition for farmers. Even if they want to diversify, farmers often face rural economic infrastructures tailored to commodity production and lacking in necessary equipment, supplies, technical expertise, cold storage warehouses, and slaughter and processing facilities. Regional food distribution chains that once accommodated a diversity of crops and livestock have been entirely eliminated in many traditional farming areas.

While our farmers grow feed grains, cotton, and oil seed crops, we are shipping our fruits and vegetables across the country or even around the world. Fruits and vegetables are the fastest growing category of U.S. food imports, increasing at an average annual growth rate of 9.7 percent.[17] So even in farm country, most of the cash residents spend on their weekly food bills leaves the region and the state. Dinner tables remain disconnected from the fields that surround them. Across the Midwest, the result is a paradox: so much agriculture, so little food.

Food deserts–low-income areas where fresh produce is in limited supply–are by no means just an urban problem. USDA defines a food desert as "a Census tract where 33 percent or 500 people, whichever is less, live more than a mile from a grocery store in an urban area or more than 10 miles away in a rural area. At least 20 percent of the residents must live below the federal poverty line, currently $22,350 for a family of four." The 2008 Farm Bill funded a $500,000 study to map food deserts across the country to find out where access to healthy foods is most urgently needed (See Figure 25, "Food Deserts.")

Many inner-city areas, particularly low-income neighborhoods, have become "fresh food-free zones," where it is often easier to find a fast food restaurant or a convenience store than a grocery store. Estimates show, for example, that one-fifth of Chicago's 3,000,000 residents lack access to healthy, affordable food outlets. Rural food deserts, even in farming areas, are also common, particularly across the Great Plains. More than half of Kansas' 675 cities and towns don't have a grocery store, a critical element of rural infrastructure that has been vanishing as populations plummet, businesses shutter, and access to healthy food means driving ever-longer distances.[18] Items purchased in a gas station or small convenience store, whether in a rural or urban area, are rarely a worthy substitute for the produce and wholesome foods a grocer offers.

If expanding access to and availability of healthy foods throughout the country becomes a Farm Bill goal, as it should, spending priorities must be drastically altered to bring about structural changes. Consider, for example, that over the course of the 2008 Farm Bill, $13 to $21 billion has been spent every year on commodity crops. Just $600,000 per year was directed toward specialty crops during the same time period, despite the fact that produce, fruits, and nuts make up one-third of the economic output of all U.S. cropland production.[19] Changes may

Figure 24

Overweight and Obesity on the Rise

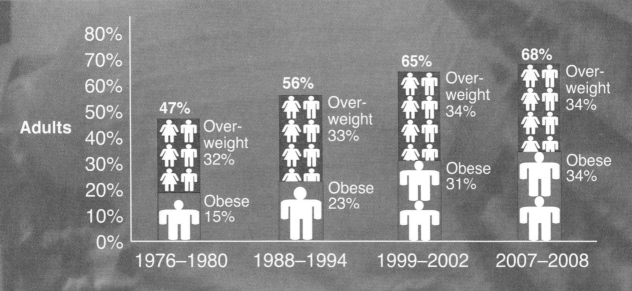

Age-Adjusted Prevalence in U.S., Ages 20–74, 1976–2008

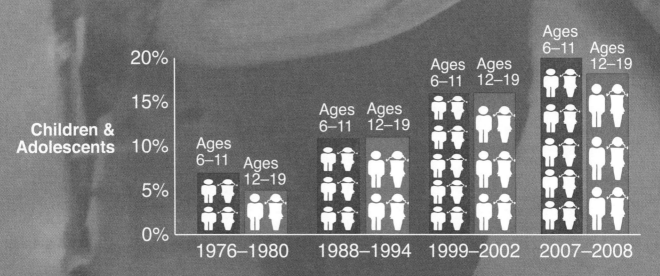

Obesity Among Children and Adolescents Ages 6–19 Years, 1976–2008

Source: Centers for Disease Control and Prevention

eventually mean removing long-standing restrictions that currently prevent commodity producers who receive crop subsidies from growing fruits and vegetables.

Environmental Health Concerns

Public health concerns don't begin on the store shelves, but in farm fields and livestock production facilities.

Aspects of industrial agriculture make living in a rural community a health hazard: water and air contamination, exposure to pesticides and antibiotic-resistant pathogens, high rates of occupational injuries in farm and food processing jobs. And the damage doesn't just stay on the farm. Harmful chemicals, hormones, and other substances make their way into the food system. Some of these are persistent and accumulate inside the food chain and inside our bodies.

Meat production is a big part of environmental and community health problems, particularly because of high concentrations of animals, but also because of the monoculture farming of feed crops. Routine dosing of antimicrobial medicines to livestock inside crowded animal factories under the guise of growth promotion, for example, has been publicly criticized by organizations and institutions such as the American Public Health Association, the American Medical Association, the Union of Concerned Scientists, the Centers for Disease Control, the Pew Commission on Industrial Animal Food Production, and dozens of others. Nearly 30

million pounds of antibiotics were used by the livestock industry in 2009 according to the Food and Drug Administration—more than 70 percent of the country's total annual consumption of these drugs.[20] Antibiotic-resistant bacteria can spread from food production facilities to the public through human contact with infected animals, consumption of contaminated foods, or animal wastes that are spewed across the landscape. Because of the overuse of antibiotics in animal production, bacteria are now resistant to important human medicines such as tetracycline, ampicillin and streptomycin.[21] During the last Farm Bill cycle, the Food and Drug Administration issued recommendations for limiting antibiotic use in food animals. But USDA has yet to implement the changes, which would ban subtherapeutic uses of antibiotics and require veterinary consultations for drug applications.

Exposure to agricultural chemicals is another serious health issue. Fertilizers and pesticides are used heavily on the vast monocultures where commodities are grown, and on many specialty crop operations as well. While low doses of pesticides are probably not harmful to most people, the long-term cumulative effects of farm chemicals include elevated cancer risks and disruption of the body's reproductive, immune, endocrine, and nervous systems. Arsenic, a known carcinogen, is regularly added to poultry feed so chickens and turkeys grow faster. Some of that winds up in the meat, as shown in a study commissioned by the Institute for Agriculture and Trade Policy in Minneapolis, where researchers consistently detected arsenic residues in retail chicken. The Food and Drug Administration, however, does not test poultry for arsenic, despite its widespread use as a growth promoter. Poultry waste also poses serious health concerns. Massive tonnages of poultry litter are dumped on agricultural lands as a fertilizer and untreated poultry waste is also routinely fed to livestock.

Nitrogen fertilizers load the air and water with toxic chemicals. It is estimated, for example, that corn plants take up just 35 percent of the nitrogen applied to the soil to nourish plants. Much of that remainder leaks out into waterways or becomes airborne in the form of nitrous oxide, a potent greenhouse gas. Bioaccumulation of chemicals becomes a serious problem as nutrients increase and interact in unexpected ways in environments and communities over time.

Albeit limited, the Farm Bill resources that are dedicated to helping reduce dependence on nitrogen, restore ecosystems and wetlands, and decrease the use of drugs in livestock production are invaluable to public health. Other beneficial programs prevent animal waste from entering waterways and mitigate respiratory diseases very common in concentrated livestock production. Pilot programs also have funded the retiring of polluting diesel engines to decrease nitrous oxide emissions and generally improve air quality. Sustainable Agriculture Research and Education programs assist farmers with important innovations in chemical reduction techniques as well as practices that benefit human health and welfare.

Of course other programs can backfire. The Environmental Quality Incentive Program (EQIP) was originally designed to help small landowners improve soil and water quality by reducing fertilizer and waste runoff into streams and waterways. Since 2002 hundreds of millions in EQIP funds have been directed toward large confinement animal facilities, or CAFOs, to help them deal with waste issues. Using taxpayer dollars to enable the CAFO industry to expand and concentrate livestock production into even fewer hands has only perpetuated an already serious health contagion. CAFOs are regularly linked to the leakage of manure from containment lagoons, increased ammonia emissions, nutrient loading in groundwater, and fish kills. If fish are dying in the waterways around livestock facilities, what can be said about water quality for humans?

Public Health: Bridge to a Healthy Farm Bill?

If the Farm Bill is to achieve its purpose, to create a secure, healthy food system from field to plate, it must support a fundamentally healthy agricultural system: fair prices for farmers, healthy rural environments, a diversity of crops and wildlife, respectable conditions for food animals, and a culture that appreciates and understands the impor-

Figure 25

Food Deserts
Low-income Areas Where Access to Healthy Food is Limited

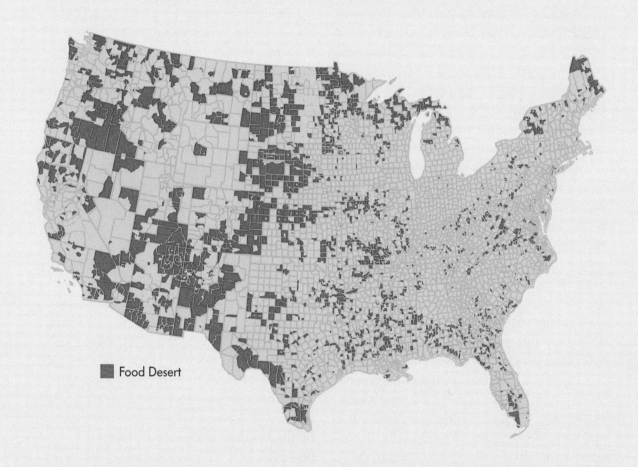

Food Desert

The problem of food deserts—low-income areas with limited access to healthy food—affects rural regions and inner city neighborhoods alike. Residents of California's Central Valley, for example, many of them farm workers, have trouble accessing fresh produce. Yet the region produces nearly half the fruits and vegetables grown in the United States. In urban areas, food desert conditions exist primarily in poor neighborhoods, where access to healthy food is limited by both availability and purchasing power. To reverse these trends, many communities are establishing partnerships with stores that traditionally don't sell fresh produce, farmers markets, and alternative food delivery methods such as mobile produce trucks and weekly deliveries to churches or libraries.

Source: USDA ERS Food Desert Locator

tance of food and farming. The Farm Bill will also need more programs that promote healthier forms of agriculture—crop diversification, grass-pasturing animals, Know Your Farmer programs that create more educated consumers—to benefit human and community health.

With refocused priorities, the Farm Bill's billions of dollars could jump-start such a transformation of the food system. Sea changes in public behavior around health are not unprecedented. In the mid-1960s, Surgeon General Luther Terry's warning against cigarette smoking changed attitudes about the long-term health effects of tobacco use. The President's Council on Physical Fitness established new protocols and standards for physical education in public schools in the 1970s. There is no reason a healthy food movement could not radiate through all levels of society. Farmers markets could serve as hubs of nutrition and culinary education and healthy food distribution.

Replacing our current high-calorie bill with a Food and Farm Bill that promotes healthy citizens, healthy lands, and healthy urban and rural economies requires voters to demand a diet that meets the nutritional and environmental challenges of the 21st century. Public health just might deliver the political bridge that unites us around those fundamental connections.

Food Stamps for Good Food

Melanie Mason

Coretta Dudley's monthly grocery shopping strategy is as finely calibrated as a combat plan. Armed with $868 in Supplemental Nutrition Assistance Program (SNAP) benefits (the fancy new name for food stamps), she stops first at FoodMaxx, a discount supermarket in East Oakland, where she stocks up on four weeks' worth of nonperishables: cases of noodles, cans of vegetables and boxes of the sugary cereals her kids like. She also buys fresh fruit—apples and pears and bananas and grapes—but those will be gone in a week. Then she swings by Wal-Mart for bread, eggs and milk. Later, she'll hit the family-owned meat market, where she chooses hamburger and cube steaks. Other than $100 she sets aside to replenish the milk, eggs and cheese later in the month, that first multipronged attack will last her and her six children, ages 4 to 16, the whole month. That's the idea, anyway.

"At the end of the month, we'll still need something," she says. "It never fails."

Almost 500 miles away, in the City Heights neighborhood of San Diego, Tsehay Gebere has developed her own shopping plan at the Saturday farmers' market. The lines are long, and the ten-pound sacks of oranges, plentiful at 9 am, will have disappeared by noon. But Gebere, a weekly fixture at the market, has the inside track. She persuades farmer Bernardino Loera to sock away four bags in his van. Forty-five minutes later, she gets back to Loera's stall and collects her hoarded prize.

Like Dudley, Gebere receives food stamp benefits, for herself and her four children. Like

Dudley, Gebere shops at discount supermarkets like Food 4 Less for most of her groceries. But while Dudley buys four bags of fruit every month, Gebere buys at least four bags every week—made possible by the free money she gets at the farmers' market.

Yes, free money—though the technical name is "double voucher." The market matches a certain amount of money from a customer's federal food assistance benefits, essentially doubling the customer's purchasing power. City Heights was one of the first double voucher markets in the country; there are now more than 160 participating farmers' markets in twenty states. They reach just a tiny fraction of the more than 43 million Americans receiving food stamps. But their very existence raises questions about SNAP's identity: is it a welfare program or, as its

recent name change suggests, a nutrition program? These questions are the subject of lively debate in USDA offices and advocacy circles, where the idea of giving extra money for fruits and veggies, innocuous as it may seem, is exposing fault lines between traditional advocates for the poor and a new coalition of healthy-food activists.

The underlying premise of the modern food stamp program, shaped in the Kennedy/Johnson years, was that the American poor were starving and in need of calories, any calories at all. But there is now a well-documented overlap between the country's staggering rate of "food insecurity" (the term used by the USDA in lieu of "hunger") and its escalating obesity rates. In 2009, 43 percent of households below the federal poverty line experienced food insecurity. And if you're poor, you're more likely to be obese. Nine of the ten states with the highest poverty levels also rank in the top ten of obesity rates.

That one can be simultaneously food insecure and obese seems like a paradox. But consider that many low-income neighborhoods have few full-service supermarkets. Grocery shopping in the neighborhood likely means buying at corner stores with limited options for healthy choices. Even if those options do exist, they are not necessarily the rational economic choice for someone on a tight budget. The cost per calorie for foods containing fats and oils, sugars and refined grains is extremely low, but these are precisely the foods linked to high obesity rates. Healthy choices like fruits and vegetables are as much as several thousand times more expensive per calorie.

In a California Department of Public Health survey of eating habits, low-income people said they knew the importance of healthy eating. But they still eat fewer fruits and vegetables than the government recommends, less than the American population as a whole. "People said they couldn't afford it," says George Manalo-LeClair, legislation director with the California Food Policy Advocates. "It's cost."

At the heart of this whole mess—poverty, hunger and declining health—is the food stamp program. Nationwide, the average SNAP beneficiary received $125.31 per month in fiscal year 2009. If food stamps constitute a person's entire food budget—as often happens, even though the program is intended to supplement recipients' own money—that translates to just under $1.40 per meal. If you're looking to buy something that will satiate you for $1.40, you probably won't be buying broccoli.

Researchers have long studied whether food stamps contribute to obesity. Previously the conclusion was, probably not. But in an Ohio State University study released in the summer of 2009 the finding was, quite possibly yes. The study found that the body mass index (BMI) of program participants is more than one point higher than nonparticipants at the same income level. The longer one is on food stamps, the higher the BMI rises.

If the link exists—and it is exceedingly difficult to prove a causal relationship between food stamps and any one physical condition—it exposes a weakness in the program. The food stamp program has certainly evolved since the "war on poverty," but fundamentally it is still operating as though the only health threat facing the poor is insufficient calories.

❀ ❀ ❀

The roots of the City Heights farmers' market date back thirty years, to an incident in 1980 Gus Schumacher calls "the case of the broken pear box." Schumacher was helping his brother, a farmer outside Boston, load a truck after the Dorchester farmers' market closed when he dropped a box of Bosc pears in the gutter. A woman passing by bent down and retrieved the damaged fruit, explaining that she was on food stamps but still couldn't afford fresh fruits and vegetables for her children. Schumacher ended up giving her an additional ten pounds of apples and pears. "People should not be picking fruit out of a gutter," he says.

A former under secretary in the USDA, Schumacher is now vice president of policy at Wholesome Wave, a Connecticut-based nonprofit that helped City Heights and similar programs get off the ground. For him, the broken pear box was a revelation: people on food assistance desperately want the products that small farmers like his brother were selling. If those pricey pears could be made affordable for these new shoppers, it could be a win-win for buyer and seller.

City Heights was an ideal community to put Schumacher's theory to the test. The average income in the neighborhood is around $26,000, as opposed to $63,000 in the county as a whole. The types of fruits and vegetables on offer are tailored to fit the cultural preferences of shoppers, mostly Latino, Vietnamese and Somali. The market's operators say more than 1,800 customers, 250 of whom are regulars, participate in their double voucher program, dubbed "Fresh Fund." In a survey of marketgoers, 90 percent said that they include more fresh fruits and vegetables in their daily diet, thanks to Fresh Fund. The market's small farmers have reaped benefits too. Bernardino Loera, Gebere's orange vendor, says Fresh Fund dollars account for three-quarters of his sales.

City Heights customers say they love the quality of the market's produce—"the food is so fresh," "it's natural," "it's organic." But it is also surprisingly economical, given the reputation farmers' markets have for designer produce. Lemons run six for $1 here; at the Albertson's down the street, lemons were selling two for $1. Other items, like kale and onions, were pretty much equal to Albertson's offerings. Loera says he adjusts his prices to match what customers can afford. The wares are made even cheaper by the Fresh Fund. Each time shoppers visit the market, their SNAP electronic benefits transfer (EBT) card is swiped, and they receive wooden tokens in $1 denominations they can use at individual stalls. The Fresh Fund is a true match program. Customers can deduct up to $20 per month from their benefit accounts; they then receive an equal amount in Fresh Fund dollars.

In three years, Wholesome Wave and its affiliated programs have secured funds from major philanthropies, including Newman's Own Foundation and the Kresge Foundation. The group had a $1.4 million operating budget last year, and Schumacher expects $1 million more in 2011. But the real money is federal money—almost $70 billion spent in fiscal year 2010 on SNAP. If just 3 percent went to fruit and vegetable incentives, that would be more than $2 billion to make healthy food affordable at farmers' markets and grocery stores.

Incentives are already on the radar at the USDA. Later this year, a fifteen-month pilot program in Massachusetts will attempt to apply the double-voucher theory—extra money for healthy foods—to the supermarket, where most food stamp purchases are made. Taking advantage of SNAP's EBT card, which functions like a debit card, the program will add 30 cents to select recipients' SNAP balance for every dollar spent on fruits and vegetables—fresh, frozen, canned or dried. The experiment cuts to the heart of nutrition incentives: would a little extra money back change people's shopping behavior—and how much money would it take to make an impact?

Food stamps have long had a vigorous network of advocates in Washington; the healthy-food advocates are the new kids in town, with backgrounds in public health with emphasis on nutrition. The convergence of the two groups has not been particularly graceful. "I have to say we got off to kind of a rocky start," says Manalo-LeClair, whose organization has worked with both types of groups. "People were pleased that the food stamp program has the ability to fight hunger, and we haven't solved that problem. So then they were saying, 'Are we asking too much to have it do more in terms of preventing obesity as well?'"

To some in the anti-hunger lobby, the emphasis on nutrition is a political Trojan horse, a pretext for cuts or restrictions to the program. "Nine times out of ten, the people in these debates who use the term 'reform' use it as a sugarcoated way of just slashing benefits," says Joel Berg, director of the New York City Coalition Against Hunger. Indeed, the link to obesity has been raised in Congress as a reason not to increase funding for the program. Also, critics worry that it's a short road from incentives to disincentives: New York City Mayor Michael Bloomberg recently suggested banning the use of SNAP benefits for sugary soda, and Schumacher once proposed a surcharge for Coke and Twinkies (he has since dropped the idea). To some, this approach smacks of paternalism, implying that low-income people cannot be trusted to make their own decisions. "The right and left said we were being nannies," says Schumacher.

The people who run City Heights argue that their initiative would actually expand choices for low-income people who want to include fruits and vegetables in their everyday diet. Imagine if everyone on food stamps enjoyed the same choice. What if there was a place like City Heights in East Oakland, where Dudley could get $20 more each month to spend on fresh produce? Is that something she'd be interested in?

"If they'd match me? Yeah…" She trails off, imagining how that would work. "Yes!" she says, getting louder now. "Oh, my God—I would love that!"

Maybe she could buy fruit all month long. Maybe fresh vegetables wouldn't just be for holidays. For a moment, Dudley adjusts her battle plan to indulge in this new fantasy.

"Twenty dollars a month," she says. "That would change a lot."

Melanie Mason, a journalist in Washington, D.C., has been published in the New York Times, Politico, *and* The Dallas Morning News. *This article originally appeared in the March 28, 2011 edition of* The Nation.

17. Ethanol:
Growing Food, Feed, Fiber, *and Fuel?*

Most analysts agree that we are rapidly approaching "peak oil," the point when the volume of global oil production begins to decline. In response, Farm Bill programs have promoted a shift to liquid "biofuels" and "biomass" energy derived from farms. The Renewable Fuels Standard of the Energy Independence and Security Act of 2007, for instance, boosted the country's ethanol production by mandating that up to 36 billion gallons be blended into gasoline by 2022.[1] But taxpayers have been investing in this industry for decades via corn subsidies, import tariffs, tax

For politicians and lobbyists, ethanol became a sacred cow, but the high costs of these policies are now being viewed in a more critical light.

credits for every gallon of ethanol blended with gasoline, loan guarantees, construction cost-shares, and gas pump upgrades. For politicians and lobbyists, ethanol became a sacred cow, untouchable, because of the belief that these public investments would 1) support farmers, 2) reduce dependence on foreign oil (currently about 60 percent of U.S. oil consumption), 3) cut greenhouse gas emissions, and 4) strengthen national defense.

The high costs of these policies–$17 billion between 2005 and 2009 alone[2]–are now being viewed in a more critical light. Voters and politicians can no longer ignore facts such as:

- In 2010, 36 percent of the U.S. corn crop was turned into ethanol, but that only constituted 8 percent of the nation's gasoline.
- A 1.1 mpg increase in passenger vehicle fuel efficiency would save as many gallons of oil as all the ethanol produced today.[3]

Feed Crop versus Cellulosic Ethanol

Ethanol can be made from feed crops such as corn, or cellulosic sources such as grasses, leftover corn stalks, and other woody materials with no food value. Today, most corn ethanol is produced in dry grind factories, which consume less energy than earlier generation wet mill plants. The corn is dried, milled, and then fermented and later distilled into ethanol. The leftover co-products, called dried distiller grains and solubles (DDGS), are fed to livestock. After a major expansion of dry-grind facilities over the course of the 2002 and 2008 Farm Bills, the United States has become the world's largest ethanol producer, even selling its surplus to Brazil, whose once prolific sugar-based biofuel industry has declined in recent years.

Making ethanol from stalks and grass is a bit more challenging. It takes an extra step to separate the plant's lignin from the cellulose. Extra energy is also required during distilling. On the plus side, the lignin can be used instead of fossil fuels as an energy source for distillation.

The notion of a sustainable ethanol industry is predicated on a massive shift from annual crops like corn, sorghum, and soybeans to perennial native plants such as switchgrass, forest "thinnings," or high-biomass perennial crops like Chinese myscanthus—cellulose sources that theoretically won't require excessive plowing or chemicals to pump up yields. It's a compelling notion. But it may be more hype than reality. Despite years of government mandates, no cellulosic ethanol plants are close to operating commercially, even as we continue to invest hundreds of millions of dollars in the effort. And in reality, cellulosic crops don't have to be made into ethanol to displace fossil fuels. A more efficient alternative might be to convert them directly into electricity, a process that is much more efficient, can be achieved with existing technology, and could displace coal and natural gas. Reports show, for example, that an electric car can go twice as far on the energy from a given quantity of wood or switchgrass as an equivalent vehicle powered by ethanol.[4]

The Mounting Case Against Corn Ethanol

By early 2011, drums were finally beating inside the nation's capital for a repeal of ethanol subsidies and tax breaks that were sucking up $7 billion per year or more from American taxpayers. Some Iowa counties were reportedly receiving up to $26,800 per rural household in ethanol subsidies, despite evidence that using corn to help fill gas tanks might not be the best use of crops, technology, and scarce taxpayer dollars.[5]

First is the simple energy in, energy out equation. In other words, the amount of power you actually get out of ethanol for what's required to grow and refine it. Recent analyses reveal that when all of the "well to wheel" inputs of growing, fertilizing, irrigating, harvesting, drying, and processing are tallied, at least two-thirds of a gallon of oil are needed to produce a gallon of ethanol (roughly a 33 percent "net energy balance").[6] The bulk of energy used to make ethanol currently comes from coal- or natural gas-fired power plants. Which makes you wonder, how renewable can the fuel be if you need nonrenewable energy to produce it?

Depending on which life cycle assessment you read (there are dozens to ponder), the shift from hydrocarbon- to carbohydrate-based fuels could either ease particulate emissions and global warming significantly or actually make things far worse. In 2005, Dan Kaman of the University of California at Berkeley's Energy and Resources Group reported a 10 to 15 percent per mile reduction in greenhouse gas emissions from corn-based ethanol. On the same campus, Tad Patzak argued that in its present form, ethanol produces 50 percent more carbon dioxide

Figure 26

The Grain Ethanol Gold Rush
U.S. Corn-based Ethanol Production 1998-2011

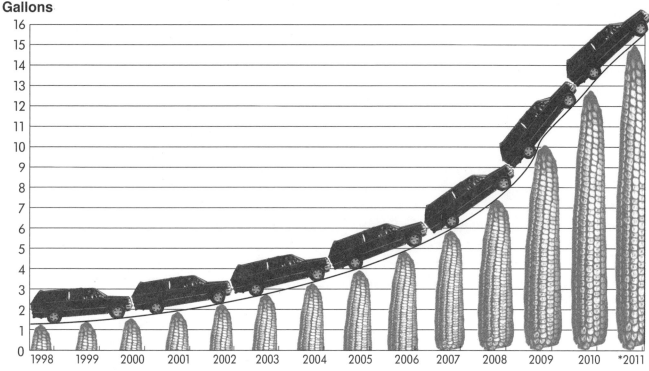

Billions of Gallons

16
15
14
13
12
11
10
9
8
7
6
5
4
3
2
1
0

1998 1999 2000 2001 2002 2003 2004 2005 2006 2007 2008 2009 2010 *2011

BTUs/gal gasoline = 115,500 BTUs/gallon

BTUs/gal ethanol = 75,700 BTUs/gallon (only 2/3 as efficient)

2003 50% of refineries majority farmer owned

2006 80% of new refineries absentee owned

8% of gas consumption displaced by ethanol in 2011

40% of the U.S. corn crop used for ethanol in 2011 (36m acres)

Sources: The American Coalition for Ethanol and the Renewable Fuels Association; American Coalition for Ethanol, March 19, 2010; Steven Rattner, "The Great Corn Con," *New York Times*, June 24, 2011. *Projected amount of ethanol to be produced in 2011.

and sulfur emissions (along with lung and eye irritants) than fossil fuels. According to Michael Bomford of Kentucky State University, the differences between studies almost entirely depend upon how researchers assess the value of the byproduct livestock feed.

The Case for Conservation

Even the most ardent proponents admit that, at best, biofuels can only ever be a part of a diversified energy future. There is simply not enough french fry grease to satisfy the world's diesel addiction, and only so much arable land. Already about 30 million acres (the equivalent of all the cropland in Iowa and then some) are dedicated to ethanol corn—but the output is displacing a mere 8 percent of gas.

The same amount of gasoline could have been displaced simply by increasing fleet-wide fuel economy just 1.1 miles per gallon.[7] (And that would have saved American taxpayers nearly $20 billion between 2005 and 2011 alone.)

Clearly, increasing fuel efficiency and cultivating a public consciousness around conservation is a more effective way to reduce gasoline use than corn ethanol. Here are some other common sense ways that the Environmental Working Group reports could improve gas mileage without a costly ethanol industry: common sense car maintenance including regular oil changes, proper tire inflation, and filter replacements; better all-around driving habits that avoid excessive speeding

How to Boost U.S. Fuel Economy

Avg. fuel economy of U.S. fleet in 2009: 20.0

Action to Boost Fuel Economy	Low Est. +MPG	High Est. +MPG
Sensible driving	1.0	6.6
Observing the speed limit	1.4	4.6
Regular engine tune-ups	0.8	0.8
Proper tire inflation	0.6	0.6
Recommended motor oil	0.2	0.4
Replacing clogged air filters	0.4	1.2

Source: Cox and Hug, "Driving Under the Influence," EWG, 2010.

and acceleration; and higher industry standards for fuel efficiency.

If helping small farmers diversify their economic portfolios was another goal of federal policy makers, ethanol has failed to deliver. What began as a movement of farmer-owned and -operated small-scale plants has given way to facilities dominated by global giants like Archer Daniels Midland, one of the most vocal ethanol advocates and most prolific beneficiaries of ethanol subsidies.[8] Spurred on by mandates and incentives from the Energy Independence and Security Act of 2007, the federal Renewable Fuels Standard, and the California Low-Carbon Fuel Standard (LCFS), engineering firms like Broin and ICM have joined the grain-based ethanol gold rush. [9] Dozens of relatively small "dry grind" plants (15 to 30 million gallons per year) have been erected in proximity to large grain supplies, thanks in no small part to a slew of government subsidies.

Ethanol's Stewardship Legacy?

Food prices are on the rise around the globe. Land values throughout the Corn Belt are skyrocketing. And the grim reality is sinking in that even if the entire U.S. corn crop were distilled into liquid fuel, it would still supply less than 20 percent of domestic demand. Conservationists worry about the vulnerability of transforming every potentially productive acre—including land set aside for conservation and protected grasslands and parklands—into some form of biofuel monoculture.

Any benefits of the ethanol boom—increased farm revenue, significant reductions in subsidy payments, lower greenhouse gas emissions, and a more diversified fuel supply—come with a potentially unaffordable environmental price tag. As the demand for fuel corn pushes farmers to intensify their land use, soil and water quality are starting to suffer.[10]

Some optimists hope that farming standards can prevent the worst damage. In 2011, European countries agreed upon standards for sustainable cultivating and harvesting of biofuel crops. Similar efforts have stalled, however, in the United States, where there is still no consensus on what constitutes "sustainable" farming practices. There are also legitimate concerns that over-harvesting "crop residues"

like wheat straw, corn stalks, etc., eventually will impoverish the soil. Sir Albert Howard, the early-20th-century pioneer of the organic and sustainable farming movements, called this "The Law of Return," where "what comes from the soil must return to the soil." Organic matter must be added back into soil for it to stay productive. Cover cropping, crop rotations, and other natural methods will become essential not just for biofuel production but for all of agriculture.

In addition, harvesting cellulose from lands now set aside to protect wildlife could have devastating consequences to biodiversity and reverse decades of gains made by Farm Bill conservation programs. Here are just a few guiding questions:

- How much further will federal mandates for biofuel production drive idled lands into production?
- Will parks, forests, and other public lands become vulnerable to energy exploitation and food production?
- How will bio-refineries manage the challenges of seasonality, storage, and transport of crops?
- What are the long-term consequences of "super weeds" now resistant to herbicides used in genetically engineered crops?
- Will food and energy shortages feed on one another?
- Can subsidies be structured to protect farmers during price falls, and to protect taxpayers from huge payouts to

Figure 27

Bio-based Energy: Pros and Cons

Purported Benefits	Challenges
Strengthens national security by displacing foreign oil. As oil supplies contract, a transition beyond a petroleum-based economy is necessary.	Replacing 8 percent of the U.S. gas consumption required 36 million acres of corn in 2010. Improving fuel efficiency standards by 1.1 MPG would have done the same.
Helps in the transition to new generations of more efficient types of biofuels, such as cellulosic ethanol.	After many years and billions of dollars in government and industry supports, there still are no commercially viable cellulosic ethanol plants on line.
Could eventually shift away from corn-based agriculture to perennial crops like switch grass, myscanthus, perennial sorghum and others that have less impact.	Challenges still remain in terms of crop storage and transport, prices required to make farming profitable, and the agricultural impacts of next-generation fuel crops.
Reduces greenhouse gas (GHG) emissions.	Studies show that ethanol from Brazil has lower GHG emissions than U.S. corn-based ethanol. Currently, tariffs prevent the import of foreign ethanol.
Becomes an economic engine for rural development.	Almost 80 percent of ethanol plants are now absentee-owned operations that have profited mightily from state and federal supports.
Helps with future development of crop "residues" such as straw, stalks, and other by-products for primary fuel source.	The use of bio-fuels to produce energy that charges batteries may be far more practical than running cars with liquid biofuels.
Biotechnology can overcome obstacles with specifically designed energy crops, innovative enzymes, and other breakthroughs.	Biotechnology's impacts include uncontrollable cross-pollination, the creation of resistant weeds and organisms, human health allergies, and concentration of wealth and seed supply.
Biofuels are just part of a larger integrated future energy strategy.	It takes 2/3 of a gallon of fossil fuel to make 1 gallon of corn ethanol. This diverts us from the real need for energy conservation and fuel reduction.
Provides farmers with new markets and opportunities for farmer-owned multinational cooperatives.	There are far more effective ways to compensate farmers fairly than to support an industry now dominated by large corporations.
Ethanol is a clean-burning fuel.	Making ethanol with coal power emits more GHGs than gasoline. Making ethanol with natural gas and biomass power has less emissions than gas.

biofuels producers that no longer need them?

• What about other sources of cellulose, such as the Municipal Waste Stream or forest thinning, that could prevent immense agricultural expansion?

Perhaps a long-term benefit will emerge from all this, once ethanol ceases to be a way for huge corporations to profitably dump excess corn, and a more logical energy order arises. A sensible biofuel movement could evolve, embracing a diversification of fuel and nonfuel crops on landscapes that include crop rotations, streamside protection, the maintenance of healthy soils, and abundant wildlife habitat and wild areas.

GMO Designer Fuels: In a Station Near You

Genetically modified (GMO) fuel crops–plants that have been altered through the gene-splicing techniques of biotechnology–are already in your gas tank. As of 2009, 85 percent of the U.S. corn crop and upward of 80 percent of all soybeans planted were genetically modified varieties, primarily approved for animal feed rather than human consumption. With consumers in Europe, Japan, Mexico, and Africa increasingly reluctant to allow GMO crops inside their borders, the rapidly expanding North American biofuels industry is set to become a convenient outlet.

Rival seed giants Monsanto and DuPont have been jockeying for market share with conventionally bred corn varieties that boast higher starch content to maximize ethanol production. But most experts acknowledge that corn has its limitations (and negative ecological implications) as a fuel source. So some are turning to biotechnology for alternatives.

"More miles to the acre" may be the new mantra of biotech agribusiness firms eager to cash in on the biofuel craze in at least two different ways: (1) modifying the genetic structure of plants to make fermentation easier; (2) boosting yields of both annual and perennial crops. Syngenta, for example, has its sights set on "self-processing" corn.

Each transgenic kernel would carry an amylase enzyme that is currently added separately to starch at the ethanol plant.[11] To pull this off, engineers have inserted a gene from a heat tolerant thermotrophic microbe that lives near hot-water vents on the ocean floor.[12] Meanwhile, DuPont and Bunge have engaged in a joint venture to genetically engineer soybeans for biodiesel and other uses.[13]

Researchers are also branching out into perennial plants such as fast-growing poplar trees and dense grasses such as the Chinese *miscanthus*, which promoters tout can grow 20 tons of biomass per acre with little fertilizer or irrigation. California-based Ceres Corporation has been breeding switchgrass, a Prairie States native, so that it would need even less fertilizer and irrigation and require infrequent replanting.

Another goal of biotech firms is to reduce the amount of lignin that holds plant cells together. Removing lignin presently complicates turning cellulose into ethanol. But it's also nature's way of endowing plants with the stiffness to grow upright. Needless to say, the prospect of unleashing a new genetic trait such as "droopiness" onto the landscape is raising the hackles of scientists, botanists, legal activists, and other observers.

Even the conventional agriculture community is cautioning against a massive increase in intensive corn farming. Many fear that the abandonment of crop rotations could strain the soil, tax water resources, and lead to a buildup of insects or vulnerability to disease. The emergence of "super weeds" resistant to the herbicide Roundup is causing a return to even more toxic herbicides.

At the same time, the spread of new and relatively untested GMO energy crops holds

17. Ethanol: Growing Food, Feed, Fiber, and Fuel?

Figure 28

Who's Growing GMOs
Percent of Global Land Area Planted in Biotechnology Varieties by Country
(2009 Total Global Land Area: 331.6 Million Acres)

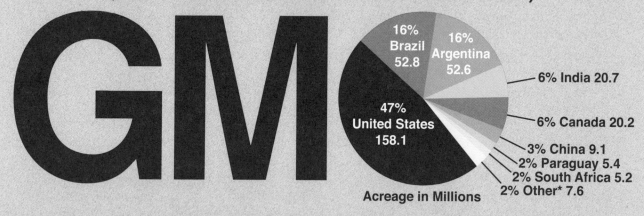

16% Brazil 52.8

16% Argentina 52.6

6% India 20.7

6% Canada 20.2

47% United States 158.1

3% China 9.1

2% Paraguay 5.4

2% South Africa 5.2

2% Other* 7.6

Acreage in Millions

*Other countries include: Uruguay, Bolivia, Philippines, Australia, Burkina Faso, Spain, Mexico, Chile, Colombia, Honduras, Czech Republic, Portugal, Romania, Poland, Costa Rica, Egypt, and Slovakia.**

Source: International Service for the Acquisition of Agri-biotech Applications, ISAAA Brief 41-2009

its own set of complications. The transfer of exotic genes and enzymes from energy crops to the human food supply or to the wild is entirely possible. Pollen transfer in open fields between the same types of crops or their wild plant relatives is a naturally occurring and uncontrollable phenomenon. The intermingling of seed is also almost impossible to prevent. This has been soundly proven with StarLink corn (approved only for animal consumption, it has surfaced in tortilla chips). More recently, herbicide-resistant Liberty Link rice contaminated conventional supplies and resulted in plummeting sales for U.S. farmers. Such contaminations—of plants and seed banks—are essentially irreversible. There are health implications as well. Bill Freese of the Center for Food Safety in Washington, D.C.,

reports that some amylase can induce allergy and requires further study.[14]

The biotech industry seems poised to go to great lengths to produce fuel from agriculture. The question we all need to ask is whether our national addiction to liquid fuels and automobiles could possibly be worth such risks.

The concentration of plant gene patents in the hands of just a few global corporations most concerns Dave Henson, an expert on genetically modified crops. "GMO biofuel conglomerates have the potential to become the next OPEC," cautions Henson. "Controlling patents and the seed supply means these giants are no longer just grain brokers and dealers, but will have the power to exercise control over growers and communities all over the world."

18. Energy and Climate Change

Energy is the driving force behind all contemporary economic activities and food systems and farming operations are no exception. From natural gas–rich nitrogen fertilizers, to power for irrigation and processing, to fossil fuels for cars, ships, semis, tractors, and laser-guided farm equipment, to the gas and electricity we use at home to cook and refrigerate, energy is gobbled up in every stage along the way. (See Figure 29, "How U.S. Agriculture Uses Energy," and Figure 30, "How the U.S. Food System Uses Energy.")

When it comes to measuring how much energy it takes to put food on our tables, however, some surprising results surface. The energy required to grow food, while significant, has been declining for decades as farmers switch to diesel power and adopt other more efficient technologies and practices. In fact, we now expend twice as much energy processing, packaging, storing, transporting, and preparing something after it leaves the farm as we use to grow it in the first place. But as energy and climate concerns converge, attention is on farms to offer solutions and adapt. The 21st century farm is viewed as an energy generator: raising crops for biofuels, installing industrial-scale wind turbines, and capturing methane gas from liquid manure pits. Pastures, woodlots, and permanent ground cover are seen as "carbon sinks," with the potential to remove carbon dioxide from an overpolluted atmosphere and store it in organic matter in the soil.

We now expend twice as much energy processing, packaging, storing, transporting, and preparing something after it leaves the farm as we use to grow it in the first place.

The Oil We Eat

As late as 1910, 27 percent of all U.S. farmland was still devoted to growing feed for horses used in transportation and cultivation.[1] Modern agriculture is so dependent on fossil fuel energy that some critics say we are literally "eating oil." Just a casual look at the facts demonstrates how intricately food and energy are inter-related:

- An estimated 15.7 percent of energy consumption in the United States in 2007 was food-related.[2]
- On average, at least 10 calories of fossil fuel are used for every calorie of industrial food eaten.[3]
- Harvesting a single bushel of corn requires the energy equivalent of one-third of a gallon of gasoline.[4]

- The average 1,200-pound steer consumes the energy equivalent of 130 gallons of oil—three barrels—over its short lifetime from cow-calf operation to conventional Midwestern feedlot.[5]
- Nitrogen fertilizers, synthesized from natural gas, are the backbone of high-yield industrial farming, consuming more than one-third of the energy used in U.S. agriculture.[6]

The Energy-Efficient Farm

One of the Farm Bill's greatest strengths has arguably resided in its capacity to serve as an economic catalyst. In 2002, the Renewable Energy and Energy Efficiency Improvements Program was launched to jump start a "clean energy" initiative within Farm Bill programs. Known as Section 9006 grants, these funds provided cost-share and loan guarantees to invest in on-farm renewable energy systems, promote energy auditing and conservation, and help to diversify energy sources in rural areas. These investments in renewable energy are recognized as Green Box payments by the World Trade Organization rules—unlike corn subsidies for ethanol—and are not limited by payment restrictions.

The 2008 Farm Bill's Energy Title quadrupled the 2002 Farm Bill's previous energy budget, adding nearly $1 billion in supports, including a number of programs geared toward making U.S. farms more energy efficient.[7] Still the ethanol industry emerged the real winner from these increases, accounting for nearly two-thirds of the funding boost: $320 million to the Biorefinery Assistance Program and $300 million to the Bioenergy Program for Advanced Biofuels.[8] The Rural Energy for America Program (REAP) superseded the Section 9006 program with an allotment of $255 million for on-farm energy improvements.[9] These grants help landowners to install renewable energy sources (wind, solar, geothermal, biomass, etc.) and make energy efficiency improvements (retrofit existing buildings, upgrade to a more efficient heating system, or replace equipment).[10]

Like many Farm Bill program categories, renewable energy funding has not been guaranteed. The Chicago-based Environmental Law and Policy Center and other groups have waged hard-fought campaigns every year to defend the annual appropriations of the Section 9006 and REAP budgets. Between 2003 and 2009, the USDA awarded $205 million in grants, but they also turned away more than half of all applicants.[11] (See Figure 31, "Demand Outpaces Supply/Renewable Priorities.") Meanwhile ethanol profits and subsidies have been soaring.

Outside of the Energy Title, on-farm energy conservation incentives have also been integrated within the Farm Bill's Conservation Title. The Environmental Quality Incentives Program (EQIP) included cost-share funds to perform energy audits, reduce energy consumption, and build methane digesters that are placed on top of liquid manure lagoons to capture gas emissions.

Figure 29

How U.S. Agriculture Uses Energy

Fertilizer Production 29%

Diesel Fuel (Nonirrigation) 25%

Electricity (Nonirrigation) 18%

Gasoline 9%

Irrigation 7%

Herbicide/Pesticide Production 6%

Liquid Petroleum Gas 5%

Natural Gas (Nonirrigation) 1%

Source: Compiled by Earth Policy Institute from USDA; USDOE; Duffield; Miranowski.

Figure 30

How the U.S. Food System Uses Energy

Home Refrigeration & Preparation 28%

Processing 20%

Wholesale/Retail 16%

Agricultural Production 14%

Food Service 12%

Packaging 6%

Transportation 4%

Source: Patrick Canning, Ainsley Charles, Sonya Huang, Karen R. Polenske, and Arnold Waters, "Energy Use in the U.S. Food System," Economic Research Service, March 2010

Under the Conservation Stewardship Program (CSP) farmers can receive financial incentives for (1) energy auditing, (2) decreasing tillage and the use of fertilizers and other fossil fuel inputs, (3) recycling used motor oil, (4) purchasing ethanol and biodiesel, and (5) generating renewable solar, wind, hydroelectric, geothermal, or methane power.

We are liable to hear more about methane digesters in coming years. Public financing for methane digesters has a lot in common with taxpayer support for corn ethanol. As with an ethanol plant, it is extremely expensive to build contraptions that capture the potent methane greenhouse gas vapors rising off cesspools on dairies or hog farms. And like the ethanol industry, CAFO operators have been increasingly relying on large infusions of taxpayer subsidies to help them build their infrastructure. Methane produced from animal waste is not extremely efficient. Most of the energy consumed in feed is used to fuel an animal's metabolism. The manure contains far less energy as a result. Producing any large quantity of energy in a methane digester requires additional biomass. In the end, government funding for industrial-scale methane digesters seems more of a policy to make the concentrated animal feeding industry look responsible (a questionable goal) than a sound energy policy. Farm Bill funds should be used for methane digester production but only on small- and medium-scale, highly efficient operations, where the numbers of animals are in balance with the amount of wastes being generated.

There are other ways to produce animal proteins that can reduce greenhouse gas releases. Animals raised on pasture spread wastes naturally without heavy concentrations of methane. Hogs raised in deep straw bedding rather than industrial confinement systems significantly reduce methane emissions as well.

Nitrogen Fertilizers—Agriculture's Achilles Heel

For more than half a century, nitrogen fertilizers have formed the backbone of industrial agriculture. Each year U.S. farmers apply over 12 million tons of nitrogen fertilizers to increase crop yields as the soil's nutrients become exhausted. As long as fossil fuels have been cheap and abundant, nitrogen fertilizers have also been relatively inexpensive. Farmers heap nitrogen on fields in increasing quantities even as gains in productivity decline. Nitrogen fertilizers have been extremely effective in maintaining ever-increasing yields, even functioning as a form of relatively cheap crop insurance.

These gains have come at considerable environmental and health costs. In fact, over-dependence on synthetic nitrogen fertilizers represents one of the most important challenges facing the food system. Fertilizers are responsible for between one-third and one-half of all energy expended in modern farming. Much of that is expended during the

Figure 31

Demand Outpaces Supply
Applications vs. Funds for Renewable Energy Grants

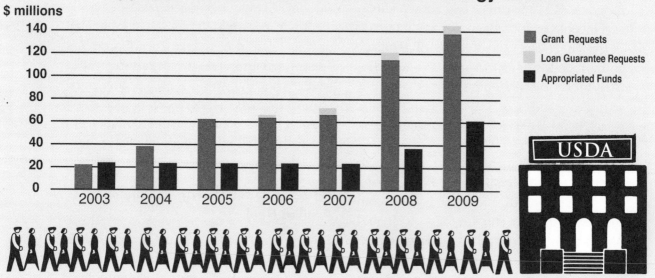

$ millions

- Grant Requests
- Loan Guarantee Requests
- Appropriated Funds

Source: Environmental Law and Policy Center

Renewable Priorities
REAP Funding Totals by Technology (2003–2009)

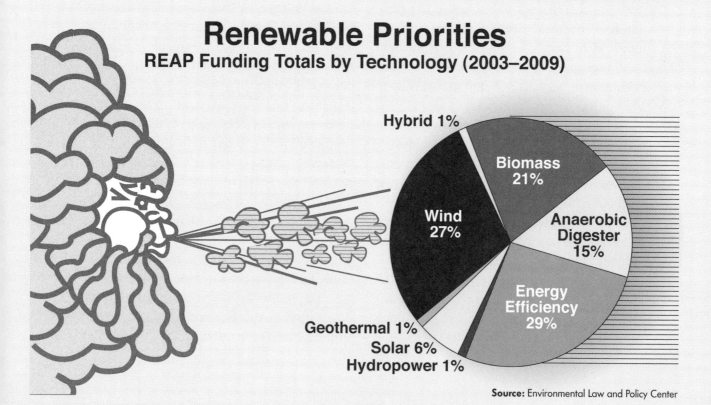

Hybrid 1%

Biomass 21%

Wind 27%

Anaerobic Digester 15%

Energy Efficiency 29%

Geothermal 1%

Solar 6%

Hydropower 1%

Source: Environmental Law and Policy Center

manufacturing process, in which nitrogen is synthesized under extremely high pressure. The energy sources that create those manufacturing conditions are frequently powered by coal or natural gas.

Nitrogen fertilizers are also extremely "leaky"—that is, they are very difficult to contain after application. Unlike wastes in a natural ecosystem that provide food and nutrients for other species, nitrogen becomes a toxic pollutant that is long lasting and takes time to break down. Only one-third to one-half of the fertilizers actually reach the crops they are intended to fortify. The rest ends up in groundwater as nitrates and in surface water as ammonia, where it fertilizes algae blooms that die off and create dead zones. Nitrous oxide is released in the atmosphere with 300 times the potency of carbon dioxide.[12] According to USDA reports, 108 million acres of U.S. cropland—two-thirds of the fields that receive synthetic nitrogen—need improved management to prevent leakage.[13]

Intentionally growing plants that absorb nitrogen out of the atmosphere—a traditional farming practice known as cover cropping—is one logical shift away from the challenge of the overloading of ecosystems with synthetic nitrogen. Unfortunately, present regulations and incentives are not sufficient to sway farmers away from nitrogen fertilizers toward other forms of fertilization such as cover cropping. The benefits could be considerable. In addition to pollution prevention and energy savings from reduced manufacture of synthet-ic fertilizers, the National Wildlife Federation estimates that planting cover crops on all suitable acreage (185 million acres) could eliminate 4 percent of annual U.S. greenhouse gas emissions. Bolstering USDA's budgets to create positive solutions to this problem represents one of the most urgent and presently underfunded Farm Bill priorities.

Adapting to Weather Uncertainty

Interconnected with critical energy issues are the ever-apparent impacts of climate change and their effects on agriculture and food security. The last five years have brought rising temperatures, radical fluctuations in precipitation patterns, extreme flooding, and drought in agricultural areas across the world. Worldwide agriculture contributes an estimated 30 percent of total greenhouse gas emissions (GHGs) although the number is far less in the United States.[14] This includes almost one-quarter of the carbon dioxide, two-thirds of the methane, and nearly all nitrous oxide emissions.[15] Most of the food system's GHGs are rooted in production methods—nitrous oxide released through soil disturbance and deforestation, and methane emissions generated by livestock—rather than in the energy-intensive activities that take place after foods leave the fields and farms. Even the modern food system's ever-lengthening "food mile" component, in which an average item travels an estimated 5,000 miles from farm to fork,[16] is dwarfed by the climate-altering impacts related to clearing land, soil tillage, and the global production of more than 50 billion food animals, increasingly in grain-fed confinement systems.

Agriculture can conserve energy and reduce the pressures of climate change in large part by increasing the food system's ability to capture carbon. This is the natural process whereby living plants take carbon dioxide out of the air, convert it to carbohydrates through photosynthesis, and tie it up in the soil in the form of organic matter. It's one way of off-setting the tremendous amounts of carbon dioxide (CO_2) humans have pumped into the atmosphere by burning fossil fuel, raising food animals, and plowing soils. Farming practices such as grass-pastured livestock production and organic agriculture are increasingly proving to be excellent ways to both produce healthy food and decrease carbon emissions related to agriculture.

A 2009 USDA report entitled "Putting Dairy Cows Out to Pasture: An Environmental Plus" demonstrated that in terms of energy use, negative climate impacts, and air quality, raising dairy cows outside on year-round pastures results in a much smaller ecological "hoofprint" than raising cows in confinement facilities.[17] This peer-reviewed study found that total emissions for greenhouse gases in year-round, grass-based systems were at least 10 percent lower than comparably sized confinement operations. More dramatically, ammonia emissions, a major source of air pollutants, were reduced by 30 percent.

Keeping cows on pastures also reduced fuel consumption and cut carbon dioxide emissions from farm equipment. Researcher Al Rotz concluded, "When farmland is transitioned from rotated crops to perennial grassland, you can build up lots of carbon in the soil and substantially reduce your carbon footprint for 20 to 30 years."[18] While the volume of milk production from grass-fed cows drops substantially compared to grain-fed, confinement dairy cows, the total output of essential ingredients of milk protein and fat content were found to be the same.

The Organic Advantage

USDA studies also show that scaling up organic grain production could significantly reduce GHG emissions and the need for nitrogen fertilizers in farming systems. The primary benefits accrue because organic farmers replace nitrogen fertilizer inputs with extensive use of cover crops that naturally accumulate atmospheric nitrogen in the soil.

Organic systems also typically increase the amount of carbon contained in the soil. Carbon performs many critical functions in building healthy soil: acting as a reservoir of plant nutrients, binding soil particles together, maintaining soil temperature, providing a food source for microbes, tying up heavy metals and pesticides, and increasing water retention capacity and aeration.[19] A UK Soil Association review of 39 studies covering 100 comparisons of organic and non-organic farming showed that, on average, organic systems yield 20 to 28 percent higher levels

Figure 32

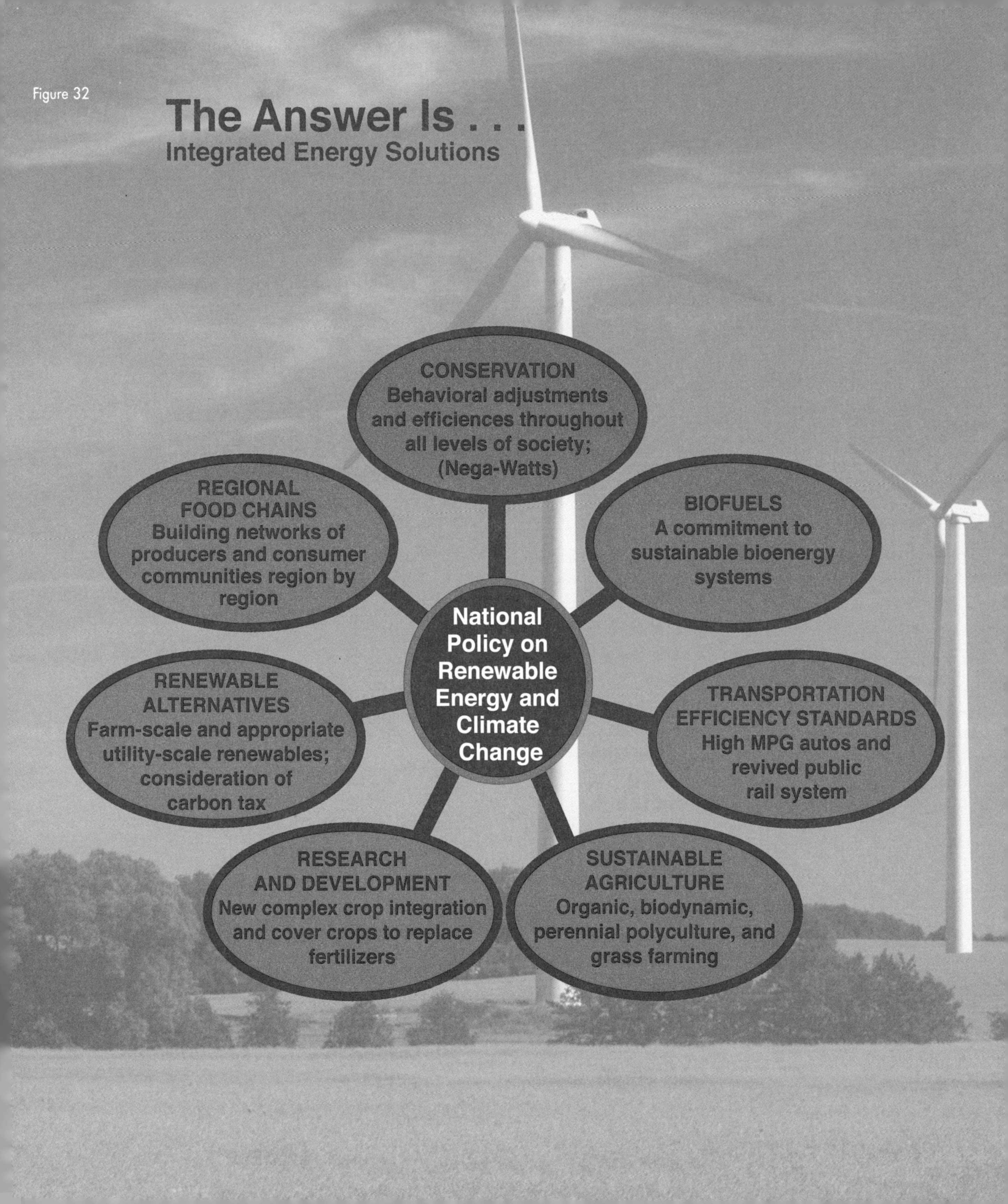

The Answer Is . . .
Integrated Energy Solutions

National Policy on Renewable Energy and Climate Change

CONSERVATION
Behavioral adjustments and efficiences throughout all levels of society; (Nega-Watts)

REGIONAL FOOD CHAINS
Building networks of producers and consumer communities region by region

BIOFUELS
A commitment to sustainable bioenergy systems

RENEWABLE ALTERNATIVES
Farm-scale and appropriate utility-scale renewables; consideration of carbon tax

TRANSPORTATION EFFICIENCY STANDARDS
High MPG autos and revived public rail system

RESEARCH AND DEVELOPMENT
New complex crop integration and cover crops to replace fertilizers

SUSTAINABLE AGRICULTURE
Organic, biodynamic, perennial polyculture, and grass farming

Energy and Climate Change Policy

The scientific consensus on global climate change predicts inevitable disruptions and potentially dire consequences. The prescriptions are equally clear: significant reductions in fossil fuel emissions are needed across the board. Agriculture differs from almost every other sector of the economy in that most of its greenhouse gas emissions are not caused by energy use. Soil disturbance, land clearing, and livestock and manure management release more than three times as much greenhouse gas as total (direct and indirect) farm energy use. Tough choices will be made in the decades ahead. Regional production of diverse renewable energy sources should be aggressively scaled up. At the same time, energy is not renewable if essential resources such as soil and water are despoiled in the process. Simply increasing the supply of renewable energy without a national strategy to make the United States "carbon neutral" may only succeed in providing more power to consumers. Across the world, and prominently in agricultural areas, large wind farms are gaining traction as alternative electricity producers. The latest generation of turbines has been criticized as noisy, visually polluting, and ultimately beneficial to investors outside of the communities where they are installed. Within an overall context of a more positive energy future, however, it should be possible to identify appropriate areas to locate utility-scale wind farms, with exceptions such as these proposed by John Davis of the Adirondack Council:

- No energy production in roadless areas.
- No windmills or energy production in wildlife migration corridors.
- No windmills in parks or protected areas.
- Keep windmills away from water bodies.
- Complement renewable energy funding with a national energy conservation platform.

of Soil Organic Carbon (SOC) in topsoil.[20] Studies show that organic production often leads to further increases of SOC deeper in the subsoil as well.

Conclusion

The Farm Bill has no Climate Change Title. Programs that help landowners adapt to climate change and energy efficiency currently reside in the Titles for Conservation and Energy. Few, if any, programs are tailored to changes in rainfall cycles, sea levels, air and water temperatures, and vegetation patterns, which scientific consensus insists will inevitably reshape agriculture and life as we know it.

It is important to keep in mind the Farm Bill's interconnectedness with broader issues and policies. Energy supports can serve broader communities as well as targeted landscape goals, rather than merely profiting absentee plant owners already thriving in the marketplace. Biological diversity, effects on soil and water, regional economic development, climate change, public health, and aesthetics, should all add to the picture of the energy future we are envisioning and investing in with taxpayer resources and the public trust.

19. Healthy Lands, Healthy People: Why Farmlands Matter to Conservation

Federal farm programs are geared to support the growth of production agriculture as well as to help conserve biodiversity on the landscape. Yet, when out of balance, these two goals can work at cross purposes. Throughout the implementation of the 2008 Farm Bill, conservation has been losing ground as market forces and government subsidies have driven commodity harvests and prices sky-high. Budget-tightening efforts have frequently targeted conservation programs as well.

Conservation on private lands remains essential to maintain a network of healthy habitats in regions throughout the country. And the Farm Bill's Conservation Title potentially provides not just millions, but billions of dollars—when appropriated—to accomplish this.

According to a 2011 USDA report, the same tools that farmers insist are essential—subsidized crop insurance, disaster assistance, marketing loans—are eroding decades of conservation gains by encouraging agricultural expansion into grasslands.[1] In the Northern Plains in particular, where half of all North American waterfowl are born every year, nearly 700,000 acres of rangeland were converted to cropland between 1997 and 2007.[2]

Across the Corn Belt, too, grassland bird populations, important indicator species, have experienced a precipitous decline. Breeding grounds have disappeared for once-common species such as the bobolink, savannah sparrow, Baird's sparrow, northern harrier, horned lark, loggerhead shrike, and eastern and western meadowlark as grasslands are converted to subsidized row crops and subdivisions. While some farmers and ranchers have adopted stewardship practices to accommodate these declining species, the critical mass needed to stem the losses has not materialized. Grasses can be reseeded, but once land is cultivated, it is extremely difficult to re-establish the full range of habitat diversity. Ornithologists warn that we have only a decade to restore perennial ground cover across what is now the corn and soybean landscape before many grassland birds disappear from their traditional ranges altogether.

Paying Farmers Not to Farm

Why pay farmers not to farm? It's a natural enough question. The answer partly lies in the value of healthy rural landscapes that are not compensated by the almighty marketplace. Water filtration and flood prevention, open space preservation, wildlife habitat, carbon storage, scenery enhancement, and species protection are just a few of the benefits of well-cared-for private lands. But farmers motivated to maximize profits through intensive production often work directly against these benefits: by diminishing biodiversity with genetically identical monocultures, mining the soil, overdrawing groundwater reserves, physically concentrating livestock in huge numbers, or continually applying agrochemicals.

Any citizen who cares about land stewardship has a stake in what happens on farmlands. Here are a few compelling reasons:

• Nearly two-thirds of the 1.9 billion acres in the continental U.S. is made up of crop, pasture, range, and forest land—about one-half of which is privately owned.
• Only one-tenth of the lower 48 states falls under some form of state or federal habitat protection, and these areas have become increasingly fragmented.
• Public lands are being exploited for resource extraction, grazing, timbering, off-road recreation, and other harmful activities.
• As of 1995, 84 percent of all endangered or threatened plants and animal species were listed in part due to agricultural activities.[3]

With the U.S. population now over 300 million and showing no signs of a plateau, agricultural lands face constant development pressure. Nationwide, an average of 1.6 million acres of farmland were lost to development every year between 1982 and 2007.[4] At the same time, an estimated 400 million acres of agricultural land will transfer to new owners in the coming decades. Without a ready generation of new farmers and ranchers willing to take over, the probability that some of this land will be converted to nonagricultural uses remains high.[5]

The outright purchase of all the land necessary to safeguard our natural heritage is simply not economically or politically feasible. (Even if purchased, many landscapes would require ongoing management, at least in the short term.) Government agencies and land trust organizations have effectively used easements to acquire rural lands (or their development rights) to fight sprawl and protect biodiversity, but they aren't enough. Conservation incentives for private landowners remain essential to maintaining a network of healthy habitats. And the Farm Bill's Conservation Title potentially provides not just millions, but billions of dollars—when properly appropriated—to accomplish this.

The best programs, says conservation biologist Randy Gray, encompass a habitat large enough to permit the recovery of a species in that area. For example, Environmental Quality Incentive Program payments to a Montana alfalfa farmer for cutting back on irrigation raised the in-stream flow of the Big Hole River, which in turn supported the threatened fluvial Arctic grayling. Utah ranchers in the Parker Mountain Adaptive Resource Management Area earned Wildlife Habitat Incentive Payments for changing

Land Cover/Use
Surface Area of the U.S. Contiguous States

	Public	Range	Forest	Crops	Pasture	Developed	Water	Other	Conservation Reserve Program
% of US land base	21%	20%	20%	19%	6%	6%	3%	3%	2%
Millions of acres	401.9 (± 0.0)	405.3 (± 1.8)	404.9 (± 1.5)	368.4 (± 1.2)	117.3 (± 0.9)	107.3 (± 0.7)	50.4 (± 0.1)	50.6 (± 0.8)	31.6 (± 0.2)

Total surface area of the 48 contiguous states by land cover/use in 2002. Margins of error defining the 95% confidence intervals are in parentheses. The total surface area of the United States is 1,937.7 million acres (NRCS 2004).

grazing practices, and as a result a quarter million acres of sage grouse habitat was restored. In the Lower Mississippi Valley, Conservation Reserve Program or Wetlands Reserve Program contracts with farmers helped return more than 600,000 acres of agricultural lands to bottomland hardwood forest habitat for the Louisiana black bear, and, with good fortune, will perhaps support the return of the ivory-billed woodpecker, thought extinct until sighted in 2004.

CRP and WRP: A Modern New Deal

The Dust Bowl—when a continent's soil and farm population were literally displaced by drought and economic depression—spurred the early Farm Bill conservation programs. In the following decades, a new ethic of soil protection gave rise to sensible practices such as cover cropping to protect the soil between harvests, field rotations to discourage pest buildup, contour strips to prevent erosion on hilly lands, and windbreaks or hedgerows to guard against weather. Federal subsidies to implement these new practices, however, came with strings attached. Farmers who got the money had to idle a portion of their land to reduce the price-crushing overproduction of crops. But during the 1970s Get Big or Get Out era, Farm Bill conservation programs took a U-turn. Farmers were encouraged to plant "fencerow to fencerow," eliminating former habitat linkages and any wild areas that might get in the way of industrial farm equipment. Drainage tiles and open ditches, used to remove water and make low-lying areas plantable, became standard management practices of USDA's conservation and farm extension outreach. Every year from the mid-1950s to the mid-1970s, more

151 19. Healthy Lands, Healthy People

than 500,000 acres of wetlands were lost to agriculture.[6]

Conservation took a more positive turn during the early 1980s. Concern among biologists about declining North American waterfowl populations, whose breeding grounds fell within farmed areas of the northern prairie states (also known as the Prairie Pothole Region or PPR), generated a new wave of reforms. Three provisions in the 1985 Farm Bill charted a new course for wildlife management on private lands.

The Conservation Reserve Program (CRP) paid yearly rental fees to farmers to idle up to 40 million total acres of critical waterfowl breeding habitat and highly erodible cropland.[7] Two "disincentive" policies– Swamp Buster and Sod Buster–revoked subsidy payments to any farmers who drained wetlands or converted prairies into cropland. Legislators strengthened stewardship incentives with the Wetlands Reserve Program (WRP) in the 1990 Farm Bill. This program contracted with landowners to restore and protect formerly converted wetlands through permanent easements.

Idling and restoring these millions of acres of erodible lands and wetlands kept the entire billion-acre agricultural landscape from turning into an ecological sacrifice zone for the production of feed, food, fiber, and fuel. While far from perfect, the CRP and WRP placed nearly 10 percent of all croplands and more than 2 million acres of wetlands under some form of protection. Among the quantifiable outcomes:

- Annual soil erosion on croplands fell from 3.1 billion tons per year in the pre-CRP era to 1.7 billion tons in 2007.[8] (See Figure 34, "Erosion on Cropland.")
- More than 26 million ducks were estimated to have been hatched between 1992 and 2003 as a direct result of CRP enrollments.[9]
- Nearly 70,000 acres of wetlands were restored each year between 1997 and 2003.[10]
- Until the recent ethanol boom, CRP and WRP were highly popular with landowners. Only one-third of applications for conservation programs are typically funded, because of budget constraints.

Unfortunately, those and other stewardship gains are in clear retreat now. Record prices for commodity crops, coupled with the expansion of the biofuels industry, and generous Farm Bill safety net programs like crop insurance, disaster assistance, and marketing loans, are drawing idled acreage back into production. Public discourse about the future of agriculture is again focused on growing more food for the world population rather than environmental sustainability.

Conservation Reserve Program (CRP) acreage actually declined by 3.4 million acres during the 2008 Farm Bill. This constituted a 10 percent loss in conservation lands despite a 10 percent increase in CRP rental payments. After record flooding and droughts, farmers wanted out of their CRP contracts (without penalty) so they could put the protected acreage into crop production. The mounting loss of soils and productive farmland to drought, flooding, and wildfire should send a signal that more, not fewer, conservation programs are needed to make the landscape more resilient to weather related catastrophes, but that message hasn't gotten through. Enrollment in CRP programs is lower than it has been in a long time mainly due to a surge in the number of expiring contracts and strong demand for feed and fuel crops. The future of the Wetlands Reserve Program is equally uncertain. WRP's acreage increased to 2.3 million acres under the 2008 Farm Bill, but still remains far below the 3 million acre limit. The decline of both these conservation and stewardship programs could bode poorly for many species.

Permanent Disaster Assistance—The Need for Conservation Compliance

Over the course of the 2008 Farm Bill, crop insurance became the largest and most popular form of federal farm support. Yet unlike traditional subsidies, there are no conservation compliance requirements for crop insurance and risk management programs. And the number of recipients of disaster-related insurance claims is on the rise.

Crop insurance in fact appears to be the new code word for crop subsidies. Commodity lobbyists have insisted that insurance be the centerpiece of future "farm safety nets." A wide range of other nonprofits, including the Izaak Walton League, Environmental Working Group, Center for a Livable Future, Sustainable Agriculture Coalition, and Wild Farm Alliance are calling for all federal risk management programs to be linked to conservation compliance. In other words, those who receive taxpayer support for crop insurance would agree not to drain wetlands, plow highly erodible lands, or plant crops with a low chance of successful harvest.

Getting Conservation Programs on Track

Beginning in 1985 and continuing with each successive Farm Bill, legislators pushed more and more money at landowners to achieve conservation goals, but other shortcomings undercut progress. Budgets for on-the-ground technical assistance didn't keep pace with conservation funds. In the words of one former top official, "NRCS staff have been turned into money obligators, pushing money out the door, frequently to the largest landowners, so that allocations aren't lost by the end of the fiscal year, without always being able to do the conservation planning they have been trained to do."

More recently, the dearth of qualified USDA NRCS field biologists has led to an increasing number of partnerships with conservation organizations. Groups such as Pheasants Forever, Ducks Unlimited, Trout Unlimited, the California Waterfowl Association—typically hunting, fishing, and wildlife associations—are working with USDA NRCS offices to help determine the best uses of valuable Farm Bill conservation dollars.

Who receives the money is a second critical problem. Paradoxically, some of the country's worst stewards have been rewarded with the most money under the premise that landowners with egregious problems deliver the highest benefit per dollar spent. Good stewards, for the most part, have been left out of this process. In the most unfortunate cases, opportunistic landowners plow up and erode intact prairie remnants, or remove functional terraces and shelterbelts that protected fields and slopes, to apply for set-aside payments. In the case of the Wetlands Reserve Program—arguably the Farm Bill's most successful conservation effort to date—only wetlands previously impacted by agricultural development are eligible for funding; you can't use the money to save pristine ecosystems. The Environmental Quality Incentives Program has doled out over $100 million per year since 2002 to help Concentrated Animal Feeding Operations comply with the Clean Water Act, even though EQIP was originally established to target small producers. Meanwhile, conservation programs generally have far more applicants than available funds.

Senate and House appropriations committees also deserve a heaping share of criticism. Their budgets are delivered months late and double-digit percentage points short of the cash promised. Even as the popularity of conservation programs has soared, congressional appropriations committees have slashed allocations during annual budget negotiations and cyclical reconciliation battles.

Conservation efforts have also suffered from years of poor regional planning. Without strategic watershed-wide, habitat-specific, or larger regional and statewide plans, efforts become catch-as-catch-can. (Conservation biologist Randy Gray criticized such approaches as "random acts of environmental kindness.") As the environmental threats have become more dire and conservation dollars more scarce, strategies are evolving. The USDA's scattershot funding is slowly being replaced by goal-oriented conservation plans to restore habitat across agricultural regions, rather than just at the individual farm or ranch level.

Yet nothing—nothing—continues to be more counterproductive than the complete disconnect between commodity crop subsidies and conservation programs. On the one hand, subsidies encourage farmers to maximize acreage, insurance programs eliminate economic risks, and disaster bailouts encourage plowing even marginal lands. Meanwhile, the USDA directs less than 7 percent of its overall spending toward conservation, much of that to right past wrongs and to clean up problems stemming from overfarming. Consider, for example, that even as 1.7 million acres were enrolled in the Conservation Reserve Program in South Dakota between 1985 and 1995, more than 700,000 acres of grassland were converted to crops. These were grasslands primarily tilled for corn and soybeans, already in excess supply.[11] The grassland alteration process only accelerated during the 2008 Farm Bill, as hay and pasture acreage was transformed into commod-

Figure 34

Erosion on Cropland

Conservation programs have reduced but not eliminated erosion on farmland

Sheet & Rill Erosion   Wind Erosion

Erosion in
Billions
of Tons
Per Year

Total = 3.06	Total = 2.79	Total = 2.17	Total = 1.89	Total = 1.81	Total = 1.73
1.38	1.30	0.99	0.85	0.80	0.77
1.68	1.49	1.18	1.04	1.01	0.96
1982	1987	1992	1997	2002	2007

3.5
3.0
2.5
2.0
1.5
1.0
0.5
0.0

Source: UDSA NRCS

Figure 35

What Will Become of CRP Contracts?

Millions of conservation acres may go under the plow 2007–2020

The Conservation Reserve Program is at a critical junction with over 30 million acres scheduled to expire between 2011 and 2020. The USDA has undertaken an initiative to re-enroll and extend some of these contracts on a short-term basis. But it remains unclear whether millions of CRP acres will remain idled and protected in the coming decade.

Number of
acres due
to expire
(in thousands)

7,000

6,000

5,000

4,000

3,000

2,000

1,000

2007 2008 2009 2010 2011 2012 2013 2014 2015 2016 2017 2018 2019 2020

Source: USDA FSA Conservation Reserve Program Monthly Summary August 2011

ity monocultures. Such a dichotomy makes Farm Bill conservation programs seem more like a distraction than a coordinated national stewardship strategy.

In fact, during a 2011 briefing, a top conservation official characterized conservation programs this way: "This is advertising. We need to grow 70 percent more food by 2030 without destroying the land base. What is good for the sage grouse is good for the rancher."

Rewarding Stewardship Rather than Yield

A recent initiative has shown that farm subsidies and conservation don't have to be at odds. Backed by Iowa Senator Tom Harkin, and referred to inside the Beltway as "the Harkin Program," it was pilot-tested in 2002, and adopted as the Conservation Stewardship Program in the 2008 Farm Bill. Rather than offering subsidies to maximize commodity output or take land out of production, the CSP rewards landowners for sound stewardship—soil protection, clean water, energy efficiency, and pesticide reduction. The CSP is crafted to support a whole new era of agriculture, allowing farmers to transition away from commodity crop production, increasing the equity of subsidy payments, and conforming to WTO rules of acceptable agricultural supports.

Designed as a full entitlement program, the Conservation Stewardship Program is available to all landowners who meet a set of environmental standards. Successful applicants must demonstrate that they are preventing manure or other fertilizer from running into streams, and that they are conserving soil and minimizing pesticide use, among other requirements. Extra points—and higher payments—are available for those who provide habitat for wildlife or protect streams and groundwater, including reducing fertilizer or pesticide use, converting crop land into permanent pasture, or installing farm-scale windmills or solar photovoltaic arrays to supply the farm with energy.

Advocates of healthy agriculture agree, hands down, that the Conservation Stewardship Program (CSP) is the most inventive idea to grace a Farm Bill in decades. Rather than encouraging damaging high-output commodity agriculture with one title, and funding remedial conservation with another, the CSP embodies a holistic approach for the first time since the New Deal. Organic farmers—who represent the fastest growing segment of the food sector and have been long ignored by Farm Bill spending—finally have an advantage in program eligibility. The CSP also holds the promise of serving as a safety net for farmers interested in transitioning from commodity row crops toward perennial grass pastures for livestock, an urgent reform required of the food and farming system.

Despite these directives, the program's funding for the next Farm Bill remains uncertain.

19. Healthy Lands, Healthy People

Figure 36

The Conservation Challenge

Ongoing Concerns	Critical Programs and Ideas
Conservation efforts are too isolated to have far-reaching effects.	Initiatives should be undertaken at the landscape scale and augmented with more on-the-ground technical staff.
Conservation programs continue to be flat-funded.	Conservation budgets should not be cut disproportionately compared to other Farm Bill titles.
Conservation Reserve Program contracts expire and millions of acres may become intensively cropped for biofuel grains.	CRP contracts protect erodible land, provide wildlife habitat, and decrease overproduction; energy crops should be produced from diverse perennial crops under sound conservation guidelines.
Conservation Security Program remains slow to roll out across the country.	Conservation Security Program has the potential to transform the farm support system and at the same time achieve far-reaching conservation and trade goals.

Healthy Lands, Healthy Economies

From a taxpayer perspective, it's hard to argue against the benefits of the Farm Bill's conservation dollars. The things humans depend upon for survival—food production, a stable climate, clean air and water, and vibrant biodiversity—are directly a function of healthy ecosystems. Recent scientific reviews show that biodiversity is particularly critical;[12] it is the wide variety of species in an area that gives an ecosystem the resilience to adapt to ever-changing conditions. In fact, signs show that the more species we keep alive in the places where we live and farm, the more successful our agricultural operations become.

Consider, for example, that one out of every four mouthfuls of the foods and beverages we consume depends on pollination. Farmers grow more than one hundred crop plants that rely on pollinators—bees, butterflies, moths, hummingbirds, bats—from apples and cherries to squashes and blueberries. According to the Xerces Society, insect-pollinated crops contributed an estimated $20 billion to the U.S. economy in 2000. If this calculation were expanded to include indirect products, such as milk and beef cattle fed on alfalfa, pollinators would be responsible for almost $40 billion worth of agricultural products each year.[13]

Due to a number of environmental factors, the number of European honeybees, the world's most relied on agricultural pollinator, has declined by 66 percent since World War II. Likewise, North America's thousands of native pollinators have suffered from the fragmentation of habitats and the extensive use of pesticides. A growing body of evidence supports the idea of restoring habitats in and around farmlands to allow native pollinator populations to rebound—if only as an insurance policy against predicted catastrophic losses of honeybees. Native habitats in and around farms can support dozens of resident pollinating species (as well as other beneficial insects) that eagerly go to work in farm fields and orchards.

Bats, too, provide invaluable services to farmers, but are under threat. A colony of just 150 big brown bats, for example, can eat over 1 million insect pests in a year.[14] Yet bats are dying en masse from a mysterious fungus known as White Nose Syndrome. These losses are compounded by the proliferation of windmills across the Midwest. With windmill blades towering above tree lines, bats are frequently struck and killed or have their lungs crushed by sudden pressure changes. Though bat mortalities due to wind energy are not officially tracked nationwide, estimates have the number reaching as high as 111,000 annually by 2020.[15] Boston University wildlife researcher Thomas Kunz estimates the economic impact of bat loss to be at least $3.7 billion a year—the pest control costs farmers would not need to spend with healthy bat populations. But Kunz says those costs could reach $53 billion, according to his estimates published in the journal *Science*.[16] Just as honeybee colony collapse has become a research priority in recent years, USDA should also pay careful attention to this impending crisis.

One might also think that clean water efforts would be a Farm Bill priority, since agriculture is responsible for 70 percent of U.S. water contamination—primarily through nutrient leaching and animal waste. USDA reports show that farmers can reduce nitrogen leakages at lower costs than sewage plants can remove it.[17] Studies show that every dollar invested in riparian vegetation (which helps to filter water and recharge groundwater) saves $7.50 to $200 in municipal water treatment.[18] Clearly, a nationwide campaign to improve habitats throughout all of the nation's waterways could have positive impacts on public health, wildlife, and regional economies. Farm Bill dollars are already at work to revegetate thousands of miles of farmland waterways throughout Pennsylvania's and Maryland's tributaries to the Chesapeake Bay. Another important regional focus is the Upper Mississippi Watershed, where fertilizer runoff is linked to the Dead Zone in the Gulf of Mexico, more than 1,000 miles away.

Conclusion

The most fundamental reason to bolster and refine conservation spending is this: Species, once lost, are gone forever, and, once they're gone, the fibers of the continent's distinct biological fabric begin to unravel. Land health and the health of the people will always be deeply interconnected. There will be no agriculture on completely degraded habitats, and the loss of one element in an ecosystem, no matter how large or small, is often a precursor to a cascading effect of further impoverishment of a landscape.

Conservation Program Landscape

Conservation Security Program (CSP—2002). The first comprehensive green payments approach to agricultural subsidies. Also, the first conservation program enacted as an entitlement program, with a budget set by the number of farmers deciding to apply and able to meet the rigorous environmental standards required. The Bush Administration flat-funded and capped the CSP far below promised levels.

Conservation Reserve Program (CRP—1985). CRP is a voluntary land retirement program in which landowners sign up for 10- or 15-year contracts, receiving annual rental payments and cost-share assistance to establish resource-conserving groundcovers on eligible, mostly highly erodible, farmland. Contracts are expiring on 28 million acres between 2006 and 2010, and biofuels advocates are eyeing CRP land for grain and cellulosic ethanol production.

Wetlands Reserve Program (WRP—1990). Helps landowners protect, restore, and enhance wetlands through long-term and permanent conservation easements. The goal is to protect priority wetland functions and values, along with optimum wildlife habitat. The 2002 Farm Bill boosted the WRP to 250,000 new acres each year, but congressional appropriators have used backdoor tactics to reduce that amount.

Environmental Quality Incentives Program (EQIP—1996). Cost-share and incentive payments to install or implement structural and management practices. From 1996 to 2002, EQIP was prohibited by law from subsidizing large-scale, regulated industrial livestock confinement operations, and payments were capped at $10,000 per farm per year. Since 2003, EQIP has funded fecal waste management on large-scale animal feeding operations, initially with a payment limitation of $450,000 per operation. These pollution subsidies were reduced to the still exorbitant limit of $300,000 in 2008.

Farm and Ranch Lands Protection Program (FRPP—1996). Matching funds (up to 50 percent of the fair market value of the conservation easement) to help purchase development rights to keep productive farm and ranchland in agricultural uses. USDA partners with state, tribal, or local governments and nongovernmental organizations to acquire conservation easements or other interests in land from landowners.

Grassland Reserve Program (GRP—2002). Helps landowners restore and protect grassland, rangeland, pastureland, shrubland, and certain other lands. Provides short- or long-term assistance for rehabilitating grasslands and protects vulnerable grasslands from development or conversion to cropland. Grasslands make up the largest land cover on America's private lands—over 525 million acres. The GRP has only enough funding for about 2 million acres.

Wildlife Habitat Incentives Program (WHIP—1996). Provides 5- to 10-year cost-share payments and technical assistance to landowners to develop and improve fish and wildlife habitat primarily on private land. Not limited to agricultural lands. WHIP can reach landowners who are not eligible for other farm conservation programs.

Agricultural Management Assistance (AMA—2000). Cost-share assistance for agricultural producers in 15 states (the northeastern states plus UT, NV, and WY) to construct or improve water management structures or irrigation structures; plant trees for windbreaks or improve water quality; and mitigate risk through production diversification or resource conservation practices, including soil erosion control, crop rotation, integrated pest management, or transition to organic farming.

Conservation Innovation Grants (CIG—2002). A subset of EQIP. Under CIG, EQIP funds are used to award competitive grants to nonfederal governmental or nongovernmental organizations, tribes, or individuals to accelerate technology transfer and adoption of promising technologies and approaches to pressing natural resource concerns.

Partnerships and Cooperation Initiative (2002). Allows USDA to designate special projects and enter into stewardship agreements with nonfederal entities, including state and local agencies and nongovernmental organizations, to provide enhanced technical and financial assistance through the integrated application of all the Farm Bill conservation programs. The partnerships help to organize landowners in particular watersheds or defined constituencies and energize them through special incentives to create flexible and efficient solutions to complex resource conservation challenges.

Conservation Technical Assistance (CTA). The CTA Program provides the technical capability, including direct conservation planning, design, and implementation assistance, that helps people plan and apply conservation on the land. A key part of the basic conservation infrastructure for all conservation programs.

Conservation compliance. Refers broadly to disincentive programs (Sod Buster, conservation compliance on highly erodible land, and Swamp Buster) created by the 1985 Farm Bill to decrease destructive practices on highly erodible cropland without adequate erosion protection and to prevent the draining of wetlands on agricultural land. Violation of these provisions can result in denial of commodity subsidies and conservation payments, though enforcement has been lax and succeeding Farm Bills have weakened the rules. Swamp Buster rules are key to achieving the national wetlands no-net-loss policy. Proposals to strengthen Sod Buster are getting renewed attention as limited remaining native prairie gets converted to cropland.

Safeguarding Sage Grouse and Their Elaborate Courtship Dance

Jim Robbins

RYEGATE, Mont.—When permanent settlement began in the West, some 16 million greater sage grouse lived on the steppes of the high plains.

There may now be as few as 200,000 of these ground-dwelling birds, famous for their elaborate courtship dance, and they are on the decline, hit especially hard by oil and gas development. Their dwindling numbers warrant protection as an endangered species, federal officials say. Because other species need listing first, though, and because protections for endangered species are widely reviled in the West, a unique way of managing the birds is under way.

The Sage Grouse Initiative, a project administered by the federal Natural Resources Conservation Service, targets for protection three-quarters of the birds on about a quarter of total sage grouse habitat. Officials call it a triage approach to conservation—protecting land where habitat is mostly intact and ignoring much of the land that has been degraded by energy development and other things.

"We're targeting like a laser beam those places where there are a lot of birds," said David E. Naugle, an associate professor of wildlife at the University of Montana and scientific adviser to the project.

The effort is also unique because it covers so much land—some 56 million acres across 11 Western states. Nothing near this scale has been done with a species in trouble. The project received $18 million last year and $30 million this year from the conservation service. Last week, the conservation service announced the addition of $23 million to buy conservation easements on core habitat.

"The federal government really stepped up in a meaningful way to keep sage grouse off the endangered species list," said Tom Remington, director of the Colorado Division of Wildlife, which is not involved in the effort. "It's mind-boggling that they did it so fast and it's as well funded as it is. And applying science in this way is unprecedented."

Noah Greenwald, a biologist with the Center For Biological Diversity, which focuses on endangered species, thinks the plan is good, but doesn't go far enough. The sage grouse initiative "is voluntary," Mr. Greenwald said. "We hope the promises are kept, but things can fall through the cracks."

Neither, he said, does the plan protect sage grouse habitat on federal land damaged by energy development, and plans to protect the birds in those areas are not nearly as strong as an endangered designation would be. The group has sued to force listing of the bird so it receives full protection under the law.

The effort began with the locations of the biggest, healthiest populations. In each state leks have been well tallied—a lek is like a sage grouse town square, a critical area where the birds carry out courtship rituals and mate. Counting birds on the lek in the spring gave biologists a solid estimate of numbers.

The spring breeding rite of the sage grouse is one of the bird world's most dramatic courtships. For a month or so dozens of males, which are the largest grouse in North America and can weigh up to seven pounds, show up at the grassy lek and jockey for territory with displays—puffing up a huge collar of white chest feathers, fanning their tail feathers and making popping sounds by slapping together two small yellow air bladders on their chests. The birds clash and feathers fly, all in an effort to prove superiority and claim a few more square feet of ground than other birds.

By April the females fly in, and some researchers joke that it's the wildlife equivalent of the bars during spring break in Florida. "It's chaos," said Dr. Naugle. As the air is filled with the popping of air bladders, "everyone starts displaying and strutting and trying to woo the females." The top male may mate with three-quarters of the females.

Within the 56 million acres, the conservation service is concentrating on ranch land with the highest numbers of birds and best habitat, called core areas, and working to improve it. It's a last, large-scale effort to stem the bird's decline, and should it fail the bird will probably receive strict protection across its range.

The program is part of the 2008 federal farm bill, and the lead agency is the conservation service, whose main mission is to provide financing and technical help to farmers and ranchers. An idea at the heart of the initiative, though, is that a better-managed ranch will also improve habitat for sage grouse, and a more profitable ranch means it's less likely to be sold for subdivisions.

The project worked to improve habitat on 1,000 square miles last year and will work with ranchers on 3,000 square miles this year. The conservation service, said Dr. Naugle, is the key to doing so much in so short a time. "They have an army already in place to create these kind of outcomes," he said.

The program, heavily based on research into the impact on grouse from such things as livestock grazing and barbed-wire fences, comes down to ranchers like Ben Lehfeldt. Mr. Lehfeldt runs sheep and cattle north of Billings, in a part of central Montana that is still rich in sage grouse. As he rides along a dirt road through his remote, wind-swept ranch across gentle sagebrush-studded swells, Mr. Lehfeldt points out plastic tags the size of playing cards affixed to miles of barbed-wire fence. Sage grouse fly low, just feet off the ground, and fences kill hundreds of birds a year. This marking of some fences and the removal of others, for a total of 180 miles of fence, should prevent 800 to 1,000 collisions annually, according to a study done at the University of Idaho. Ranchers have also put ramps in the tanks they use to water cattle to allow a bird that falls into a tank to climb out.

Mr. Lehfeldt said he liked the approach. An endangered species designation would have meant restrictions and no financing. So it would have been a lot more contentious. "It would have made things a lot harder if they did," Mr. Lehfeldt said. The energy industry has also fought the designation.

The forests of silver-green sagebrush are vital to every aspect of the grouse's life. The birds need heavy grass beneath the two- to three-foot-high sagebrush, for cover from predators during nesting and brood rearing, so eight new water tank locations will enable Mr. Lehfeldt to let his cattle and sheep range more widely in this dry country, which will allow prairie grasses to grow taller. Where land has been tilled, ranchers are paid to reseed to native prairie.

The program began last year, and this spring biologists will begin monitoring to see what effect the changes have had.

"We're expecting an 8 to 10 percent increase in nest success," based on these steps, Dr. Naugle said. "If it doesn't increase we'll tweak the habitat management to reach those benefits. It's adaptive management, and we monitor every step of the way."

While the Endangered Species Act would protect the bird by law, this program is voluntary. It can have hefty incentives. Ranchers can receive a total from farm programs of up to $450,000 over 10 years, but have to match some of that. Still, it is enough for ranchers to make changes in management right away that may otherwise have taken years, or may never have been made.

In some places, especially on federal land, efforts to protect the birds will not be made. Energy development has turned much of Wyoming's sagebrush steppes into a network of roads, power lines and other development. Because the birds don't tolerate disturbance, their numbers have suffered badly. A boom in wind power turbines and subdivisions are problems as well because of the roads and traffic associated with them. A wild card in this project is West Nile virus. Where Dr. Naugle has studied grouse, there is 25 percent mortality during outbreak years. Moreover, settling ponds that the energy industry uses to store water extracted with the gas breed mosquitoes, carrier of the virus, and the industry is searching for ways, including mosquito-eating fish, to cope with the problem.

Canada's experience with sage grouse has been a dark lesson for biologists here. Western Canada once had flourishing populations. Primarily because of energy development there are now just 200 birds in Saskatchewan and fewer than a hundred in Alberta, and there are concerns the Alberta population will soon disappear.

Because of their strong flavor, sage grouse are not a widely hunted game species. They are important as an umbrella species—if their diverse habitat is protected, it protects other prairie species, from migratory song sparrows to pygmy rabbits and mule deer.

"This initiative is one of the most important I have seen in a decade, to preserve high-quality habitat," said Ben Deeble, sagebrush coordinator for the National Wildlife Federation in Missoula. "They are bringing in the best new science to analyze impacts."

This article originally appeared in the February 7, 2011 New York Times.

20. National Security: Food on the Front Lines

Although "agriculture" and the "War on Terror" rarely appear in the same sentence, Americans have long recognized the critical role that agriculture plays in keeping the nation safe. Until the Organic Act of 1862 established the USDA, the Department of State handled agriculture policy. Today, in issues as varied as military preparedness, the vulnerability of concentrated production systems, and helping soldiers relate to rural citizens in foreign war zones, food and farm policy are on the front lines of national security debates.

During World War II, malnourishment plagued the military, contributing to the rejection of 40 percent of draftees due to poor health. Today, the opposite has occurred: obesity has become the top medical basis for refusing young Americans for military service.

In both cases, the nation has looked to school lunches as at least a partial solution. Right after the war, Congress passed the School Lunch Act of 1946. In creating the federally subsidized school meal program, Congress declared it "a measure of national security, to safeguard the health and well-being of the Nation's children." More than half a century later in 2010, a group of over 100 retired generals and admirals under the banner "Mission Readiness" issued a letter to Congress, urging bigger budgets for child nutrition to improve kids' access to healthy foods like fruits and vegetables. The Child Nutrition Act mandates the spending of $10 billion per year to provide lunches for 31 million American kids in public schools and serves as a companion to the Farm Bill's nutrition programs. It was reauthorized in 2010 with only a modest budget increase. The military leaders group urged changes in child nutrition spending and policy because obesity "is limiting the pool of available recruits and eroding our military readiness."

Healthy food production, access, and affordability must be acknowledged and fully funded as essential parts of a forward-looking defense strategy.

In a report entitled "Too Fat to Fight: Retired Military Leaders Want Junk Food Out of America's Schools" the authors state that between 1995 and 2008, 140,000 candidates nationwide failed their physical exams due to weight problems. More than one of every four Americans ages 17 to 24 is too overweight to enlist. Col. Gaston Bathalon, an army nutrition expert, says that the problem "is quickly becoming a national security issue for us. The pool of recruits is becoming smaller."[1] Active troops are also struggling with diet problems. Thousands have been relieved of service because they couldn't control their weight.[2]

America's Soft Underbelly

The concept of "agroterrorism"–attacks against agricultural targets–received national attention in December 2004 when then-Secretary of Health and Human Services Tommy Thompson delivered this bombshell in his resignation speech. "For the life of me, I cannot understand why the terrorists have not attacked our food supply, because it is so easy to do."[3]

Indeed many experts are pointing to vulnerabilities in highly concentrated as well as hard to defend food and farming systems–whether animal feeding operations, thousand-acre monoculture fields, or mega-processing facilities.

One microbe can contaminate tens of millions of eggs in a modern facility where a quarter million hens are crammed six to a battery cage. One strain of wheat rust can devastate 5,000 acres of a genetically identical grain crop, when the airborne fungus sucks the life out of plant stems and rapidly spreads.

In 2004, the National Defense Research Institute (NDRI) assessed the susceptibility of the agricultural sector and modern food chain to biological terrorism in a report titled "Hitting America's Soft Underbelly."

Among many concerns, it describes problems associated with contagious diseases spreading in dairies crowded with 10,000 animals: the frequent commingling of herds,

as well as the tremendous speeds at which animals are processed and foods are distributed throughout the population. It warns that "the rapid transfer of livestock in this manner increases the risk that pathogenic agents will spread well beyond the locus of a specific outbreak before health officials become aware that a problem exists."

The Congressional Research Service prepared a separate report entitled "Agroterrorism: Threats and Preparedness" that further outlines risks to the nation's economy, health, and food security from attacks on agriculture. Animals and plants represent hard to secure secondary targets with critical shock factor. Contamination is highly possible, the authors suggest, in concentrated animal operations, in shipments of food grains, and through food ingredients that are routinely mixed together during food processing and preparation. It specifically states that "diseases may infect herds more rapidly in modern concentrated confinement livestock operations than in open pastures." Other perceived perils are economic. Because agricultural exports contribute significantly to the U.S. economy, some warn about potential impacts to national security if foreign consumer confidence in the safety of American foods is shaken. A weakening economy could lead to civil unrest. These are but two of dozens of reports addressing food within the larger scenario of national security.

Trends in concentration of production and ownership also present national defense concerns. First is the small number of operations producing most of the output, along with food distribution and processing. Modern feeding operations commonly house 100,000 beef cattle, 500,000 laying hens, 10,000 hogs, and 60,000 broiler chickens. The packing plants that process those animals have become increasingly consolidated, with the slaughter lines running at alarming speeds. Agricultural activities have also become geographically specialized. The top three hog-producing states (Iowa, North Carolina, and Minnesota) produce 53 percent of U.S. hogs. The top three chicken-producing states (Georgia, Arkansas, and Alabama) produce 41 percent of U.S. chickens. Over half of the leafy greens in the United States are grown in the Salinas Valley and are packaged in warehouses that many compare to massive salad bowls. The spread of disease is just one concern in heavily concentrated production systems. Unpredictable weather events such as flooding, drought, heat, or cold could also present major disruptions in the food supply.

Despite mounting evidence about dangers of an overly centralized and industrialized food system, most recommendations follow predictable lines. None address the root problems of scale, lack of diversity, unhygienic production conditions in animal factories, geographic concentration of food production, or heavy dependence on fossil fuels. Instead they advocate increasing monitoring capabilities to detect outbreaks before they spread out of control.

One exception might be the Know Your Farmer, Know Your Food (KYF[2] from the 2008 Farm Bill) initiative, which has emphasized support for local food production throughout all departments of the USDA. Know Your Farmer has already focused attention and resources on increasing regional infrastructure, with projects such as food hubs or mobile slaughter workshops that aim to facilitate small-scale meat production throughout the country.

Return to the Victory Garden?

Today's grocery stores typically turn over their entire inventory an average of 12.7 times per year.[4] If national food distribution networks were disrupted, supermarkets would have less than one month's worth of stock on hand to sustain local residents. In such a scenario, regional and local farms would have to become primary food sources. Taking food security into account, Farm Bill programs might also encourage citizens to supply part of their own food with home gardens.

Prior to the industrialization of agriculture after World War II, local food production was regarded as an invaluable part of daily life on the home front. Following First Lady Elanor Roosevelt's example of installing a garden on White House grounds, "victory gardens" became popular installations in backyards, vacant lots, public parks, and apartment rooftops. Citizens were motivated to take pressure off the public food supply by growing produce of their own. Extension agents provided gardeners with seed, fertilizer, and tools.[5]

Sow the seeds of Victory!

plant & raise your own vegetables

WRITE TO THE NATIONAL WAR GARDEN COMMISSION — WASHINGTON, D.C. for free books on gardening, canning & drying.

JAMES MONTGOMERY FLAGG

"Every Garden a Munition Plant"

Charles Lathrop Pack, President

By 1943, the USDA exceeded its target of 18,000,000 victory gardens. At the program's peak, home gardeners supplied 40 percent of the nation's produce, generating roughly 125 pounds of food for every American.[6]

Future Farm Bills could likewise advance food security by launching a modern-day victory garden program—or a home-garden

extension program—with a goal of inspiring 20 million new suburban and urban gardens by 2018.

From the Front Lines to the Fields

Rural areas are home to just one-sixth of the country's population, yet provide nearly one-half of all military recruits—who return as veterans. New programs and policies are using farming and local food production as a tool for rehabilitation, re-entry into civilian life, and career changes.

Farming's physical activity and working with nature are found to be profoundly therapeutic and healing. Growing food and connecting with consumers provides farmers with a positive mission and sense of responsibility and purpose.

To that end, 2008 Farm Bill dollars from the Risk Management Agency have been used to fund a series of veterans-to-farmers educational retreats around the country.

Local foods are beginning to be used to rehabilitate veterans inside military hospital dining halls. Veterans Administration Hospitals in Martinsburg, Virginia, and San Francisco, California, are purchasing fresh produce from local farmers to supply their cafeterias. By replacing frozen, canned, and dehydrated fruits and vegetables with local produce, VA cafeterias are attempting to maximize the healing qualities—superior vitamins and micronutrients—of fresh, particularly organic, foods. They may also be contributing to a more diversified and resilient food system in their areas. The next logical step would be to encourage the purchase of local food from veteran farmers for these institutions.

Conclusion

Farm Bill negotiators are well positioned to aid the military in its national security battles with programs that increase the consumption and availability of healthy foods, decentralize livestock production, and expand regional food production and distribution capabilities. But USDA is not the only government agency with the powers to do something about the lasting effects of preventable nutritional diseases. If the Department of Defense truly believes an upgrade in school nutrition programs is in the best interests of national security, perhaps it could contribute the necessary funding. It certainly has the largest budget at its disposal. And in fact, there is a recent precedent. Since 2002, the Department of Defense Farm to School Program has been offering financial, administrative, and other assistance to public school cafeterias to provide fruits and vegetables produced within the state.[7] It's time that food and agriculture systems are not only perceived as potential risks to national security. Healthy food production, access, and affordability must be acknowledged and fully funded as essential parts of a forward-looking defense strategy.

21. The Next 50 Years: Perennialization and Ecosystem-based Agriculture

Rural America today is in an Age of Monoculture. Farmers reap ever-growing harvests of annual crops by planting hybrid varieties, pumping them up with fossil fuel fertilizers, and managing them with pesticides, herbicides, and industrial machinery. A drive through monoculture farm country can appear eerily sterile–feed corn, soybeans, wheat, or cotton as far as the eye can see, uninterrupted by so much as an acre of natural habitat. Annual crops farmed so intensively exact a steep toll: the elimination of biodiversity and the continual erosion and impoverishment of soil.

A perennial food system would essentially mimic the ecosystems that existed long before sod busting and swamp draining and clean farming became the norm.

In response to grave concerns that the industrial food system will eventually collapse, a new vision for agriculture is emerging: the Age of Perennials. This idea rests on a transition to deep-rooted, diverse communities (polycultures) of long-lived perennial plants that cover and permanently protect the soil, and don't need to be re-seeded annually. Rather than being industrially imposed on the landscape, a perennial mixture would be designed to capture the ecosystems' processes of the wild that existed long before sod busting and tile as well as swamp draining became the norm. Renewable resources like sunshine, groundwater management, and nutrient cycling would drive the production process.

According to the Salina, Kansas-based Land Institute, the goals of perennial farming include:
- Extending the productive life of soils from the current tens or hundreds of years to thousands or tens of thousands of years;
- Developing resilience to extreme rainfall events, droughts, and insect and pest pressures;
- Reducing land runoff that creates coastal dead zones with disastrous effects on fisheries;
- Maintaining quality of surface and ground water;
- Building food security as we deal with intersecting issues of climate, population, water, and biodiversity loss.[1]

Starting with Grass

Already we have one common perennial agriculture system: hay and pasture-based grazing operations. Pastures can be comprised of a variety of perennials such as timothy, orchard grass, clover, and alfalfa. Some farms and ranches are exclusively devoted to grass-fed livestock production, while others rotate pastures with row crops to restore the soil, prevent pest buildups, and diversify their food and crop output. Increasingly, orchards and vineyards are turning to permanent ground cover and incorporating livestock grazing during certain times of the year. A broad range of experts see an expansion of farming systems like these as essential for regions like the Upper Mississippi watershed, where decades of massive soil loss and leaching of nutrients from industrial corn and soybean operations have resulted in one of the world's largest dead zones in the Gulf of Mexico.

A 12-year research program conducted by Minnesota's Chippewa River Watershed Project has been studying this problem. Scientists have documented that where there are concentrations of perennial plants, significant reductions in soil sediments and agricultural nutrients in surrounding watersheds follow. Their findings suggest that if just 10 percent of critical lands in the Chippewa watershed were converted to rotations of pastures and other perennial crops and habitats, measurable improvements in water quality would result throughout surrounding waterways.[2]

Critics frequently argue that shifting to such diversified agricultural methods is a luxury the world can no longer afford; that only chemical- and technology-intensive farming can provide the food necessary for a growing population. Peer-reviewed studies increasingly show the opposite, however. Sustainable agriculture systems are not just highly productive but also have other benefits—such as a reduced carbon footprint, the elimination of toxic chemicals, prevention of soil loss, habitat protection, and beauty.

Modern organic, biodynamic, and rotational grazing practitioners have developed sophisticated and profitable farming systems—gains made possible by a growing base of knowledge about the interplay of ecology and farming. This marriage of specialties is referred to as *agroecology*. One of the defining principles of agroecology is designing food production around on-farm renewable energy exchanges rather than the extractive energy resources like petroleum-based fuels and agrochemicals so important in the age of monoculture. Great strides have been made in the production of dairy and beef cattle, swine, and poultry on small- and large-scale pasture operations. Animals are being raised in appropriate numbers and are not solely dependent on faraway sources of subsidized feeds. As in a healthy ecosystem, their wastes become soil nutrients rather than toxic byproducts that overflow into watersheds, communities, and the food system. These innovations have been achieved with just a fraction of the research budget allocated to conventional agriculture over the last five decades.

The Next Step: Perennial Grains

Science is now on taking on a new agroecological frontier: perennial grains. Perennials have many ecological advantages over annual crops. Because they live longer and develop deep roots over time, perennial plants have greater access to ground water. Also, those deep root systems make them less susceptible to wind and rain, protecting the soil from erosion. This is critical as agriculture has been expanded to steep hillsides and low lying wetlands not suitable to annual crops.

Innovative research has been underway for decades at the Salina, Kansas-based Land Institute, Washington State University, and other institutions around the world to breed food crops with close wild perennial relatives. The goal is to develop commercially viable perennial grains, oil seeds, and other crops that would form the foundation of enduring farming practices that don't compromise the soil, poison the environment, or degrade water quality. One can imagine, for example, a farm field dominated by perennial wheat or sunflowers that can remain productive for many years, without the need for annual tilling, reseeding, or applying heavy doses of chemicals.

The next leap forward in agroecology may not be that far off. According to the Land Institute, research in Canada, Australia, China, and the United States suggests that perennialization of major grain crops like wheat, rice, sorghum and sunflowers can be developed within the next several decades.

The perennialization of animal agriculture and cropping systems, while critical, is not an ending point. In order to be truly sustainable, farms must appropriately fit the land they occupy, and cannot fall into the same land-abuse patterns that monocultures have. Just as in native grasslands or rainforests, future farming systems must be made up of combinations of perennials that function as a whole, and are both highly productive and resilient to drought, floods, and pest pressures. This will mean understanding how agriculture can be adapted to the unique structure and functions of local ecosystems.

An ecosystem can remain healthy only if its species and habitats have not been picked apart by the excessive expansion of agriculture. Watersheds must remain functional without overdrafting of groundwater or discharging of nitrogen and other nutrients. Woodlands, shrublands, and other contiguous habitats must continue to flourish as perennial agriculture is adapted to an area's natural ecology.

Toward a 50-Year Farm Bill

To spark this systemic shift in food production, we need to re-imagine the landscape itself: corn and soybean fields steadily replaced by permanent ground cover, much of it used for the grazing of animals. And in the long run, newly developed perennial crops will increasingly replace annual grains and oil seeds. These complex perennial food production systems will be less dependent on fossil fuels, more resilient to weather impacts, and also capture soil carbon from the atmosphere and increase wildlife habitat.

Just as in the days of the Dust Bowl, when the country faced devastating losses of soils, the Farm Bill presents the country's primary tool for ushering in a new generation of agricultural policy and stewardship. It is, after all, the main economic mechanism we have for accounting for things that the market does not address: stewardship and health. Because it is renewed regularly every five to seven years, the Farm Bill also presents a path that can be assessed and updated at regular intervals. And with its countrywide reach and mission to safeguard the food system, USDA is poised to take on a forward-thinking effort like the perennialization of food production.

A coalition of organizations and sustainable farming advocates, led by Land Institute founder Wes Jackson and author Wendell Berry, and farmer-philosopher Fred Kirschenmann, has called for perennialization to become a focus of Farm Bill spending over the next 50 years.[3] USDA funding, drawn from budgets for crop subsidies, conservation, and research, could jump-start this urgently needed transition. The U.S. Department of Agriculture, which has a network of research and extension services, sizable budget, and interactions with tens of thousands of farmers and landowners, could take the lead, as it previously did with the industrialization of farming, and more recently with its hefty investments in the ethanol industry. Just as cellulosic ethanol is now viewed as the next generation of sustainable biofuels, the perennialization of food crops can certainly shape the USDA's research

agenda for many decades to come.

Of course this will entail a major course correction in the mission of the Farm Bill itself. This will mean confronting inevitable outcomes of continuing to mine the soil and pollute waterways as if they are unlimited resources. Finally it will acknowledge the Farm Bill's unique potential to engage in long-term solutions to problems of food production. Jackson and the 50-year Farm Bill Coalition outline the following goals to drive future food and farm policy:

- No net loss of soil, soil fertility, or soil biodiversity;
- Net reductions in greenhouse gas emissions;
- Conservation and detoxification of water supplies;
- Minimal nitrogen runoff;
- More profitable farms, more farm families, and more vital rural communities;
- Healthful food; and
- High yields.[4]

Transitioning from the age of monoculture to the age of perennials and ecosystem-based farming will be a long process. Acreage for pasture and forage-crop rotations will increase. Annual feed grain crop acreage will decline, to be gradually replaced by land devoted to new perennial grains as they become commercially viable and widely available. The Land Institute's June 2009 report "A 50-Year Farm Bill" asserts that such a revolution in farming is attainable if only we choose to realign priorities to achieve it.

They are changes that lie well within the capacities of American farmers working the world's best soils. All can be achieved on current levels of federal funding. It is a question of realigning incentives so that the self-interests of the farmer coincide with the collective long-term interests of the nation.[5]

Our diets must eventually adapt to perennial agriculture as well. Health advocates already concur that we simply can't continue eating and producing food the way we have for the last 50 years. Pasture-raised animals are higher in nutritional components that are favorable to human health than grain-fed animals. These include omega-three fatty acids, conjugated linoleic acids, beta carotene, and other vitamins.[6] Perennial grains and forages might also offer nutritional advantages as well.

Fifty years may not be enough time for a complete transformation of the food system, though many argue that the challenges are so urgent we simply have no time to waste. A large-scale shift away from confinement livestock systems to grass-based perennial pasture systems, however, is a crucial starting point. The next revolution in agriculture—perennial food crops that function sustainably over time like grasslands or forest ecosystems—is also within reach, and federal policy makers would be wise to invest heavily in turning this research into an on-the-ground reality.

A 50-Year Farm Bill

Wes Jackson and Wendell Berry

The extraordinary rainstorms in June 2008 caused catastrophic soil erosion in the grain lands of Iowa, where there were gullies 200 feet wide. But even worse damage is done over the long term under normal rainfall—by the little rills and sheets of erosion on incompletely covered or denuded cropland, and by various degradations resulting from industrial procedures and technologies alien to both agriculture and nature.

Soil that is used and abused in this way is as nonrenewable as (and far more valuable than) oil. Unlike oil, it has no technological substitute—and no powerful friends in the halls of government.

Agriculture has too often involved an insupportable abuse and waste of soil, ever since the first farmers took away the soil-saving cover and roots of perennial plants. Civilizations have destroyed themselves by destroying their farmland. This irremediable loss, never enough noticed, has been made worse by the huge monocultures and continuous soil-exposure of the agriculture we now practice.

To the problem of soil loss, the industrialization of agriculture has added pollution by toxic chemicals, now universally present in our farmlands and streams. Some of this toxicity is associated with the widely acclaimed method of minimum tillage. We should not poison our soils to save them.

Industrial agriculture has made our food supply entirely dependent on fossil fuels and, by substituting technological "solutions" for human work and care, has virtually destroyed the cultures of husbandry (imperfect as they may have been) once indigenous to family farms and farming neighborhoods.

Clearly, our present ways of agriculture are not sustainable, and so our food supply is not sustainable. We must restore ecological health to our agricultural landscapes, as well as economic and cultural stability to our rural communities.

For 50 or 60 years, we have let ourselves believe that as long as we have money we will have food. That is a mistake. If we continue our offenses against the land and the labor by which we are fed, the food supply will decline, and we will have a problem far more complex than the failure of our paper economy. The government will bring forth no food by providing hundreds of billions of dollars to the agribusiness corporations.

Any restorations will require, above all else, a substantial increase in the acreages of perennial plants. The most immediately practicable way of doing this is to go back to crop rotations that include hay, pasture and grazing animals.

But a more radical response is necessary if we are to keep eating and preserve our land at the same time. In fact, research in Canada, Australia, China and the United States over the last 30 years suggests that perennialization of the major grain crops like wheat, rice, sorghum and sunflowers can be developed in the foreseeable future. By increasing the use of mixtures of grain-bearing perennials, we can better protect the soil and substantially reduce greenhouse gases, fossil-fuel use and toxic pollution.

Figure 37

Farm Bill: 2060 Vision
Protecting Our Soils with Perennials

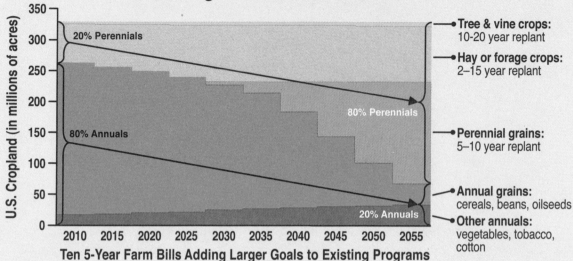

2010: Hay or grazing operations will continue as they exist. Preparations for subsidy changes begin.

2015: Subsidies become incentive to substitute perennial grass in rotations for feed grain in meat, egg, and milk production.

2020: The first perennial wheat, Kernza™, will be farmer-ready for limited acreage.

Source: Land Institute, "A 50-Year Farm Bill," 2009.

2030: Educate farmers and consumers about new perennial grain crops.

2045: New perennial grain varieties will be ready for expanded geographical range. Also potential for grazing and hay.

2055: High-value annual crops are mainly grown on the least erodible fields as short rotations between perennial crops.

Carbon sequestration would increase, and the husbandry of water and soil nutrients would become much more efficient. And with an increase in the use of perennial plants and grazing animals would come more employment opportunities in agriculture—provided, of course, that farmers would be paid justly for their work and their goods.

Thoughtful farmers and consumers everywhere are already making many necessary changes in the production and marketing of food. But we also need a national agricultural policy that is based

upon ecological principles. We need a 50-year farm bill that addresses forthrightly the problems of soil loss and degradation, toxic pollution, fossil-fuel dependency and the destruction of rural communities.

This is a political issue, certainly, but it far transcends the farm politics we are used to. It is an issue as close to every one of us as our own stomachs.

This op-ed originally appeared in the January 4, 2009 New York Times. Wes Jackson is a plant geneticist and president of The Land Institute in Salina, Kansas. Wendell Berry is a farmer and writer in Kentucky.

22. Local Food: The Emerging Agricultural Economy

More Americans today care about the source of their food than ever before. As part of a burgeoning local food movement, they are seeking out organically grown fruits and vegetables, pasture-raised meat, eggs, and dairy products. They want to leverage their food dollars to support their local economy, family farmers, and high standards of animal welfare, and to consume the best tasting foods. They are turning farmers markets and community gardens into dynamic social hubs in urban areas, and pushing municipalities to change laws to allow for urban farming.

Local food is a dynamic vehicle for public health, job creation, resource protection, and food security—but Farm Bill policies have been relatively slow to catch on.

Local food is a dynamic vehicle for public health, job creation, resource protection, and food security—but Farm Bill policies have been relatively slow to catch on. Soon, though, it will be impossible for Washington policy makers to ignore a cultural phenomenon sweeping across cities throughout the country. Consider some of the trends in the rapidly evolving local food movement:

- America had more than 7,000 farmers markets in 2011, up from 2,746 in 1998.[1]
- By 2009 more than 2,000 schools had Farm-to-School (F2S) programs to purchase locally grown food snacks and lunches for students. In 2001, there were just six such programs.[2]
- According to USDA, sales of local foods totaled over $5 billion in 2010; 20 percent of those sales were direct to consumers.
- Cities and rural areas around the country have developed over 100 "food hubs" that serve as centers for storing, processing, and distributing foods grown in surrounding rural areas.[3]

Shortening Food Supply Chains

New business models have vastly increased the amount of local food consumed, particularly in urban areas. Community Supported Agriculture arrangements engage members who pay a monthly or annual fee to a farm in return for regular deliveries of seasonal produce and foods like eggs, grassfed meats, and honey. Farm-to-School programs are changing schools' purchasing priorities to give preference to local farmers so that lunch and snack programs include fresh fruits and vegetables, rather than frozen and processed ingredients. Farmers markets have expanded customer bases for producers and offered opportunities for consumers to participate in a local food economy by reaching into areas previously untapped by this model. Local producers in northern climates are using high-tunnel greenhouse systems to extend the growing season for local greens and other high value crops.

Some Farm Bill grants and loans are helping stimulate these new, shorter supply chains. Programs like the Farmers Market Promotion Program, Seniors Farmers Market Nutrition Program, and Value Added Producer Grants have been around for at least a few Farm Bill cycles, long enough to sizably increase the number of markets and the production necessary to supply them. But truly scaling up local food capacity will require significant investment in infrastructure: processing facilities where produce can be prepared, dried and packaged; multi-species slaughter facilities where regional livestock can be processed; hubs where foods can be stored centrally until distributed; and new retail outlets, especially in areas where fresh food access is limited. USDA funding sources such as Specialty Crop Block Grants and Community Facilities Grants are just beginning to address such needs with programs to get more fresh foods into inner-city convenience stores, for example. Revolving loan funds and forgivable loan funds are just a few means that policy makers have to spur innovation and build infrastructure at the state and local levels.

In fact, the local food movement is challenging the Farm Bill's underlying conception of rural development. Is an urban farmers market that opens new business opportunities for producers who live outside the city technically "rural development"? What about a grant that helps a rural dairy set up a cheese-making facility in a county that is heavily urbanized? Current Farm Bill definitions around rural development pose funding limitations for counties that have both dense urban populations as well as a balanced rural sector capable of diversified local food production. The very idea of "rural development"—long a goal of Farm Bill program promoters—may become a pressure point for change as the clamor for increased local food production gains steam.

Underlying regional food production efforts is a broader public discussion about the best way to feed a surging global population. The conventional agriculture industry has for the most part shunned (and sometimes aggressively attacked) the regional food movement as elitist and boutique. They argue that local agriculture is unable to meet the needs of a rapidly changing world. Local food advocates are pushing against that charge. They view diversified regional food production as a necessary shift away from a food system that is almost totally reliant on heavily centralized large-scale producers and distributors. Rather than a threat, local food advocates see regional production as an essential complement to an industrial food system that is both vulnerable and overly centralized.

The ramping up of regional food production can be an engine for reviving economic development as well as an important evolution in a more diversified U.S. agriculture. The specialization of fruit and vegetable crops in just a few states—California and Florida in particular—offers important opportunities for job creation in communities around the country. One wonders what the effects of severe weather in either of those states could be on fresh produce supplies, for example. Similarly, the costs of shipping foods across the country could easily escalate as petroleum becomes more scarce. Diversification of fruit and vegetable production to the local level also has community development potential. An estimated 13 million acres of fruit and vegetable production would be required if people increased their consumption to satisfy USDA's dietary recommendations and that food was grown in the U.S.[4]

With increased exposure to risks from uncertain weather, rising energy costs, contamination, and a host of other factors, urban areas are looking at the scaling up of local food production as an integral element of basic food security. Motivated by public health concerns and the desire to enhance community development, local governments, food councils, NGOs, and others are working to boost local supplies of fruits and vegetables and to establish food outlets in neighborhoods where access is limited.

Know Your Farmer, Know Your Food

The public's growing interest in connecting consumers with farmers hasn't been entirely lost on the USDA. Over the course of the 2008 Farm Bill, Deputy Secretary of Agriculture Kathleen Merrigan launched the Know Your Farmer, Know Your Food (KYF2) initiative to put the promotion of local agriculture on USDA's agenda. KYF2 was a task force charged with breaking down traditional inter-agency silos in an attempt to identify opportunities to support local food production capabilities. Even though the program had no office, staff, or distinct budget, it immediately began to breathe new air into a bureaucracy gripped by the inertia of decades of supporting commodity agriculture. The KYF2 task force used its resources and skill sets to connect the dots between USDA programs and the revitalizing local food economy. Specific goals included:

- Stimulating food- and agriculture-based community economic development;
- Fostering new opportunities for farmers and ranchers;
- Promoting locally and regionally produced and processed foods;
- Cultivating healthy eating habits and educated, empowered consumers;

- Expanding access to affordable fresh and local food; and

- Demonstrating the connection between food, agriculture, community and the environment.

Memos were compiled to identify existing programs that could fund local food initiatives, such as Value Added Producer Grants and Business and Industry Guaranteed Loan Programs. Already, efforts that fall under the Know Your Farmer, Know Your Food directive are having tangible impacts on citizens' daily lives. A growing number of farmers markets now accept electronic SNAP benefits, spreading the local food movement to new sectors of the population.

Government grants and credit programs are spawning local businesses that create jobs and add value to farm products: jam, cheese, and vinegar facilities, and mushrooms raised in agroforestry operations. Disadvantaged farmers, young people, and high school students are all getting involved in agriculture as a result of USDA outreach and education programs. Crucial mapping has been done to identify productive livestock regions that lack nearby slaughter and processing facilities—a critical need in an era of ever-concentrated meat packing and processing.

The Know Your Farmer, Know Your Food Initiative's Regional Food Hub Subcommittee focused on studying and promoting one of the most dynamic developments in local food system work. Food hubs are central locations where local or regional crops are aggregated, stored, processed, and distributed. The business management structures for food hubs vary widely: some are private, others are nonprofits, some are extensions of food cooperatives. Food hubs service farmers on the one hand—many of whom may be too small to supply traditional wholesalers—and wholesale consumers on the other—restaurants and schools, for example, interested in sourcing local products that aren't always readily available from wholesalers. For small growers that don't own refrigerated trucks or warehouse spaces, food hubs can be a godsend, providing much needed infrastructure and marketing support. Likewise, for purchasers seeking local foods, a food hub can provide a steady supply of otherwise hard to source products.

According to a USDA survey, food hubs in existence for an average of five years, for example, typically employ six or more people, work with 40 farmers and ranchers, and generate $700,000 in total gross annual sales. In addition, 40 percent of food hubs are specifically targeting areas with limited access to fruits and vegetables. One can expect the food hub to rapidly expand and evolve in municipalities around the country as a crucial nervous system for regional food production.

The Know Your Farmer initiative has also spawned partnerships outside of USDA. Nonprofit organizations across the nation, for example, are designing nutrition incentive programs to connect low-income families with small farmers through farmers markets. These programs help people receiving federal nutrition assistance in the form of SNAP or WIC vouchers to attend farmers markets and to use their assistance dollars to purchase healthy food—in many cases doubling their purchasing power when they buy fruits and vegetables. In California, Roots of Change (ROC) helped create the Farmers Market Consortium, which includes 8 local NGOs in 16 counties, benefiting 754 individual small farmers selling specialty crops at 124 farmers markets, 70 of which offer incentives. Over a two-year period, ROC and its regional partners raised nearly $250,000 in matching money, which has been distributed in $5 and $10 contributions to SNAP and WIC recipients who buy fresh fruits, vegetables and nuts at participating farmers markets.[5] This not only puts healthy food on people's tables but boosts local farmer income as well. Similar networks are managed by Market Umbrella in New Orleans, Fair Food Network in Michigan, and Wholesome Wave in several states on the East Coast. Together, these organizations are collecting data—such as weight loss and other health indicators—to share with Congress in order to create a permanent federal program that ushers in an effective approach to nutrition assistance across the nation.

Cities Taking Charge

In 2010, Seattle took a unique approach to Farm Bill organizing. Richard Conlin, president of the Seattle City Council, assembled a group that included health care practitioners, farmers, retailers, and other civic leaders such as Dennis Hayes, organizer of the first Earth Day. They drafted a set of food system principles, beginning with the idea that the Farm Bill could be an economic and policy driver of such concerns as social justice and community development. The resulting "Seattle Farm Bill Principles" reflected their circumstances

By taking on the Farm Bill as a local priority, cities may soon challenge the USDA with a whole set of new priorities around urban agriculture.

in the Pacific Northwest: fighting an obesity crisis, supporting knowledge about healthy foods, building Farm to School and school garden programs, and increasing availability of locally sourced foods.

The exercise was intended as a learning experience and teaching tool rather than an extended campaign. But the idea caught fire. In May 2011 the City of Seattle officially ratified the principles.

Cities across the country immediately began taking notice. Duluth, Minnesota, adapted the principles for itself. Philadelphia, Salt Lake City, New York City, and Minneapolis established Farm Bill working groups in the lead-up to the 2012 Farm Bill reauthorization. In November 2011, the National League of Cities passed a resolution supporting healthy food, public health, and sustainability based on the Seattle Farm Bill Principles. This organization serves as a resource for more than 1,600 dues-paying members and reaches tens of thousands of other cities and towns through advocacy and networking programs.

These efforts to develop a vibrant agriculture at the interface of urban and rural areas are moving swiftly. By taking on the Farm Bill as a local priority, cities may soon challenge the USDA with a whole set of new priorities around urban agriculture. These discussions are already extending far beyond SNAP benefits and healthy food access. New York, for example, has been providing conservation incentives to farmers in surrounding rural areas for nearly a decade to ensure that their water supply is cared for far upstream, a policy that saves millions of dollars in mechanical filtration costs. Air pollution from farms and animal feeding operations is another critical issue with city policy makers, as is the preservation of beauty and wildlife in a region. Many cities are working on a variety of levels to contain urban growth boundaries and prevent future sprawl and subdivisions from gobbling up remaining productive lands. Farm Bill funding sources like the Farm and Ranch Lands Protection Program could help urban areas to protect surrounding farmland and open space, work already being led by land trusts and other organizations in many areas of the country.

Conclusion

Healthy foods produced locally–the kinds of efforts championed by the Know Your Farmer initiative, the Seattle Farm Bill Principles, and numerous food policy charters–are the tip of a burgeoning agriculture revolution. The motivation is not about expanding farmers markets so that elite urban consumers can buy expensive organic foods. It's about saving small farms before they disappear altogether, and making good-tasting food a centerpiece of the debate around issues of health, environmental sustainability, and social equity. Rural and urban constituencies need one another. By supporting regional food production, we become healthier, happier, more engaged, more secure citizens.

Expanding local food production capabilities does not mean the end of trade or the end of supports to large-scale production. As the world's food and health needs intensify and we are challenged by all kinds of unpredictable and unimaginable situations, we will need a wide range of sustainable food systems thriving and functioning properly.

If our Farm Bill dollars are limited, as they are and no doubt will be for the foreseeable future, our question should be how to best spend them. As more and more city dwellers and suburbanites realize how federal food and agriculture policies actually impact them, the Farm Bill may no longer be perceived as an arcane program to help Midwestern corn farmers and provide SNAP benefits to the poor. The Farm Bill may become, in the very near future, a local food bill too.

Figure 38

Seattle Farm Bill Principles
Supporting Healthy Farms, Food and People

Guidance for the 2012 Farm Bill

1 Health-centered Food System

The driving principle of the Farm Bill must be the relationship of food and ecologically sound agriculture to public health. Food that promotes health includes fruits, vegetables, whole grains, nuts, seeds, legumes, dairy, and lean protein. Improving the health of the nation's residents must be a priority in developing policies, programs, and funding.

2 Sustainable Agricultural Practices

Promote farming systems and agricultural techniques that prioritize the protection of the environment so that the soil, air, and water will be able to continue producing food long into the future. Integral to both domestic and global agricultural policies should be agricultural techniques and farming practices that enhance environmental quality, build soil and soil fertility, protect natural resources and ecosystem diversity, improve food safety, and increase the quality of life of communities, farmers, and farm workers.

3 Community and Regional Prosperity and Resilience

Enhance food security by strengthening the viability of small and mid-scale farms, and increasing appropriately scaled processing facilities, distribution networks, and direct marketing. Develop strategies that foster resiliency, local innovation, interdependence, and community development in both rural and urban economies. Opportunities that create fair wage jobs are key to a strong economy.

4 Equitable Access to Healthy Food

Identify opportunities and reduce barriers by developing policies and programs that increase the availability of and improve the proximity of healthy, affordable, and culturally relevant food to urban, suburban, and rural populations. Protect the nation's core programs that fight food insecurity and hunger while promoting vibrant, sustainable agriculture.

5 Social Justice and Equity

The policies reflected in the Farm Bill impact the lives and livelihoods of many people, both in the U.S. as well as abroad. Develop policies, programs, and strategies that support social justice, worker's rights, equal opportunity, and promote community self-reliance.

6 Systems Approach to Policymaking

It is essential to reduce compartmentalization of policies and programs, and to approach policy decisions by assessing their impact on all aspects of the food system, including production, processing, distribution, marketing, consumption, and waste management. Consider the interrelated effects of policies and align expected outcomes to meet the goal of a comprehensive health-focused food system.

The Seattle Farm Bill Principles were initiated by Seattle City Council President Richard Conlin as part of the Seattle Local Food Action Initiative. www.SeattleFarmBillPrinciples.org

TURNING

THE TABLES

23. Turning the Tables

The Farm Bill is one of those topics where once you start pulling the string, you find the whole world attached. That's because the Farm Bill sets the rules of the game, influencing not only what we eat, but also who grows it, under what conditions, and how much it costs. The agribusinesses and food manufacturing lobbying organizations that have in essence written those rules for our legislators in recent decades deserve the lion's share of the responsibility for shaping the present state of our food system and its tangle of critical problems.

The good news is that, to a large extent, the ideas needed to turn the tables and create a health-focused food and farming system already exist. They share a common condition:

Many of the models we need to turn the tables and advert a collision course for the food and farming system already exist. They all share a common condition: Most are either ignored, marginalized, or largely underfunded by Farm Bill programs, yet they surface, a testament to their resilience, tenacity, and, ultimately, their solution-oriented wisdom.

Most are ignored, marginalized, or underfunded by current Farm Bill programs. And yet, momentum is there. The movement to create a nourishing, environmentally sustainable, and affordable food system is becoming one of the unifying issues of our time. Food and farm policy is an ongoing cultural and political process, a series of give-and-takes that stretches from the checkout stand to the voting booth. People from all walks of life have enormous influence—as citizens, food consumers, business owners, professionals, doctors, nurses, students, teachers, parents. Every day, many of us can choose to support, or not, a particular aspect of the food and farming sector through our purchases. Every day, we can speak up for improving land stewardship or basic nutritional health in our workplaces, schools, and communities. Every Farm Bill cycle, we can demand that our representatives not barter away their votes.

We can join or take active leadership positions with advocacy organizations. Plenty of early efforts that, at the time, seemed minimally effective or even symbolic, later emerged as models, reproduced in one place after another. Some have inspired mainstream movements—such as organic farming or pasture-based livestock production—that are influencing food policy at state, national, or even international levels.

Conditions now call for a bold new Farm Bill—a true Food Bill. Program titles must become more deeply integrated, and subsidies should stop undermining the nation's nutrition goals. Indeed, all government subsidies—whether for crops, insurance, research, marketing, or anything else—should come with related social obligations for commitment to the health of our citizens and our natural resources.

Common sense demands that the narrow self-interests of corporate agribusiness yield to an updated and broader vision. Local and regional production and distribution capabilities should be expanded immediately, if not to cut down on food miles, then to preserve family farms and create jobs. Concentrated animal production should be reduced, if not to curb global warming, then to halt the onslaught of waste on the environment and to provide more nutritious foods to local and regional markets. Real eligibility limits should be levied on subsidy recipients, if not to end corporate welfare for undeserving landowners, then to encourage more geographic equity among subsidy recipients, and

to strengthen both national security and local food security. Funding to help communities preserve farmland should be increased, if not to prevent sprawl and the loss of open space, then to invest in the potential for rural areas as tourist destinations.

It's time to seriously question whether the far-away industrial mega-farm model is indeed the only way to feed a growing global population, or whether it's even possible without costly government supports and unsustainable environmental practices. It's time that citizens begin to see that Farm Bill politics are local politics. A farm and food policy that is taking a toll on the land, making the building blocks of unhealthy food unrealistically cheap, and tearing away at the fabric of rural communities, requires an era of new solutions.

The time has arrived for a food fight.

25 Ideas Whose Time Has Come

1. Aligning Farm Bill crop supports to USDA dietary guidelines.

2. Conservation programs that reward stewardship and sound farming rather than surplus production.

3. Subsidies that function as safety nets, loans, strategic crop reserves, and stewardship incentives, not direct giveaways.

4. Income eligibility limits on farm supports with no loopholes.

5. Expanded infrastructure for local and regional food supply chains, including small-scale livestock processing.

6. Affordable, high-quality, healthy foods for everyone.

7. Healthy school lunch programs tied to nearby farms, and school gardens that teach children where food comes from.

8. Fair prices for all crops maintained by a re-established grain reserve and other supply management.

9. Farm and ranchland preservation to buffer communities against sprawl, save wildlife habitat, and prevent agricultural lands from being developed.

10. Preserve native prairies and functional grasslands, and penalize those who plow them up.

11. Incentives for a grass-based livestock economy with a goal of shifting 50 percent away from feedlots within 30 years.

12. Reduce farm-related global warming emissions with a wholesale shift to organic and perennial agriculture.

13. Food labeling that informs consumers how an item was produced, including whether it contains genetically modified organisms or animals raised in confinement systems (such as eggs from hens in battery cages).

14. New farmer programs, including training, incentives, and start-up loans.

15. Elimination of corn ethanol subsidies; conservation standards for bio-energy crops.

16. End anti-competitive practices in livestock, including Captive Supply, which allows meat-packer monopolies to own and slaughter their own animals.

17. Fund more on-the-ground technical conservation assistance and enforcement.

18. Tying conservation compliance to taxpayer-funded crop or revenue insurance.

19. Farm-direct distribution, including farm-to-school, farm-to-hospital, farm-to-health care provider, CSAs, farmers markets, and more.

20. Farm-scale renewable energy and energy efficiency projects.

21. Crop rotation, cover crops, and other alternatives for synthetic fertilizers.

22. Improved conditions for all food system workers.

23. A 50-year Farm Bill focused on perennial, ecologically based farming.

24. Restoration of native pollinator habitat (and invasive species removal) added to conservation goals.

25. Food aid reform that enables recipient nations to purchase local or regional crops rather than commodities purchased from U.S. agribusinesses.

Somewhere in America's Future...

It is not that difficult to imagine a time in America's future when the sun rises over vastly different agricultural landscapes. Out of vision, and out of necessity, citizens will begin to see and value food and farm policy as part of a much larger orbit of social, economic, and environmental concerns. Government support for food and agriculture may remain significantly high, (and may even exceed current levels), but spending programs will pass rigorous tests for costs and benefits.

In such a future, citizens, consumers, and food producers understand they are bound by similar fates. The nutrition of the body reflects the health of the land. American farmers and ranchers produce an abundance of some of the finest crops and livestock in the world, but they are more fairly rewarded for their efforts. And the farms, ranches, and forests that cover nearly two-thirds of the contiguous United States supply far more than food. With incentives for proper management, they also provide clean air and water, renewable energy, wildlife habitat, diverse forests, and open space.

Healthy, locally produced foods form the basis of a modern disease prevention strategy. With ever-escalating fuel prices and other concerns, the need for relative autonomy in food production becomes an organizing principle in nearly every region of the country. In public schools, children have direct contact with numerous farms that provide their cafeterias with organically raised fruits, vegetables, grains, and grass-fed milk, meat, and eggs. A similar transformation sweeps hospitals and universities, corporate campuses, and government agencies. Obesity rates eventually begin to decline, while the costs of Medicare, Medicaid, and public health fall. Worker productivity rebounds.

Traveling through the countryside, one sees that a new vision has taken hold. Monoculture fields that once blanketed entire counties and regions instead include large areas of polycultures of perennial grasses, restored prairies, and cover crops. Wooded field margins and vibrant creek banks transect row crop and orchard operations. Large set-aside areas of protected wildlands and natural habitats serve as buffer zones against extreme storm events. Organic agriculture, a preferred farming method in many regions, requires more people than strategies used in agriculture at the turn of the 21st century, but also reduces energy inputs and harmful air emissions and raises the nutritional content of foods. Greenhouses extend growing seasons for types of fresh produce that can withstand cooler temperatures, such as salad greens and root crops.

No single reform more dramatically transforms the landscape than the large-scale conversion from confinement animal feedlot operations to diversified farms that include grass-pastured livestock. Under a national grassland recovery campaign, grass farmers are emblematic of a new family farm movement. On-farm generated incomes also begin to rise among family farmers. Soil erosion significantly stabilizes while agricultural runoff and farm-related water pollution decreases. Grassland bird species become common again as nesting habitats return. Herds of bison even return to vast areas of the Great Plains that for decades were fragmented by artificially green crop circles. Formerly threatened species such as the sage grouse and prairie chicken rebound because of collaborative stewardship efforts.

"Food deserts" lacking in fresh locally grown fruits and vegetables may still exist in intensive agricultural production zones, though healthy food oases have also sprung up across the country in rural and urban areas. A new generation of supply networks makes this possible. Regional economies emerge as powerful supporters of family farmers, with a variety of innovative methods for storing, transporting, processing, and distributing locally grown foods. The Food Stamp Program remains a front line of defense against hunger and food insecurity. Yet it too evolves through a heightened

awareness that delivering not just calories, but nutritious foods to those in need best serves the long-term interests of citizens and the country alike. Thanks to nearly heroic community organizing and the difficult work of forging of public and private partnerships, access to healthy foods expands into neighborhoods most at risk for nutritionally preventable diseases such as hypertension, obesity, and diabetes.

Such a transformation has only been made possible by a transformation inside the Washington, D.C., beltway. Food and farm policy, still subject to politicking and opportunism, is less of a Matrix-like parallel universe in which the corporations control and dominate the subsidy system in the name of the small farmer. The Food and Farm Bills that lawmakers debate and reauthorize every five to seven years are more transparent and accessible to the average citizen. Research and development efforts focus on finding solutions to urgent goals facing the country: decreasing energy inputs, reducing global warming emissions, protecting declining wildlife species, developing perennial polycultures, and encouraging the next generation to take up the challenge. The United States finds itself in a leadership role in the development of locally adapted small- and medium-scale methods and technologies that produce food, fiber, feed, and energy in response to ongoing environmental challenges and ever-changing conditions and awareness.

Looming challenges persist, to be sure. The tug of war between global economics, the inclination to farm industrially, a continually growing population, and the fragility of wild nature continues. We still eat too many french fries. But a chapter has been closed and a new one begun. The critical moment occurs when previously isolated voices join ranks to challenge the status quo by insisting on a healthier, more hopeful, and secure future for themselves, their children, and grandchildren. Farm and food policy becomes an integrated economic engine that not only encourages long-term environmentally viable crop production but truly supports health and nutrition, renewable energy, entrepreneurial development, stewardship, fair trade, living wages, and regional food security.

Activist Tool Kit:
Local Farm Bill Organizing

Become a Farm Bill organizer. Inform yourself about the bill. Get together with local groups working on the bill. Set up a table at your farmers' market. Include the Farm Bill in your teaching about food policy, food studies, or agriculture. Here are some solid suggestions gathered from experienced Farm Bill organizers. Get busy!

Learn about the Farm Bill. This will require "cracking the code" of Farm Bill lingo. The USDA has a lot of useful information, including the full text of the bill itself and specialized reports.

Adopt a local food charter. Check out the Seattle Farm Bill principles, the Healthy Food Declaration, or draft a new one of your own.

Bring local officials up to speed. A local Farm Bill agenda can easily begin with a community group. Perhaps political leaders will engage once they understand the movement is legitimate.

Communicate with your representatives. Meet with them to discuss your commitment to local food and see if you can work together. Members of the Senate and Congressional agriculture committees have to hear clearly and often from their districts about emerging priorities.

Be clear about the connections. What foodshed are you discussing? What are the specific needs? How will buying locally help to solve local needs?

Create outreach and educational opportunities. Communicate to your community why they have an interest in the outcome of Farm Bill debates. Look over Environmental Working Group Farm Subsidy databases and other search engines to familiarize yourself with spending in your state.

Build coalitions. Identify the many constituencies affected by local food systems: family farms, public health offices, economic development groups, local schools, government agencies, charities, food policy councils, social justice movements. Develop partnerships to spread the word.

Think beyond Washington. Solicit funds from a number of different sources, including private, nonprofit, and state, that could multiply the impact of Farm Bill dollars.

Take the long view. Change rarely happens over the span of just one Farm Bill. Learn about how previous gains were made—and realize that they must be supported and defended through the long process of appropriation, implementation, rule making, and so on.

Activist Tool Kit: USDA Agencies and Farm Bill Programs Worth Looking At

Familiarize yourself with the work of agencies and programs from recent Farm Bills that have a record of achievement. Over the past two decades, a number of important programs have been created to promote a healthy food and farming system. See if they can be applied or expanded to your area of influence.

Agricultural Marketing Service

- Farmers Market Promotion Program
- Federal-State Marketing Improvement Program
- Specialty Crop Block Grants

Farm Service Agency

- Farm Loan Programs
- Farm Storage Facility Loans

Food and Nutrition Service

- Senior Farmers' Market Nutrition Program
- Supplemental Nutrition Assistance Program
- Special Supplemental Nutrition Program for Women, Infants, and Children
- WIC Farmers' Market Nutrition Program

National Institute of Food and Agriculture

- Agriculture and Food Research Initiative– Improved Sustainable Food Systems
- Agriculture and Food Research Initiative– Agricultural Economics and Rural Communities
- Beginning Farmer and Rancher Development Program
- Community Food Projects
- Small Business Innovation Research
- Sustainable Agriculture Research and Education

Natural Resources Conservation Service

- Conservation Stewardship Program
- Conservation Technical Assistance
- Environmental Quality Incentives Program
- Farm and Ranch Lands Protection Program
- Grassland Reserve Program
- Wetlands Reserve Program

Risk Management Agency

- Risk Management Education and Outreach

Rural Development

- Business and Industry Guaranteed Loan Program
- Community Facilities
- Rural Business Enterprise Grants
- Rural Business Opportunity Grants
- Rural Cooperative Development Grants
- Rural Microentrepreneur Assistance Program
- Value-Added Producer Grants

Activist Tool Kit:
Get Connected

Step 1

Stay up to date. The Food and Farm Bill field is complex and constantly evolving. Check these websites to learn more about the issues and stay up to date with the latest news and changes:

Center for Rural Affairs
Lyons, NE
(402) 687-2100
www.cfra.org

Environmental Working Group
Washington, D.C.
(202) 667-6982
www.ewg.org

Farm Bill Budget Visualizer
Baltimore, MD
http://www.jhsph.edu/clf/programs/visualizer/

FarmPolicy.com
www.farmpolicy.com

Institute for Agriculture and Trade Policy
Minneapolis, MN
(612) 870-0453
www.iatp.org

National Sustainable Agriculture Coalition
Washington, D.C.
(202) 547-5754
www.sustainable agriculture.net

Watershed Media
Healdsburg, CA
(707) 431-2936
www.farmbill2012.org

Step 2

Get involved. Assembled here is a list of organizations, agencies, educational institutes, and other entities to help you find organizations in your field of interest or your area to work with.

Conservation Groups

Defenders of Wildlife
Washington, D.C.
(800) 385-9712
www.defenders.org

Environmental Defense Fund
New York, NY
(800) 684-3322
www.edf.org

Green Cities California
www.greencities california.org

Izaak Walton League of America
Gaithersburg, MD
(301) 548-0150
www.iwla.org

Natural Resources Defense Council
New York, NY
(212) 727-2700
www.nrdc.org

Soil and Water Conservation Society
Ankeny, IA
(515) 289-2331
www.swcs.org

Wild Farm Alliance
Watsonville, CA
(831) 761-8408
www.wildfarmalliance.org

Xerces Society
Portland, OR
(503) 232-6639
www.xerces.org

Sustainable Agriculture

Alabama Sustainable Agriculture Network
Birmingham, AL
(559) 546-1090
www.asanonline.org

American Farmland Trust
Washington, D.C.
(202) 331-7300
www.farmland.org

California Climate & Agriculture Network
Sebastopol, CA
www.calclimateag.org

Dakota Rural Action
Brookings, SD
(605) 697-5204
www.dakotarural.org

Ecological Farming Association
Soquel, CA
(831) 763-2111
www.eco-farm.org

Florida Organic Growers
Gainesville, FL
(352) 377-6345
www.foginfo.org

Glynwood Center
Cold Spring, NY
(845) 265-3338
www.glynwood.org

GRACE Communications
New York, NY
(212) 726-9161
www.gracelinks.org

Land Stewardship Project
Minneapolis, MN
(612) 722-6377
www.landstewardship project.org

Marin Carbon Project
Nicasio, CA
(415) 536-9408
www.marincarbon project.org

Michael Fields Agricultural Institute
East Troy, WI
(262) 642-3303
www.michaelfields aginst.org

National Center for Appropriate Technology
Butte, MT
(800) ASK-NCAT
www.ncat.org

NCAT Sustainable Agriculture Project
www.attra.ncat.org

National Family Farm Coalition
Washington, D.C.
(202) 543-5675
www.nffc.net

National Information System for Regional IPM Centers
Raleigh, NC
www.ipmcenters.org

Northeast-Midwest Institute
Washington, D.C.
(202) 544-5200
www.nemw.org

Northeast Sustainable Agriculture Working Group
Belchertown, MA
(413) 323-9878
www.nesawg.org

Northern Plains Sustainable Agriculture Society
LaMoure, ND
(701) 883-4304
www.npsas.org

Organic Trade Association
Brattleboro, VT
(802) 275-3800
www.ota.com

Pesticide Action Network North America
San Francisco, CA
(415) 981-1771
www.panna.org

Rural Advancement Foundation International–USA (RAFI)
Pittsboro, NC
(919) 542-1396
www.rafiusa.org

Socially Responsible Agriculture Project
(208) 634-8776
www.sraproject.org

Worldwatch Institute
Washington, D.C.
(202) 452-1999
www.worldwatch.org

Healthy Food Systems and Anti-Hunger

Ample Harvest
www.ampleharvest.org

Feeding America
Chicago, IL
(800) 771-2303
www.feedingamerica.org

Bread for the World
Washignton, D.C.
(202) 639-9400
www.bread.org

California Food Policy Advocates
Oakland, CA
(510) 433-1122
www.cfpa.net

Center for Food Safety
Washington, D.C.
(202) 547-9359
www.centerforfood safety.org

Community Food Security Coalition
Portland, OR
(503) 954-2970
www.foodsecurity.org

Congressional Hunger Center
Washington, D.C.
(202) 547-7022
www.hungercenter.org

Fair Food Network
Ann Arbor, MI
(734) 213-3999
www.fairfoodnetwork.org

Farmers Market Coalition
www.farmersmarket coalition.org

Food & Water Watch
Washington, D.C.
(202) 683-2500
www.foodandwater watch.org

Food Animal Concerns Trust
Chicago, IL
(773) 525-4952
www.foodanimal concerns.org

Food Change
New York, NY
(212) 566-7855
www.foodchange.org

Food Routes
Troy, PA
(570) 673-3398
www.foodroutes.org

Growing Power
Milwaukee, WI
(414) 527-1546
www.growingpower.org

National Catholic Rural Life Center
Des Moines, IA
(515) 270-2634
www.ncrlc.com

National Council of Churches
New York, NY
(212) 870-2227
www.ncccusa.org

Northwest Farm Bill Action Group
Seattle, WA
www.nwfoodfight.org

Roots of Change
San Francisco, CA
(415) 391-0545
www.rootsofchange.org

Slow Food USA
Brooklyn, NY
(718) 260-8000
www.slowfoodusa.org

The Food Trust
Philadelphia, PA
(215) 575-0444
www.thefoodtrust.org

Wholesome Wave
Bridgeport, CT
(203) 226-1112
www.wholesomewave.org

Why Hunger Food Security Learning Center
New York, NY
(800) 548-6479
www.whyhunger.org/fslc

Education and Beginning Farmer Programs

Agriculture and Land-based Training Association (ALBA)
Watsonville, CA
(831) 758-1469
www.albafarmers.org

California FarmLink
Santa Cruz, CA
(831) 425-0303
www.californiafarmlink.org

Center for Ecoliteracy
Berkeley, CA
(510) 845-4595
www.ecoliteracy.org

Community Alliance with Family Farmers
Davis, CA
(530) 756-8518
www.caff.org

Leopold Center for Sustainable Agriculture
Aimes, IA
(515) 294-3711
www.leopold.iastate.edu

Midwest Organic and Sustainable Education Service (MOSES)
Spring Valley, WI
(715) 778-5775
www.mosesorganic.org

National Young Farmers' Coalition
Tivoli, NY
www.youngfarmers.org

Sustainable Agriculture & Food Systems Funders (SAFSF)
Santa Barbara, CA
(805) 687-0551
www.safsf.org

UC Sustainable Agriculture Research and Education Program
Davis, CA
(530) 752-7556
www.sarep.ucdavis.edu

USDA Sustainable Agriculture Research and Education
College Park, MD
www.sare.org

International Trade and Globalization

Global Development and Environment Institute at Tufts University
Medford, MA
(617) 627-3530
www.ase.tufts.edu/gdae

International Forum on Globalization
San Francisco, CA
(415) 561-7650
www.ifg.org

International Society for Ecology and Culture
Berkeley, CA
(510) 548-4915
www.isec.org.uk

Oxfam
Oxford, UK
44 (0) 1865 47 3727
www.oxfam.org.uk

World Trade Organization
Geneva, Switzerland
41 (0) 22 739 51 11
www.wto.org

Renewable Energy

Alternative Energy Resources Organization
Helena, MT
(406) 443-7272
www.aeromt.org

Clean Coalition
Palo Alto, CA
www.clean-coalition.org

Climate Central
Palo Alto, CA
(877) 425-4724
Princeton, NJ
(609) 924-3800
www.climatecentral.org

EARTHWORKS
Washington, DC
(202) 887-1872
www.earthworksaction.org

Energy Foundation
San Francisco, CA
(415) 561-6700
www.ef.org

Environmental Law & Policy Center
Chicago, IL
(312) 673-6500
www.elpc.org

Rocky Mountain Institute
Boulder, CO
(303) 245-1003
www.rmi.org

The Minnesota Project
St. Paul, MN
(651) 645-6159
www.mnproject.org

Union of Concerned Scientists
Cambridge, MA
(617) 547-5552
www.ucsusa.org

Government Agencies

Association of State and Interstate Water Pollution Control Administration
Washington, D.C.
(202) 756-0600
www.acwa-us.org

Congress
Washington, D.C.
www.congress.org
See above site for instructions on how to write to your representative.

Congressional Research Service
Washington, D.C.
www.loc.gov/crsinfo/
CRS reports can be found at these websites:
University of North Texas
www.digital.library.unt.edu/govdocs/crs/
National Council for Science and Environment
www.ncseonline.org/programs/science-policy/crs-reports

Economic Research Service
Washington, D.C.
(202) 694-5050
www.ers.usda.gov

Natural Resources Conservation Service
Washington, D.C.
See website for contact info
www.nrcs.usda.gov

United States Department of Agriculture
Washington, D.C.
See website for contact info
www.usda.gov

USDA Farm Bill
www.usda.gov/farmbill

Policy

Agricultural Policy Analysis Center
Knoxville, TN
(865) 974-7407
www.agpolicy.org

American Farm Bureau Federation
Washington, D.C.
(202) 406-3600
www.fb.org

California Institute for the Study of Specialty Crops
San Luis Obispo, CA
(805) 756-5014
www.cissc.calpoly.edu

Chicago Council on Global Affairs
Chicago, IL
(312) 726-3860
www.thechicagocouncil.org

Farm Aid
Cambridge, MA
(800) FARM-AID
www.farmaid.org

Food First
Oakland, CA
(510) 654-4400
www.foodfirst.org

Food Research and Action Center
Washington, D.C.
(202) 986-2200
www.frac.org

Organic Farming and Research Foundation
Santa Cruz, CA
(831) 426-6606
www.ofrf.org

Public Citizen
Washington, D.C.
(202) 588-1000
www.citizen.org

Public Health Law & Policy
Oakland, CA
(510) 302-3380
www.phlpnet.org

Rudd Center for Food Policy and Obesity
New Haven, CT
(203) 432-6700
www.yaleruddcenter.org

Southern Legislative Conference
Atlanta, GA
(404) 633-1866
www.slcatlanta.org

W.K. Kellogg Foundation
Battle Creek, MI
(269) 968-1611
www.wkkf.org

World Resources Institute
Washington, D.C.
(202) 729-7600
www.wri.org

Health and Nutrition

American Dietetic Association
Chicago, IL
(800) 877-1600
www.eatright.org

American Public Health Association
Washington, D.C.
(202) 777-2742
www.apha.org

Center for a Livable Future
Baltimore, MD
(410) 502-7578
www.jhsph.edu/clf

Center for Science in the Public Interest
Washington, D.C.
(202) 332-9110
www.cspinet.org

Food Democracy Now
Clear Lake, IA
*www.fooddemocracy
now.org*

Healthy Eating Network
*www.healthyeating
network.com*

MIT Collaborative Initiatives
Cambridge, MA
(617) 252-0003
*www.collaborative
initiatives.org*

Network for a Healthy California
*www.dhs.ca.gov/ps/cdic/
cpns/network*

New York City Farm Bill Coalition
New York, NY
*www.foodbillnyc.
wikispaces.com*

Physicians Committee for Responsible Medicine
Washington, D.C.
(202) 686-2210
www.pcrm.org

Prevention Institute
Oakland, CA
(510) 444-7738

Robert Wood Johnson Foundation Center to Prevent Childhood Obesity
Little Rock, AR
(501) 526-2244
*www.reverse
childhoodobesity.org*

Society for Nutrition Education
Indianapolis, IN
(800) 235-6690
www.sne.org

United Fresh Produce Association
Washington, D.C.
(202) 303-3400
www.unitedfresh.org

Step 3

Take it to The Hill. Tell the people in charge of the Farm Bill what you want our country's food policy to look like. Check to see if your senators or representative sit on one of the key committees listed below. Remember committee membership changes each election cycle, so keep checking back!

House Committee on Agriculture – Oversees all U.S. policy related to agriculture.

House Subcommittee on Conservation, Energy, and Forestry – Soil, water, and resource conservation, small watershed program, forestry, and energy.

House Subcommittee on Department Operations, Oversight, and Credit – Agency oversight, special investigations, and agricultural credit.

House Subcommittee on General Farm Commodities and Risk Management – Programs and markets related to cotton, cottonseed, wheat, feed grains, soybeans, oilseeds, rice, dry beans, peas, lentils, the Commodity Credit Corporation, risk management, including crop insurance, commodity exchanges, and specialty crops.

House Subcommittee on Nutrition and Horticulture – Food stamps, nutrition and consumer programs, fruits and vegetables, honey and bees, marketing, plant pesticides, quarantine, adulteration of seeds and insect pests, and organic agriculture.

House Subcommittee on Livestock, Dairy, and Poultry – Livestock, dairy, poultry, meat, seafood and seafood products, inspection, marketing, and promotion of such commodities, aquaculture, animal welfare, and grazing.

House Subcommittee on Rural Development, Research, Biotechnology, and Foreign Agriculture – Rural Development, farm security and family farming matters, research, education and extension, biotechnology, foreign agriculture assistance, and trade promotion programs, generally.

House Committee on Appropriations – Determines how much funding should be allocated for specific programs during each fiscal year.

Senate Committee on Agriculture, Nutrition and Forestry – Oversees all U.S. policy related to Agriculture.

Senate Subcommittee on Commodities, Markets, Trade and Risk Management – The production of agricultural crops, commodities, and products, farm and ranch income protection and assistance, safety net programs and farm credit, commodity price support programs, insurance and risk protection, fresh water food production, agricultural trade, and foreign market development.

Senate Subcommittee on Conservation, Forestry and Natural Resources – Conservation, protection and stewardship of natural resources and the environment, state, local, and private forests, general forestry, and pesticides.

Senate Subcommittee on Jobs, Rural Economic Growth and Energy Innovation – Rural economic revitalization and quality of life, rural job and business growth, rural electrification, telecommunications, and utilities, renewable energy production and energy efficiency improvement on farms and ranches, and innovation in the use of agricultural commodities and materials.

Senate Subcommittee on Livestock, Dairy, Poultry, Marketing and Agriculture Security – Animal welfare, inspection and certification of plants, animals and products, plant and animal diseases and health protection, domestic marketing and product promotion, marketing and regulation of agricultural markets.

Senate Subcommittee on Nutrition, Specialty Crops, Food and Agricultural Research – Domestic and international nutrition, food assistance and hunger prevention, school and child nutrition programs, local and healthy food initiatives, and food and agricultural research, education, economics, and extension.

Senate Committee on Appropriations – Determines how much funding should be allocated for specific programs during each fiscal year.

Food and Farm Bill Glossary

Adjusted Gross Income – An income formula that determines eligibility for subsidy payments. At present, millionaires and non-farmers are welcome.

Appropriations – The annual process of allocating funds to specific programs within the Farm Bill and all other legislation. Programs can be funded at any level, regardless of what was authorized by the legislation.

Authorization – The writing and approval of legislation, theoretically determining how funds should be allocated. However, programs may or may not actually be funded at the authorized level.

Base Acreage – Historical plating records calculated by averaging the previous five years for wheat or feed grains, or the previous three years for cotton and rice, plus land idled through an acreage-reduction or -diversion program. The result determines the amount of subsidy payments.

Beginning Farmer/Rancher – A person with less than ten years of experience operating a farm or ranch.

Budget Reconciliation – The process of changing authorized spending levels without re-authorizing an entire bill. This process can take place at any time, even in legislation intended to last for a set number of years.

Cellulosic Ethanol – Ethanol made from inedible plants or inedible parts of edible plants, including grasses, leftover corn stalks, and woody materials.

Change in Mandatory Program Spending (ChIMPS) – A political term for when committees revise promised budgets for a program, usually to a lower amount.

Child Nutrition Act – A federal law originally passed in 1966 to assure the health of the nation's children. The School Breakfast Program, Special Milk Program, and Special Supplemental Nutrition Program for Women, Infants, and Children are among the programs included in the act.

Conservation Reserve Program (CRP) – A program offering financial incentives to eligible farmers who agree to idle part of their land in order to prevent soil erosion, increase wildlife habitat, improve water quality, and reduce the damage of floods and other natural disasters.

Conservation Stewardship Program (CSP) – A green payment program that rewards landowners for habitat protection, chemical reduction, energy conservation, and other environmentally directed efforts.

Contained Animal Feeding Operation (CAFO) – An EPA term for an animal factory farm, which is regulated as a potential point source of pollution under the Clean Water Act.

Counter-Cyclical Payments – A program that provides financial stability and security to farmers producing certain crops like wheat, corn, upland cotton, and peanuts by making up any gap between the market price of the crop and a set target price.

Cover Cropping – Crops planted between harvests to restore and protect the soil.

Crop Rotation – A practice of changing crops between seasons to break disease cycles and naturally restore organic matter and nutrients to the soil.

Direct Payments – Automatic payments formally established in 2002 for landowners who formerly produced commodity crops. They do not need to be farming or producing commodity crops to receive the payments.

Disaster Assistance – Payments to compensate growers for weather-related losses.

Disincentive Programs – Penalties that deny landowners or farmers federal subsidies if they plow erosion-prone grasslands (Sod Buster) or drain or alter wetlands (Swamp Buster) to expand crop acreage.

Dried Distiller Grains and Solubles (DDGS) – The residual grains left over after corn ethanol production that are fed to livestock.

Environmental Quality Incentives Program (EQIP) – Financial and technical assistance to farmers to improve soil, water, plant, animal, and air related resources on agricultural land; unfortunately, a majority of these funds go to CAFO operations.

Farmers Market Nutrition Program (FMNP) – A program associated with the Special Supplemental Nutrition Program for Women, Infants, and Children (WIC), with an emphasis on providing access to local fresh produce.

Flat-Funding – See **ChIMPing.**

Food Crop Ethanol – A biofuel made from feed crops grown on arable land that could otherwise be used to grow food for humans.

Food Desert – A fresh-food-free zone with (1) a poverty rate of 20 percent or higher or where 2) at least 500 people or 33 percent of the population lives more than one mile (in an urban area) or more than ten miles (rural area) from the nearest supermarket or large grocery store.

Food Hub – A central location for the aggregation, processing, storage, and distribution of locally or regionally produced foods.

Food Security – The USDA's classification for households that frequently experience hunger to varying degrees: High Food Security, Marginal Food Security, Low Food Security, Very Low Food Security.

Genetically Modified Organisms – Crops given specific attributes, such as resistance to herbicides, by being implanted with genes from another species.

Green Payments – Subsidies to support conservation efforts.

Know Your Farmer, Know Your Food (KYF2) – An effort within the USDA to promote the strengthening of local and regional food systems and to cultivate a national awareness of the value of local food systems.

Loan Deficiency Payments – Subsidies that provide an influx of cash when market prices are typically at harvest-time lows, allowing the producer to delay the sale of the commodity until more favorable market conditions emerge.

Marker Bill – A legislative bill used to introduce specific measures or issues into a larger legislative debate. While not intended to ever come to a vote on the floor, a marker bill is proposed as a "placeholder" for specific aspects of a larger bill.

Monoculture – A large area planted with one single crop, usually with detrimental effects on biological diversity.

Omnibus – A single piece of legislation that addresses several measures or diverse subjects.

Peak Oil – The point at which half of the world's petroleum has been tapped, after which supplies begin to rapidly decline.

Principal Farm Operator – The person designated as *most* responsible for making daily decisions about the farm business and running the farm, in the case that there is more than one person performing these tasks.

Production Agriculture – An agribusiness term describing commodity-based industrial agriculture: predominantly corn, cotton, wheat, rice, soybeans, animal foods, and sugar.

Rural Energy for America Program (REAP) – Grants to fund on-farm renewable energy and energy conservation projects, formerly known as Section 9006 grants.

SNAP-Ed – A program that provides nutrition education to recipients of Supplemental Nutrition Assistance in order to help them make healthier choices.

Sod Buster – A disincentive program included in the 1985 Farm Bill that withdrew federal payments from farmers who plowed up protected grasslands.

Sod Saver – A provision to deter landowners from converting grasslands, particularly native sod, to cropland in the drought- and flood-prone lands of the Prairie Pothole Region.

Special Supplemental Nutrition Program for Women, Infants, and Children (WIC) – A program that provides nutrition and other health assistance to pregnant and postpartum low-income women and children up to five years of age found to be nutritionally at risk.

Specialty Crops – Farm Bill term for fruits, nuts, vegetables, dried fruits, and nursery crops.

Supplemental Nutrition Assistance Program (SNAP) – A program that helps people who cannot afford sufficient nutrition for themselves and their families to purchase food.

Swamp Buster – A disincentive program included in the 1985 Farm Bill that withdrew federal payments from farmers who drained wetlands.

Three Boxes – The World Trade Organization's three classifications of government supports to agriculture: Amber, Blue, and Green.

Target Price – A price floor established by Congress for agricultural products. When the price of a good falls below this point, deficiency payments kick in.

Trade Distorting Subsidy – A subsidy that artificially depresses prices for a given good, giving that country's exports a market advantage over the competition.

Wetlands Reserve Program (WRP) – A voluntary easement program that pays farmers to preserve wetlands, aiming to achieve greatest wetland function and wildlife habitat.

Wildlife Habitat Incentive Program (WHIP) – Financial and technical support for farmers to establish practices that improve fish and wildlife habitat.

Select Bibliography

Ahearn, Mary, and Doris Newton, "Beginning Farmers and Ranchers," USDA Economic Research Service, May 2009, web edition.

"Austerity, Farm-Style," *Chicago Tribune*, April 2011.

Baker, David R. "Got Gas? PG&E Considers Using a Natural Energy Source That Comes from Cows—And It Sure Isn't Milk." *San Francisco Chronicle*, July 12, 2006, pp. C1–C5.

Berry, Wendell and Wes Jackson, "A 50-Year Farm Bill," *New York Times*, January 4, 2009, web edition.

Bittman, Mark, "Don't End Agricultural Subsidies, Fix Them," *New York Times*, March 2, 2011, web edition.

Blumenauer, Earl, "Growing Opportunities: Family Farm Values for Reforming the Farm Bill," 2011.

Bovard, James, "The Food Stamp Crime Wave," *Wall Street Journal*, June 23, 2011, web edition.

Bowers, Douglas, Wayne Rasmussen, and Gladys Baker. "History of Agricultural Price-Support and Adjustment Programs, 1933–84." Agricultural Information Bulletin No. AIB485, December 1984.

Charles, Dan. "Going Green in Agriculture: Calls Grow to Subsidize Green Farming." National Public Radio Morning Edition, April 13, 2006, transcript.

——. "Going Green in Agriculture: EU Shifts Subsidies from Crops to Land Stewardship." National Public Radio Morning Edition, April 13, 2006, transcript.

Cleeton, James. "Organic Foods in Relation to Nutrition and Health: Key Facts." Information Sheet summary of "Coronary and Diabetic Care in the UK 2004," by the Association of Primary Care Groups and Trusts, Soil Association, United Kingdom.

Conkin, Paul, *A Revolution Down on the Farm: The Transformation of American Agriculture Since 1929*. The University Press of Kentucky, 2008.

Cook, Christopher. "Business as Usual." *The American Prospect On-line*, April 8, 2006.

Deutch, John. "Biomass Movement," Commentary. *Wall Street Journal,* May 10, 2006, web edition.

Eilperin, Juliet, "The Unintended Ripples from the Biomass Subsidy Program," *Washington Post*, January 10, 2010, p. A3.

Environmental Law and Policy Center, "An American Success Story: The Farm Bill's Clean Energy Programs."

"The Ethanol Myth: Consumer Reports' E85 Tests Show that You'll Get Cleaner Emissions but Poorer Fuel Economy… If you Can Find It." *Consumer Reports*, October 2006, pp. 15–19.

Food and Water Watch and the Public Health Institute, "Do Farm Subsidies Cause Obesity? Dispelling Common Myths About Public Health and the Farm Bill," A White Paper, October 2011.

Foskett, Ken, and Dan Chapman. "Farmers Accused of 'Scheme' Wind up Keeping Millions." *Atlanta Journal-Constitution*, Oct. 3, 2006 web edition.

Foskett, Ken, Dan Chapman, and Megan Clarke. "How Savvy Growers Can Double, or Triple, Subsidy Dollars." *Atlanta Journal-Constitution*, Oct. 2, 2006, web edition.

——. "How Your Tax Dollars Prop Up Big Growers and Squeeze the Little Guy." *Atlanta Journal-Constitution*, Oct. 1, 2006 web edition.

Gerson, Michael, "In Malawi, the Toll of U.S. Budget-Cutting," *Washington Post*, March 24, 2011, web edition.

Gilbert, Curtis, "American Crystal has Outsized Influence in DC" Minnesota Public Radio, January 25, 2011.

Heilprin, John. "U.S. Reports Increase in Wetland Acreage: Bush Administration Figures Are Disputed as Being Misleading." *San Francisco Chronicle*, March 31, 2006, p. A2.

Kasler, Dale. "Ethanol Boom Lures Investors: Some Put Their Money into In-State Production Plants." *Sacramento Bee*, March 22, 2006, pp. A1, A20.

Knittel, Christopher, "The Costs and Benefits of U.S. Ethanol Subsidies," in *American Boondoggle: Fixing the 2012 Farm Bill*, American Enterprise Institute, 2011.

Kotschi, Johannes, and Karl Müller-Sämann. "The Role of Organic Agriculture in Mitigating Climate Change: A Scoping Study." International Federation of Organic Agriculture Movements, May 2004.

Krueger, Jill, Karen R. Krub, and Lynn A. Hayes, "Planting the Seeds of Public Health: How the Farm Bill Can Help Farmers to Produce and Distribute Healthy Foods," Farmers' Legal Action Group, February 2010.

Kunstler, James Howard. *The Long Emergency: Surviving the Converging Catastrophes of the Twenty-first Century*. New York: Atlantic Monthly Press, 2005.

Javers, Eamon, "Peanuts in Storage," CNBC, November 18, 2010.

Land Institute, "A 50-Year Farm Bill, June 2009.

Lilley, Ray. "A Real Job: End to Subsidies Improved Farming in New Zealand." December 20, 2005, *The Associated Press,* web edition.

Lynch, Sarah, and Sandra Batie, eds. "Building the Scientific Basis for Green Payments." A Report on a Workshop Sponsored by the U.S. Department of Agriculture, CSREES, World Wildlife Fund, and the Elton R. Smith Endowment at Michigan State University, April 14–15, 2005, World Wildlife Fund, Washington, D.C.

Manning, Richard. *Against the Grain: How Agriculture Highjacked Civilization*. North Point Press, 2004.

——. "The Oil We Eat: Following the Food Chain Back to Iraq." *Harper's* Magazine, February 2004.

Marlow, Scott. "The Non-Wonk Guide to Understanding Federal Commodity Payments." The Rural Advancement Foundation International, 2005.

Marshall, Liz, and Suzie Greenhalgh. "Beyond the RFS: The Environmental and Economic Impacts of Increased Grain Ethanol Production in the U.S." WRI Policy Note, World Resources Institute, Washington, D.C., September 2006.

Martin, Andrew, "In the Farm Bill, a Creature from the Black Lagoon," *New York Times,* January 13, 2008, web edition.

Millman, Joe. "Labor Movement: As U.S. Debates Guest Workers, They Are Here Now in Construction 'Subidos.'" *The Wall Street Journal*, September 18, 2006, p. A1.

Mission: Readiness, Military Leaders for Kids, "Too Fat to Fight: Retired Military Leaders Want Junk Food Out of America's Schools," A Report, April 2010.

Morgan, Dan, "The Farm Bill and Beyond," The German Marshall Fund of the United States, Policy Paper, 2010.

Morgan, Dan, and Gilbert M. Gaul. "No Farm? No Crop? No Problem–Subsidies Still Grow." *Washington Post*, July 2, 2006, web edition.

Moss, Michael, "While Warning About Fat, U.S. Pushes Cheese Sales," *New York Times*, November 6, 2010, web edition.

Muller, Mark, and Heather Schoonover. "U.S. Farm Policy Contributes to Obesity, New Report Finds Policies Drive Production of Unhealthy Foods." Institute for Agriculture and Trade Policy, 2006.

National Policy and Legal Analysis Network to Prevent Childhood Obesity, "Farm Bill 2012: Building Coalitions for Change," Yale Law School, 2010.

Neuman, William, "High Prices Sow Seeds of Erosion," *New York Times,* April 12, 2011, web edition.

O'Brien, Doug, Halley Torres Aldeen, Stephanie Uchima, and Errin Staley. "Hunger in America: The Definitions, Scope, Causes, History and Status of the Problem of Hunger in the United States." America's Second Harvest, Public Policy and Research Department, 2004.

Peine, Emelie, "US Subsidizing Brazilian Cotton Protects Monsanto's Profits," Institute for Agriculture and Trade Policy.

"Out of Balance: Marketing of Soda, Candy, Snacks, and Fast Foods Drowns Out Healthful Messages." Consumers Union and California Pan-Ethnic Health Network, September 2005

Physicians Committee for Responsible Medicine, "Agricultural Subsidies: Conflicts with Policies on Nutrition and Health," A White Paper, 2011.

Planck, Nina. "Leafy Green Sewage." *The New York Times*, September 21, 2006.

Pollack, Andrew. "Redesigning Crops to Harvest Fuel: Scientists as Custom Tailors of Genetics." *New York Times*, September 8, 2006, pp. C1–C4.

Pollan, Michael, "Farmer in Chief," *New York Times Magazine*, October 12, 2008.

Pretty, Jules. "The Real Costs of Modern Farming: Pollution of Water, Erosion of Soil and Loss of Natural Habitat, Caused by Chemical Agriculture, Cost the Earth." *Resurgence*, issue 205, web edition.

Reginold, John, et. al. "Transforming U.S. Agriculture: Achieving Sustainable Agricultural Systems Will Require Transformational Changes in Markets, Policies, and Science," *Science*, May 2011, pp. 670-671.

Robbins, Jim, "Safeguarding Sage Grouse and their Elaborate Courtship Dance," *New York Times*, February 7, 2011, web edition.

Roberts, Susan, and Thomas Forster, "Planting the Seeds for a Healthier Food System: Public Health and the 2008 Farm Bill," The Johns Hopkins Center for a Livable Future," April 2011.

Rooney, William, ed. *Fish and Wildlife Benefits of Farm Bill Conservation Programs, 2000–2005 Update.* USDA Natural Resources Conservation Service and Farm Service Agency.

Roth, Dennis. "Food Stamps: 1932–1977: From Provisional and Pilot Programs to Permanent Policy." Economic Research Service, web edition.

Schumacher, Gus, Michel Nischan, Daniel Bowman Simon, "Healthy Food Access and Affordability," *Maine Policy Review*, Winter/Spring 2011.

Shepherd, Matthew, Stephen L. Buchman, Mace Vaughn, and Scott Hoffman Black. *Pollinator Conservation Handbook.* The Xerces Society, 2003.

Starmer, Elanor, "Big Beef with Some in Congress," *San Francisco Chronicle*, May 23, 2011, web edition.

Starmer, Elanor, and Timothy Wise, "Feeding at the Public Trough: Industrial Livestock Firms Saved $35 Billion from Low Feed Prices," Global Development and Environment Institute, Tufts University, December 2007.

Stiglitz, Joseph. "The Tyranny of King Cotton." *Atlanta Journal-Constitution*, October 24, 2006.

Thicke, Francis, *A New Vision for Iowa Food and Agriculture: Sustainable Agriculture for the 21st Century*, Mulberry Knoll, 2010.

Trauner, Carol. "Leaves of Grass: The Growing Popularity of Grass-fed Beef and What You Should Know About It," *Chefs Collaborative Communiqué*, November 2003.

Wall Street Journal, "The Madness of Cotton: The Feds Want U.S. Taxpayers to Subsidize Brazilian Farmers," May 21, 2010.

Weiss, Rick. "Gene-Altered Profit-Killer: A Slight Taint of Biotech Rice Puts Farmers' Overseas Sales in Peril." *Washington Post*, September 21, 2006.

Wellman, Nancy S., and Barbara Friedberg. "Causes and Consequences of Adult Obesity: Health, Social and Economic Impacts in the United States." *Asia Pacific Journal of Clinical Nutrition* 11(2002): S705–S709, web edition.

Wen, Dale. "China Copes with Globalization: A Mixed Review." International Forum on Globalization, 2005.

Wilkins, Jennifer. "The Oil We Eat: Fossil Fuels Consume Big Portion of Food Costs." *Times Union*, May 7, 2006, web edition.

Williamson, Elizabeth. "Some Americans Lack Food, But USDA Won't Call Them Hungry." *Washington Post*, November 16, 2006, p. A01, web edition.

Winne, Mark. "Growing a Healthy Food System– Food and Agriculture in New Mexico." New Mexico Food and Agriculture Policy Council, January 2005.

Wise, Timothy. "Identifying the Real Winners from U.S. Agricultural Policies." Working Paper No. 05-07, Global Development and Environment Institute, Tufts University, 2005.

Notes

1. We Reap What We Sow

1. Paul K. Conkin, *A Revolution Down on the Farm: The Transformation of American Agriculture Since 1929,* University Press of Kentucky, 2008, pp. 147, 164.

2. Timothy A. Wise, "Agricultural Dumping Under NAFTA: Estimating the Costs of U.S. Agricultural Policies to Mexican Producers," Global Development and Environment Institute at Tufts University, Working Paper No. 09-08, 2010.

3. "Food Security in the United States," USDA, web edition, Updated April 26, 2011.

2 Why the Farm Bill Matters

1. Essayist and farmer Wendell Berry has written: "The global 'free' market is free to the corporations precisely because it dissolves the boundaries of the old national colonialisms, and replaces them with a new colonialism without restraints or boundaries. It is pretty much as if all the rabbits have now been forbidden to have holes, thereby 'freeing' the hounds." (from "The Total Economy," in *Citizenship Papers,* 2003.)

2. According to Congressman Ron Kind, (D-WI), most people in agriculture realize that changes have to be made, and that current farm policy is distorting the real market. He contends that there are a lot of acres being planted with a few commodities. "The only reason they're planting that is for the government paycheck, not because of the market-place."

3. What Is the Farm Bill?

1. Jasper Womach, Coordinator, "Previewing a 2007 Farm Bill," Congressional Research Service, Order Code RL33037, August 18, 2005, CRS-1.

2. Ferd Hoefner, Sustainable Agriculture Coalition, "Farm Bill Primer," PowerPoint Presentation, September 2005.

3. The American farm lobby is politically secure thanks to the overrepresentation of rural America in the Senate, and makes slightly more than $50 million worth of political donations in each election cycle. The food and nutrition programs–with backing from urban representatives–historically have provided the "critical mass" of political support for the omnibus bill from outside of Farm Belt states.

4. "United States Subsidy Concentrations for 1995-2010," Environmental Working Group, web edition, Accessed July 21, 2011

5. "FY 2011 Budget Summary and Annual Performance," USDA, web edition, accessed September 27, 2011.

6. According to the USDA, 1.73 billion tons of soil was lost in 2007, the most recent year for which there is data. However, there are concerns that this number does not represent the true amount of soil loss. Many believe major crop expansion for ethanol and export markets may be contributing to increased soil loss. "RCA appraisal 2011: Soil and Water Resources Conservation Act," United States Department of Agriculture, March 2011, p. 3-2 web edition.

7. Jill E. Krueger, et al., "Planting the Seeds for Public Health: How the Farm Bill Can Help Farmers to Produce and Distribute Healthy Foods," Farmers' Legal Action Group, Inc. February 2010, 3-1

8. According to Charles Benbrook's analysis, the U.S. ranks 23 out of 34 countries, spending $2.28 per person for each 1,000 calories consumed. The countries that spent the least for every 1,000 calories consumed were Sierra Leone, 39 cents; Mali, 46 cents; Tanzania, 51 cents; and Kenya, 63 cents. The countries that spent the most per 1,000 calories consumed were Korea, $4.43; Japan, $3.68; Argentina, $3.47; Australia, $3.28; and the United Kingdom, $2.96. Americans buy lots of convenience, packaging and services with their food dollars, and as a result, pay a lot more for it.

4. Promises Broken: The Two-Lives of Every Farm Bill...

1. According to one long-time Farm Bill observer, about one-third of the members of the agriculture committees are new representatives that have been assigned to the task and are eager to be released as soon as possible.

2. Alan Guebert reports, for example, that as chairman of the Appropriations subcommittee on agriculture Republican Henry Bonilla, (R-TX) "raked in $250,414 of his $1.05 million in 2001 and 2002 Political Action Committee money from agribusiness."

3. Known also as the Harkin plan, after Iowa Democratic Senator Tom Harkin, chairman of the Senate Agriculture Committee, who championed the program in an effort to reform the problems of subsidies and monoculture factory farming.

4. Data from "Agriculture Appropriations Chart Financial Year 2011," National Sustainable Agriculture Coalition, web edition. Ironically, Slashing EQIP funding hurts relatively environmentally friendly operations more than the worst offenders. See "Paying the Polluters" in Chapter 8.

5. Where It All Started

1. Quoted in David Morris, "Ownership Matters: Three Steps to Ensure a Biofuels Industry that Truly Benefits Rural America," based on a speech to the Minnesota Ag expo in Morton, Minnesota, January 25, 2006.

2. Elizabeth Corcoran, "The Answer on the Wind," San Francisco Chronicle, Sunday January 8, 2006, p. M1.

3. Quoted in "Self-Help in Hard Times," in Howard Zinn, *A People's History of the United States,* p. 389.

4. The longest period of relative parity between farm prices and manufacturing prices was in the years leading up to World War I (1911-1914). These prices were used to determine the price parity index. See John C. Culver and John Hyde, *American Dreamer: The Life and Times of Henry A. Wallace,* p. 56 for an extended analysis.

5. John C. Culver and John Hyde, *American Dreamer,* p. 99.

6. Michael Pollan, *The Omnivore's Dilemma,* p. 48.

7. An excellent account of this period can be found in American Dreamer: A Life of Henry A. Wallace, by John C. Culver and John Hyde.

8. Pollan, Ibid., p. 49.

9. It was estimated that Farm Bill spending during these troubled times had a multiplier effect of seven. That is, for every dollar of government funds spent on farm and food policies, it generated seven dollars in the overall economy. See American Dreamer for more details.

10. Richard Manning, Against the Grain: How Agriculture Hijacked Civilization, North Point Press, New York, 2004, p. 171.

11. Bernard De Vito, quoted in Mark Arax and Rick Wartzman, *The King of California: J.G. Boswell and the Making of a Secret American Empire,* p. 186.

12. Written in 1924, referenced in Arax and Wartzman, ibid, p. 375.

6. Family Farms to Mega-Farms

1. Paul Conkin, *A Revolution Down on the Farm: The Transformation of American Agriculture Since 1929,* p. 98

2. The Soviets, with the cooperation of large grain companies, quietly purchased large amounts of grain at a pre-inflationary prices in the early 1970s. Prices soared after The Russian Grain Deal was announced, but most farmers had already sold their grain at low prices.

3. Daniel Imhoff, ed, *CAFO: The Tragedy of Industrial Animal Factories,* 2011.

4. One of the most notorious incidents of this era involved the shooting of banker Rudy Blythe and chief loan officer Deems Thulin by James and Steven Jenkins in Ruthton, Minnesota in 1983. The bank had foreclosed on the father and son's dairy operation and James and Steven Jenkins took their rage out on unsuspecting bank officials. See "Twenty Years After the Ruthton Banker Killings: Desperation Still Simmers," Paul Levy, *Star Tribune* October 20, 2003.

5. Michael Pollan, *The Omnivore's Dilemma,* pp. 52-53.

6. Ibid.

7. Paul Conkin, *A Revolution Down on the Farm: The Transformation of American Agriculture Since 1929,* pp. 132-133.

8. Paul Conkin, *A Revolution Down on the Farm: The Transformation of American Agriculture Since 1929,* p.150.

9. Mary Hendrickson and William Heffernan, "Concentration of Agricultural Markets," April 2007, Department of Rural Sociology, University of Missouri, web edition.

10. Ibid

11. Mark Drabenstott , "Do Farm Payments Promote Rural Economic Growth?" *Main Street Economist,* March 2005, Federal Reserve Bank of Kansas City.

7. The Farm Bill's Hunger Connection

1. Dennis Roth, "Food Stamps: 1932-1977: From Provisional and Pilot Programs to Permanent Policy," Economic Research Service.

2. Ibid, p. 8.

3. The USDA's "Thrifty Food Plan" is a tool intended to help individuals on food assistance to have a healthy diet. TFP is meant to "represen[t] a minimal cost diet based on up-to-date dietary recommendations, food composition data, food habits, and food price information." Additionally, TFP is the basis for maximum food assistance allotments. See Andrea Carlson et al. "Thrifty Food Plan 2006," United States Department of Agriculture Center for Nutrition Policy and Promotion, April 2007, web edition.

4. Jay L. Zagorsky and Patricia K. Smith, "Does the U.S. Food Stamp Program Contribute to Adult Weight Gain?" *Economics & Human Biology* 7(2009): 246-258.

5. "Food Stamps Offer Best Stimulus–Study," CNN, January 29, 2008, Web edition.

8. The Conservation Era Begins—Again

1. Ronald Reynolds, "The Conservation Reserve Program and Duck Production in the U.S. Prairie Pothole Region," in *Fish and Wildlife Benefits of Farm Bill Conservation Programs, 2000-2005 Update,* USDA NRCS and Farm Service Agency, p. 35.

2. The 2002 Farm Bill provided funding for an additional 1,000,000 acres of wetland set asides and restoration, mostly in the Southeastern bottomland forests that should never have been farmed in the first place.

3. "The lower 48 states had an estimated 220 million acres of wetlands and streams in precolonial times, but 115 million acres of them had been destroyed by 1997." In "U.S. Reports Increase in Wetland Acreage: Bush Administration figures are disputed as being misleading," John Heilprin, March 31, 2006, *San Francisco Chronicle*, p. A2.

4. Over 80 percent of species use aquatic habitats at some point in their life cycle. Creek corridors are probably the single most important wildlife linkages, as they connect all other habitats and lie at the heart of an ecosystem.

5. Congressman Ron Kind's "Healthy Farms, Foods, and Fuels Act of 2006" calls for a doubling of water protection incentives to $2 billion per year and a restoration of 3 million acres of wetlands.

6. 60 percent of EQIP funds were committed to livestock operations.

7. National Sustainable Agriculture Coalition, "Congress Releases Draft 6-Month Continuing Resolution," April 12, 2011, web edition.

8. Suzie Greenlaugh, Mindy Selman, and Jenny Guiling of the World Resources Institute quote the following sources for Conservation program spending: (1) EQIP funding allocation: www.nrcs.usda.gov/programs/eqip/; Personal communication: Edward Brzostek (USDA Natural Resources Conservation Service (NRCS), June 2006; (2) Conservation Reserve Program funding allocation 29th signup: www.fsa.usda.gov/dafp/cepd/29th/ TheConservationReserveProgram29thSignup.pdf; (3) Grassland Reserve Program funding allocation: www.nrcs.usda.gov/programs/grp/; (4) Wetlands Reserve Program funding allocation: www.nrcs.usda.gov/programs/wrp/; (5) Wildlife habitat Incentives program funding allocation: www.nrcs.usda.gov/programs/whip/; Personal communication: Albert Cerna (USDA-NRCS), June 2006.

9. According to the World Resources Institute, "in 2005, USDA NRCS changed operating systems for EQIP applications and NRCS suspects that many states were not able to submit all their applications because of the workload to migrate data from the old system to the new system. Therefore, the percent of applications funded in 2005 may seem artificially high. (Personal communication: Edward Brzostek, USDA-NRCS, June 5, 2006)."

10. FAO Newsroom, "Livestock a Major Threat to Environment: Remedies Urgently Needed," November 29, 2006, web edition.

9. Freedom to Farm and the Legacy of Record Payoffs

1. Scott Marlow, "The Non-Wonk Guide to Understanding Federal Commodity Payments," The Rural Advancement Foundation International–USA, 2005 edition, page 3.

2. Ibid.

3. Dan Morgan, "The Farm Bill and Beyond," The German Marshall Fund of the United States, Economic Policy Paper Series, January 2010, p. 13

10. The Beginnings of a Food Bill?

1. Dottie Rosenbaum, "Farm Bill Contains Significant Domestic Nutrition Improvements," Center on Budget and Policy Priorities, July 1, 2008, web edition.

2. Ibid

3. Ibid

4. "Farmers' Market Promotion Program: Program Basics," National Sustainable Agriculture Coalition, web edition, Accessed August 5, 2011.

5. The Department of Agriculture defines a food desert as a Census tract where 33% or 500 people, whichever is less, live more than a mile from a grocery store in an urban area or more than 10 miles away in a rural area. At least 20% of the residents must live below the federal poverty line, currently $22,350 for a family of four.

6. "Industry Statistics and Projected Growth," Organic Trade Association, web edition, Updated June 2011.

7. Conkin, *A Revolution Down on the Farm*, p. 140.

8. A sustainable rate of erosion is five tons per acre per year or less according to the National Sustainable Agriculture Coalition.

11. Who Gets the Money?

1. 2011 Farm Subsidy Database, Environmental Working Group, web edition.

2. Dan Morgan, "The Farm Bill and Beyond," The German Marshall Fund of the United States, Economic Policy Paper Series, January 2010, p. 13

3. Robert Hoppe and David Banker, "Structure and Finances of U.S. Farms: Family Farm Report, 2010 edition," Economic Research Service, U.S. Department of Agriculture, July 2010

4. Timothy Wise, "Understanding the Farm Problem: Six Common Errors in Presenting Farm Statistics," Global Development and Environment Institute, Tufts University, March 2005, p. 12.

5. "United States Top Recipients 1995-2010," Environmental Working Group 2011 Farm Subsidy Database, web edition, Accessed August 8, 2011.

6. Dan Chapman, Ken Foskett, and Megan Clarke, "How savvy growers *can double, or triple, subsidy dollars*," *Atlanta Journal-Constitution*, Oct. 2, 2006

7. Dan Chapman, Ken Foskett, and Megan Clarke, "How your tax dollars prop up big growers and squeeze the little guy," *The Atlanta Journal-Constitution*, Oct. 1, 2006.

8. Forrest Laws, "GAO Report Sheds Little Light on Payment Limit Rules," Southwest Farm Press, July 1, 2004.

9. Morgan and Gaul, "No Farm? No Crop? No Problem—Subsidies Still Grow," *Washington Post*, July 2, 2006. These reporters specifically mention Mary Anna Hudson, from River Oaks near Houston who received $191,000 and Houston surgeon Jimmy Frank Howell, who received $490,709 since the 1996 Farm Bill.

10. "Methodology Used to Identify Members of 112th Congress Receiving Farm Subsidies," Environmental Working Group, March 2011, web edition.

11. Food and Water Watch and Public Health Institute, "Beyond Subsidies: Dispelling Common Myths about Public Health and the Farm Bill," Summer 2011.

12. Tim Hearden, "Farm Subsidies: Industry Defends Need for Rice Aid," Capital Press, July 28, 2011, web edition; California Department of Food and Agriculture, "Agricultural Statistical Review," California Agricultural Resource Directory 2010-2011.

13. "Florida Summary," Environmental Working Group Farm Subsidy Database 2011, web edition.

14. Environmental Working Group, "After Hong Kong, Redraw America's Subsidy Map," December 13, 2005, web edition.

15. Ibid.

12. Who Will Grow Our Food?

1. Central Intelligence Agency, CIA World Factbook: United States Economy, web edition, updated July 26, 2011.

2. "2007 Census of Agriculture: Farmers by Age," web edition.

3. "Farming Opportunities" National Sustainable Agriculture Coalition, web edition, accessed August 9, 2011.

4. USDA, ERS, Data Set: Foreign Agricultural Trade of the United States (FATUS), web edition.

5. For instance, Tyson, Cargill, Swift, and National Beef Packing Co. control 83.5 percent of beef packing market. Smithfield, Tyson, Swift and Hormel control 64 percent of pork packing. Cargill, Archer Daniels Midland (ADM), ConAgra, and Cereal Food Processor control 63 percent of flour processing. ADM, Bunge, and Cargill control 71 percent of soybean crushing market. Similar statistics unfold for corn, soybean oil, poultry, turkey, and many other markets. Richard Longworth, *Caught in the Middle: America's Heartland in the Age of Globalism*, Bloomsbury Publishing USA, 2009.

6. Conkin, *A Revolution Down on the Farm*, p. 98.

7. Jim Barham, "Regional Food Hubs: Understanding the Scope and Scale of Food Hub Operations," USDA Agricultural Marketing Service, April 19, 2011.

8. Jean Buzby et al, "Possible Implications for U.S. Agriculture from Adoptions of Select Dietary Guidelines," USDA Economic Research Service Report Number 31, November 2006.

13. The World Trade Organization and the International Community

1. Joseph Stiglitz, "Cotton Bailout: King Cotton's tyranny: U.S. subsidies unfairly cut," *Atlanta Journal Constitution*, October 8, 2006.

2. U.S. cotton farmers receive an average of $230 per acre in subsidies.

3. Ferd Hoefner "WTO Panel Rules Against COOL Regulations," National Sustainable Agriculture Coalition, November 21, 2011.

14. New Zealand: Still Subsidy-free After All These Years

1. John Pickford, "New Zealand's Hardy Farm Spirit," BBC, New Zealand, October 16, 2004, web edition.

2. Ibid

3. Laura Sayre, "Farming Without Subsidies? Some Lessons from New Zealand," *The New Farm*, March 2003.

4. Ibid

5. Ibid

16. Public Health and Nutrition: Building 21st Century Food Systems, Fighting Chronic Disease

1. Let's Move, "Learn the Facts," web edition, accessed August 29, 2011.

2. Five recommendations for a healthy diet include: 1) achieve an energy balance and a healthy weight; 2) limit intake of fats; 3) increase consumption of fruits, vegetables, legumes, and whole grains; 4) limit intake of sugar; 5) limit salt/sodium intake.

3. Ann Cooper, "For Healthier Kids, Increase the School Lunch Budget," Washington Post, March 5, 2010.

4. Mark Bittman, "Bad Food? Tax It, and Subsidize Vegetables," New York Times, July 23, 2011

5. Food Insecurity means that a household had limited or uncertain availability of food, or limited or uncertain ability to acquire acceptable foods in socially acceptable ways (i.e. without resorting to emergency food supplies, scavenging, stealing, or other unusual coping strategies.) Mark Nord et al, "Household Food Security in the United States, 2009," USDA Economic Research Service, web edition.

6. "The Heavy Toll of Diet-Related Diseases," USDA, Dietary Guidelines for Americans 2010.

7. "Out of Balance: Marketing of Soda, Candy, Snacks, and Fast Foods Drowns Out Healthful Messages," Consumers Union and California Pan-Ethnic Health Network, September 2005.

8. United Health Foundation, American Public Health Association and the Partnership for Prevention, "The Future Costs of Obesity: National and State Estimates of the Impact of Obesity On Direct Health Care Expenses," November 2009, p. 2.

9. Gary Paul Nabhan, *Why Some Like it Hot: Food, Genes, and Cultural Diversity*, Island Press, 2004, pp. 175-177.

10. "Agriculture Fact Book 2001-2002," USDA, Economic Research Service, chapter 2, web edition.

11. "Dietary Guidelines for Americans, 2010," USDA, Center for Nutrition Policy and Promotion, January 2011, A-2.

12. Food and Water Watch and Public Health Institute, "Beyond Subsidies: Dispelling Common Myths about Public Health and the Farm Bill," White Paper, 2011.

13. Physicians Committee for Responsible Medicine, "Agriculture Subsidies: Conflicts with Policies on Nutrition and Health," 2011, p. 8.

14. Michael Moss, "While Worrying About Fat, U.S. Pushes Cheese Sales," *New York Times*, November 6, 2010, web edition.

15. Mark Muller, "Food Without Thought:

16. Janet Raloff, "Money Matters in Obesity," *Science On-Line*, July 16, 2005, Vol. 168. No. 3.

17. "Making the Case fort Local Food Systems," A Farm and Food Policy Project Learning Paper, p. 2.

18. "Rural Ks. Grocery Stores Closing," *The Capital-Journal*, May 22, 2010, web edition.

19. Mechel S. Paggi and Jay E. Noel, "The U.S. 2008 Farm Bill: Title X and Related Support for the U.S. Specialty Crop Sector," Choices, 3rd Quarter 2008, web edition.

20. Leah Zerbe, "Factory Farms Use 30 Million Pounds of Antibiotics a Year (and You're Eating Some of It)," Rodale News, December 21, 2010, web edition.

21. "EMU Finds Multi-drug-resistant bacteria near CAFOs here: Bacteria resistant to five antibiotics found in waters of Rice Lake Drain," Environmentally Concerned Citizens of South Central Michigan, Summer 2011 Newsletter.

17. Ethanol: Growing Food, Feed, Fiber, and Fuel?

1. "The Energy Independence and Security Act: Charting a New Direction for America's Energy Policy," United States Senate Committee on Energy & Natural Resources, web edition, Accessed September 21, 2011.

2. Craig Cox and Andrew Hug, "Driving Under the Influence: Corn Ethanol & Energy Security," Environmental Working Group, June 2010.

3. Frances Thicke, *A New Vision for Iowa Food and Agriculture*, Mulberrry Knoll, 2010, p. 95.

4. J.E. Campbell, D.B. Lobell, C.B. Field, "Greater Transportation Energy and GHG Offsets from Bioelectricity Than Ethanol," *Science*, May 22, 2009, 324:5930 pp. 1055-1057.

5. Christopher R. Knittel, "Corn Belt Moonshine: The Costs and Benefits of U.S. Ethanol Subsidies," American Enterprise Institute, 2011.

6. John Deutch, "Biomass Movement," *Wall Street Journal*, May 10, 2006.

7. Thicke, Ibid.

8. Tom Philpott, "Archer Daniels Midland: The Exxon of Corn," *The Daily Grist*, February 2, 2006.

9. USDA biofuels expert, personal communication.

10. Liz Marshall and Suzie Greenhalgh, "Beyond the Renewable Fuels Standard: The Environmental and Economic Impacts of Grain Ethanol Production in the United States," World Resources Policy Institute, September 2006, p. 5.

11. Andrew Pollack, "Redesigning Crops to Harvest Fuel," New York Times, Friday, September 8, 2006, p. C1-C-4.

12. Ibid.

13. Ibid.

14. Ibid.

18. Energy and Climate Change

1 Peter Huber and Mark Mills, *The Bottomless Well: The Twilight of Fuel, the Virtue of Waste, and Why We Will Never Run Out of Energy*. Basic Books, 2005, p. 7.

2 Patrick Canning et al, "Energy Use in the U.S. Food System," USDA Economic Research Service, Economic Research Report Number 94, March 2010.

3 Estimates of this ratio vary from 6:1 to over 20:1. The average of all these estimates is around 10:1, which has become the most commonly cited figure. See: Simon Fairlie, *Meat: A Benign Extravagance*, Chelsea Green Publishing, 2010.

4 Personal correspondence with Michael Bomford

5 Personal correspondence with Michael Bomford, interpreting Nathan Pelletier et al, "Comparative Life Cycle Environmental Impacts of Three Beef Production Strategies in the Upper Midwestern United States," *Agricultural Systems* 103:6 July 2010 pp. 380-389.

6 J.A. Miranowski, "Energy Consumption in U.S. Agriculture," In J. Outlaw, K. Collins, and J. Duffield eds. Agriculture as a Producer and Consumer of Energy, CABI, 2005. See also: Michael Bomford, "Will Natural Gas Power the 21st Century?" Post Carbon Institute, May 2011.

7 Megan Stubbs, "Renewable Energy Programs in the 2008 Farm Bill," Congressional Research Service, December 20, 2010.

8 "2008 Farm Bill Side-By-Side: Title IX: Energy," USDA Economic Research Service, web edition, Accessed September 14, 2011.

9 Ibid

10 Andy Olsen et al, "Farm Energy Success Stories," Environmental Law & Policy Center.

11 Ibid

12 Francis Thicke, Ibid., p. 41.

13 Mark Ribaudo, "Reducing Agriculture's Nitrogen Footprint: Are New Policy Approaches Needed?" Amber Waves, September 2011, web edition.

14 Personal correspondence with Michael Bomford. Some estimate Agriculture contributes as much as 40 percent of GHGs worldwide. See: Vandana Shiva, "Resisting the Corporate Theft of Seeds," The Nation, September 14, 2011, web edition.

15 Johannes Kotschi and Karl Müller-Sämann, "The Role of Organic Agriculture in Mitigating Climate Change: A Scoping Study," International Federation of Organic Agriculture Movements," May 2004.

16 Michael Bomford, "Beyond Food Miles," Post Carbon Institute, March 9, 2011.

17 "Putting Dairy Cows Out to Pasture: An Environmental Plus," *Agricultural Research* May-June 2011, pp. 18-19.

18 Ibid, p. 19.

19 Paul Hanley, "Study Debunks Myths on Organic Farms," *The Star Phoenix*, September 27, 2011, web edition.

20 "Soil Carbon and Organic Farming," Soil Association, November 2009, web edition.

19. Healthy Lands, Healthy People: Why Farmlands Matter to Conservation

1. Roger Classen, "Do Farm Programs Encourage Native Grassland Losses?" *Amber Waves*, USDA Economic Research Service, September 2011, p. 2.

2. Ibid., p. 7.

3. David Wilcox cited in "Our Precious Heritage," Nature Conservancy, 2000.

4. American Farmland Trust, "Farming on the Edge Report: What's Happening to Our Farmland?" web edition, Accessed August 26, 2011.

5. Sustainable Agriculture Coalition, "No Time for Delay: A Sustainable Agriculture Agenda for the 2007 Farm Bill," p.10.

6. Ibid, p.49.

7. Arthur Allen addresses this in "The Conservation Reserve Enhancement Program," in *Fish and Wildlife Benefits of Farm Bill Conservation Programs, 2000-2005 Update*, NRCS, p. 123.

8. "2007 Natural Resources Inventory," Natural Resources Conservation Service, April 2010, page 1, web edition.

9. Ronald E. Reynolds, "The Conservation Reserve Program and Duck Production in the U.S. Prairie Pothole Region," *Fish and Wildlife Benefits of Farm Bill Programs 200-2005 Update*, pp. 34-35.

10. Stephen J. Brady, "Highly Erodible land and Swampbuster Provisions of the 2002 Farm Act," in Fish and Wildlife Benefits of Farm Bill Conservation Programs, 2000-2005 Update, USDA Natural Resources Conservation Service and Farm Service Agency, p. 12.

11. Douglas Johnson, "Grassland Bird Use of Conservation Reserve Program Fields in the Great Plains," in *Fish and Wildlife Benefits of Farm Bill Conservation Programs, 2000-2005 Update*, NRCS, p. 26.

12. "Biodiversity Critical for Maintaining Multiple 'Ecosystem Services,'" *Science Daily*, August 19, 2011, web edition.

13. Pimental, D., et al., "Economic and Environmental Benefits of Biodiversity," *Bioscience* 47 (11): 747-757.

14. Tim Lloyd, "Bats' Decline Could Cost Midwestern Farmers Billions," The Kansas City Star, September 12, 2011, web edition.

15. Ibid.

16. Ibid.

17. Marc Ribaudo, "Reducing Agriculture's Nitrogen Footprint: Are New Policy Approaches Needed?" USDA ERS, Amber Waves, September 2011, p. 4.

18. Marc Ribaudo, "Reducing Agriculture's Nitrogen Footprint: Are New Policy Approaches Needed?" USDA ERS, Amber Waves, September 2011, p. 4.

19. 60 percent of EQIP money must be spent on livestock operations. According to the NRCS, large feedlot operations receive about 25 percent of all EQIP dollars. Feedlots can be compensated up to $450,000 for the construction of manure lagoons and animal waste processing facilities. Equating basic environmental compliance with conservation is quite a stretch.

20. National Security:
Food on the Front Lines

1. "Obesity Takes Its Toll on the Military," Associated Press, July 5, 2005.

2. Ibid.

3. Robert Pear, "U.S. Health Chief, Stepping Down, Issues Warning," New York Times, December 4, 2004.

4. James E. Deitz and James L. Southam, *Contemporary Business Mathematics for Colleges,* Mason, Ohio: Cengage Learning, 2008.

5. USDA National Institute of Food and Agriculture website.

6. Endres, AB, Endres JM. U. of Illinois, "Homeland Security Planning: what victory gardens and Fidel Castro can teach us in preparing for food crises in the United States."

7. Marion Kalb, "Department of Defense Farm to School Program: Frequently Asked Questions," Community Food Security Coalition.

21. The Next 50 Years: Perennialization and Ecosystem-based Agriculture

1. The Land Institute, "A 50-Year Farm Bill," June 2009.

2. Judy Swenson, "CRWP, LSP Test New Strategy," MonteNews.com, October 4, 2010.

3. Early coalition members included Wendell Berry, Fred Kirschenmann, Herman Daly, David Orr, Dan Imhoff, Owsley Brown, Laura Jackson, etc.

22. Local Food:
The Emerging Agricultural Economy

1. "Farmers Market Growth: 1994-2011," USDA Agricultural Marketing Service, modified August 8, 2011.

2. "Farm to School Chronology," Farm to School, web edition.

3. Kathleen Merrigan, "Food Hubs: Creating Opportunities for Producers Across the Nation," USDA Blog, April 19, 2011.

4. Jean Buzby et al, "Possible Implications for U.S. Agriculture from Adoption of Select Dietary Guidelines," USDA Economic Research Service, Economic Research Report Number 31, November 2006.

5. Personal correspondence with Michael Dimock.

Photography Credits

Page 36:	Migrant mother, Nipomo, California, 1936 ©Dorothea Lange
Page 41:	Coon Creek Watershed, USDA; inset photo, ©Dan Imhoff
Page 46:	Columbines, NRCS
Page 51:	Kennedy, West Virginia, ©Cecil Stoughton/JFK Presidential Library
Page 52:	"We Need Food", ©Martha Tabor
Page 61:	Manure lagoon, NRCS
Page 62:	Cows, Helen Reddout, Socially Responsible Agriculture Project
Page 63:	Mailbox, ©Roberto Carra
Page 64:	Chesapeake Bay, Antietam, Maryland, ©Dan Imhoff
Page 83:	USA Today
Page 84:	Farm Sanctuary
Page 94:	ALBA
Page 104:	Sheep, NZ Ministry of Agriculture and Forestry
Page 121:	Obesity on the rise, ©Scott Vaughn
Page 126:	Roots of Change
Page 147:	Windmill, ©Doug Tompkins
Page 155:	Farm, Iowa, 1999 ©Lynn Betts
Page 156:	Grassland, ©Dan Imhoff
Page 168	National Archives and Records Administration, Records of the U.S. Food Administration, ARC Identifier 512498
Page 184:	School lunch program, Thousand Oaks Elementary School, ©Craig Lee

Watershed Media is an award-winning nonprofit publisher and resource center that produces action-oriented books and education campaigns about under-reported contemporary issues.
Watershed Media, 513 Brown Street, Healdsburg, California 95448, 707.431.2936, www.watershedmedia.org

OUR BOOK AND OUTREACH CAMPAIGNS INCLUDE:

The Guide to Tree-free, Recycled, and Certified Papers (1999)

Building with Vision: Optimizing and Finding Alternatives to Wood (2001)

Farming with the Wild: Enhancing Biodiversity on Farms and Ranches (2003)

Paper or Plastic: Searching for Solutions to an Overpackaged World (2005)

Farming and the Fate of Wild Nature: Essays in Conservation-Based Agriculture (2006)

Food Fight: The Citizen's Guide to a Food and Farm Bill (2007)

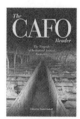

The CAFO Reader: The Tragedy of Industrial Animal Factories (2010) Edited by Daniel Imhoff

The Post Carbon Reader: Managing the 21st Century Sustainability Crises (2010) Edited by Richard Heinberg and Daniel Lerch

Smart By Nature: Schooling for Sustainability (2009) Written by Michael Stone, Center for Ecoliteracy, Foreword by Daniel Goleman